Made-from-Bone

▸ ▸ ▸ ▸ *Interpretations of Culture in the New Millennium*

Norman E. Whitten Jr., General Editor

A list of books in the series appears
at the end of the book.

Made-from-Bone

*Trickster Myths, Music, and History
from the Amazon*

Jonathan D. Hill

University of Illinois Press · Urbana and Chicago

©2009 by Jonathan D. Hill
Manufactured in the United States of America
1 2 3 4 5 C P 5 4 3 2 1

∞ This book is printed on acid-free paper.

Library of Congress Cataloging-in-Publication Data
Hill, Jonathan David
Made-from-bone : trickster myths, music, and history from the Amazon /
Jonathan D. Hill.
p.   cm. — (Interpretations of culture in the new millennium)
Includes bibliographical references and index.
ISBN-13 978-0-252-03373-5 (cloth : alk. paper)
ISBN-10 0-252-03373-6 (cloth : alk. paper)
ISBN-13 978-0-252-07570-4 (pbk. : alk. paper)
ISBN-10 0-252-07570-6 (pbk. : alk. paper)
1. Curripaco Indians—Folklore. 2. Curripaco mythology.
3. Curripaco Indians—Songs and music. 4. Tricksters—Venezuela.
I. Title.
F2270.2.C87H56   2009
398.208998'39—dc22   200802

Contents

Illustrations

Made-from-Bone

Preface:
Introducing Made-from-Bone,
the Trickster-Creator

My goal in the following pages is to provide a complete set of English translations of Wakuénai narratives about the mythic past and its transformations.
Wakuénai storytellers refer to these narratives by the phrase *yákuti úupi pérri*,
or "words from the primordial times," and they are set in an unfinished space-
time before there were any clear distinctions between humans and animals,
men and women, day and night, old and young, and powerful and powerless.
The central character throughout these primordial times and the ensuing
transformations that open up into the world of distinct peoples, species, and
places is a trickster-creator who survives a prolonged series of life-threatening
attacks and who ultimately defeats all his adversaries.

The Wakuénai refer to this trickster-creator as "Made-from-Bone" (*Iñápirríkuli*) because of the way he was created from the finger bones of his slain father. Unlike the buffoonish, comical tricksters of better-known North American
mythologies (Radin 1972 [1956]), the trickster-creator in Wakuénai society is
an omniscient, powerful being who always anticipates the treachery and deceit
of other beings and who skillfully manipulates words and other signs as tools
for deceiving and defeating these other beings.[1] From the very beginning of
mythic times, Made-from-Bone must struggle against powerful adversaries
who try to kill him and his brothers by shooting them with arrows and darts,
poisoning their food, drowning them in rivers and streams, or burning them
alive. However, Made-from-Bone always knows in advance about his enemies'
lethal traps and finds ways to escape, often turning the tables on his enemies
in the process.

One of Made-from-Bone's most potent weapons of self-defense is verbal deception, or ways of speaking that cannot be interpreted literally. The
trickster-creator always has superior knowledge of his enemies' intentions
and uses words and other signs as ways of misleading and defeating them.[2]
Made-from-Bone embodies the principle that nothing people say or do can

be taken at face value but must always be interpreted symbolically in relation to secret knowledge that does not form part of the immediate situation.[3]

I first learned about Made-from-Bone during fieldwork in the upper Río Negro region of Venezuela in 1980, when I was a twenty-six-year-old doctoral student at Indiana University. The main purpose of my fieldwork with the Arawak-speaking Wakuénai (also called Curripaco) was to record and study their traditions of musical performance. It became clear that understanding the indigenous experience of musical artistry required me to learn about events from the mythic past that are related in complex cycles of narratives.

I was privileged to work with a generous and talented elder, Horacio Ló-pez Pequeira, who was a highly respected master of sacred chanting (*malikái limínali*) and extraordinarily knowledgeable storyteller. Horacio and I spent many hours transcribing and discussing sacred chants and songs (*malikái*), shamanic songs (*malirríkairi*), and collective dance music played on a variety of flutes and trumpets. Horacio taught me about the connections between ritual chanting and mythic narratives and that some of the spirit names invoked in *malikái* are especially powerful because they "have stories" (photo 1).

Many times during my fieldwork in 1980 and 1981, Horacio warned his family in my presence that he was not going to live forever and that it was time for the next generation to learn how to sing and chant *malikái*. My graduate training in ethnomusicology and special interest in Wakuénai musical performances converged with Horacio's desire that these musical genres be recorded and studied so that future generations would not lose them. Horacio's efforts to explain to me the meanings of chanting, singing, and ceremonial dance music led us deeper and deeper into the realm of mythic narratives, or stories about the original coming-into-being of a fully human social world.

When I returned to Horacio's community during a postdoctoral research project in July 1984, I found him recovering from a serious injury that had happened while he was felling trees in a new manioc garden in late 1983. It was during this brief visit that Horacio and I made recordings of several mythic narratives that are directly related to understanding ritual and ceremonial performances and closely associated topics, such as the spiritual causes of sickness, healing, and death.

During the months of his recuperation prior to my arrival in July, Horacio had begun teaching his son, Félix López Oliveiros, how to perform *malikái* chanting and singing. Félix had been present when Horacio and I had worked with cassette tape recordings of *malikái*, listening to the chanting and singing over and over in the course of transcribing their texts and discussing their mythic meanings. I was pleased that my fieldwork had sparked Félix's interest

*Photo 1. Horacio chanting and
blowing tobacco smoke during
childbirth ritual, 1981. Photo taken
by Jonathan D. Hill.*

in his father's chanting and singing. When it was time for me to leave again, Horacio asked me if I could leave a cassette tape recorder with a supply of batteries and blank tapes so that Félix could use them to memorize *malikái* chants and songs before my return a year later. I was happy to comply and asked Félix to record any new performances of *malikái.*

When I returned to the community in July and August 1985, Horacio had fully recovered from his injuries, and Félix had become proficient in many, though not all, of the chants and songs. In addition, Félix had done an outstanding job of recording all the songs, chants, speeches, and instrumental performances of a male initiation ritual held in March 1985. We spent many hours listening to, transcribing, and discussing these tapes with Horacio over the remaining weeks of my stay.

I also continued to record Horacio's stories about events that took place in the mythic past. By the time I left the upper Río Negro in August, I had made detailed field notes summarizing twenty-five narratives and had recorded about half of them. Although I did not know it at the time, this was to be the last opportunity I would have to work with Horacio, who died in 1991, several years before I next returned to the upper Río Negro.

The idea of making the narratives themselves into the subject of a separate study did not take shape at a single moment in time but emerged over the next decade as I studied my fieldnotes and listened to recordings of various performances of *malikái* and other genres of Wakuénai musical performance. Making the narratives themselves into primary objects of attention required me to search for new ways of approaching the mythic figure of Made-from-Bone, the trickster-creator whose powerful and enigmatic character is predominant in nearly all the narratives.

Since the time of Columbus's first encounter with the Taíno and other Arawak-speaking peoples of the Caribbean, the Western world has been aware that these indigenous Caribbean and South American peoples have developed highly complex narratives explaining the origins of life and death, rivers and oceans, animals and plants, day and night, men and women. Like the Taíno stories recorded by Friar Ramón Pané (1999) on the island of Hispañola in the 1490s, the indigenous narrative traditions about Made-from-Bone translated in this book are highly metaphorical and poeticized cycles of shamanic history that do not translate easily into English and have largely eluded Western ways of knowing and experiencing the world. The vast interpretive gaps between diverse worldviews that went into the making of contemporary South America and the Caribbean can only be bridged through ethnographically based studies that document complete cycles of narratives and demonstrate how the cataclysmic events and transformations of mythic creation enter into contemporary social worlds and historical memories.

The closest anyone had come to achieving such a synthesis of ethnography and mythology was David Guss's English translation of the complete cycle of creation narratives among the Carib-speaking Ye'kuana.[4] However, the Ye'kuana would not allow Guss to record their mythic narratives, so his translations in *Watunna: An Orinoco Creation Cycle* (Civrieux 1980) had to be based on narratives that had been collected and pieced together in the 1950s by a French scientist named Marc de Civrieux. Guss later wrote an excellent ethnographic study of Ye'kuana basket making (1989) that allows us to understand how the epochal struggles between Wanadi, the good creator-god, and his evil twin Odosha enter into ritual, ceremony, and basketry.[5]

There were no English translations of complete cycles of mythic narratives for Arawak-speaking peoples of South America when I returned to the upper Río Negro region in June through November of 1998 to conduct an intensive study of narratives about Made-from-Bone.[6] The project resulted in

complete, line-by-line transcriptions and translations of trickster narratives.⁷
I brought along field recordings of narratives that I had made with Horacio
in the early 1980s. Listening to, transcribing, and translating these recordings
of narratives served as a point of departure for making new recordings and
documenting as completely as possible the entire set of narratives making
up *yákuti úupi pérri*.

After Horacio's death in 1991, the community where I had worked with
him in the 1980s had disbanded. One group of families had moved to a new
site on the Venezuelan side of the Río Negro (or Guainía as it is known above
the mouth of the Casiquiare River near San Carlos de Río Negro). Horacio's
son Félix and several other families had relocated to an island-village several
kilometers downstream. I went to visit Félix on the afternoon of June 16,
1998, in order to explain my new research project to him and to find out if
he would be willing to work with me on it. After getting reacquainted with
each other after such a long absence, Félix agreed to work with me on the
new project on narratives about the mythic trickster.

Félix asked me if I still had copies of all the tape recordings that I had made
of his father singing and chanting *malikái* back in the early 1980s. I asked
him which of these performances he needed and made him copies during my
return to the United States in late July and early August. After noting a list
of such performances, I asked if he needed a copy of the important *malikái*
song for curing victims of witchcraft. "No," Félix replied, "I already have
that one written down in my notes." That brief exchange set the tone for
my fieldwork over the remaining months of 1998. The adult leaders of the
community were struggling to revitalize their shamanic practices of chanting
and singing in rapidly changing historical conditions, and they saw tape recordings and written texts as vital components of this process of recovery.

The most striking change at the local level was that the generation of elders and senior ritual specialists with whom I had studied in the early 1980s
had died in the early 1990s, and a new generation of adults had replaced
them in positions of leadership. Félix and several other members of this new
generation were keenly interested in continuing to perform the rich genres
of narrative discourse, ritual chanting, and musical dancing of their parents'
and earlier generations. My project on indigenous narratives became part of
a collaborative process of cultural recovery in which my field notes and tape
recordings from the early 1980s became key resources.

For the next six months, I worked with Félix in transcribing narratives in
the Curricarro dialect and translating them into Spanish. We began with the
narratives that I had previously recorded with his father, Horacio, in the early

1980s. I had brought a laptop and a portable inkjet printer to the field, which allowed us to print a draft of each day's transcriptions during the evening hours when the diesel-powered electric generator was running in the village. Having electricity in the evenings also gave me just enough time to fully recharge three batteries for my laptop so that we could use it again on the following day. Each morning we began by studying and revising the printed draft of the previous day's transcriptions before turning to the more difficult and time-consuming labor of transcribing and translating (photo 2).

Félix and I developed a strong working relationship through transcribing and translating the lengthy set of recordings of his late father's narrations. Félix was fluent in the local Spanish and had good basic reading and writing skills. He became increasingly skilled at transcribing and translating narratives. Within a few weeks, we were able to work through lengthy, complicated passages of recorded speech with far greater ease and speed. Humor, gravity, beauty, cleverness, and other qualities of Made-from-Bone began to permeate our thoughts and spill over into our everyday conversations during afternoon fishing expeditions. We worked in the open, public space of the local schoolroom, so everyone in the village overheard fragments of our discussions. Made-from-Bone, the name of the trickster-creator, along

Photo 2. Félix correcting printed drafts of narratives, 1998. Photo taken by Jonathan D. Hill.

with the names of his numerous enemies and allies began to circulate again through the local community.

I had hoped that this initial stage of transcribing and translating recordings from the 1980s would serve as a springboard for moving smoothly into the recording of other narratives about the trickster-creator. However, it became clear that Félix was not as comfortable at verbally performing the narratives as he was at transcribing and reading them. So we began working on specific narratives by studying the detailed written accounts of them that I had made during my conversations with Horacio in the 1980s. In these first experiments at working from written texts to spoken words, Félix's speech was somewhat tentative and halting. By the time we had worked through several narratives in this manner, Félix was no longer reading from the transcribed texts but performing the narratives by using the written texts only as a guide to remembering the general ordering of narrative events and episodes (photo 3).

As this second stage of the project gained momentum, I began to discuss with Félix the possibility of producing a bilingual Curripaco and Spanish edition of the narratives as a contribution to the Venezuelan Ministry of Education's Program of Bilingual Intercultural Education. During a meeting in August 1998, at the Office of Indigenous Affairs in Caracas, officials at the Ministry of Education expressed a strong interest in publishing a collection

Photo 3. Félix recording narratives, 1998. Photo taken by Jonathan D. Hill.

of mythic narratives as part of a broader process of developing a bilingual curriculum for the Wakuénai living in Venezuela. When I got back to the Río Negro, Félix agreed that his deceased father, Horacio Lopez Pequeira, should be listed as the book's principal author to reflect the central importance of my recordings and field notes with him from the early 1980s for our ongoing project. The resulting manuscript, called *Yákuti Úupi Pérri (Palabras de los Primeros Tiempos)*, was submitted to the Office of Indigenous Affairs in the Venezuelan Ministry of Education in December 1998 for use in its program of bilingual intercultural education (López Pequeira, López Oliveros, and Hill 1998).

In the course of preparing the bilingual collection of narratives in 1998, Félix and I spent many hours discussing how to order the narratives and organize them into general categories. From these conversations, we agreed to arrange the narratives into three groupings, running from "The Primordial Times" (*Úupi Pérri*) through "The World Begins" (*Hekuápi Ikééñuakawa*) to "The World Opens Up" (*Hekuápi Iʰméetakawa*). This ordering is not a simple, linear chronology. Although the arrangement of narratives tends to move from earlier, undifferentiated times to later periods of cultural separateness, there are many cultural practices, such as shamanic curing rituals and *pudáli* ceremonies, that allow for movements backward and forward in mythic space-times.

The ordering of chapters in this book follows the arrangement of Wakuénai narratives into the three groupings that emerged from my discussions with Félix Oliveros in 1998. Part 1, "Words from the Primordial Times," includes nine narratives that describe the origins of the trickster-creator (Made-from-Bone, or *Iñápirríkuli*), sickness, and death. This first set of narratives centers around the figure of Made-from-Bone, whose struggles against various adversaries resulted in the creation of natural and social worlds. Overall, "The Primordial Times" was a period of unceasing violence between Made-from-Bone and his in-laws. Made-from-Bone anticipated the treachery and deceit of his enemies and skillfully manipulated words and other signs as tools for deceiving and defeating them. Made-from-Bone always managed to find ways to cope with difficult, even life-threatening situations, not by directly confronting adversaries but through self-concealment and use of secret knowledge to imagine a future way to break out of present dangers.

Part 2, "The World Begins," encompasses six narratives that explain the origins of night and sleep, cooking fire, manioc gardens, peach-palm fruits, and the musical dancing of *pudáli* ceremonial exchanges. The beginning of *pudáli* marks a major turning point in Wakuénai mythic history, for Made-from-Bone and his younger brother, Manioc-Man (*Káali*), created *pudáli* as a way to teach their children how to give and receive food and other things from their in-laws in a nonviolent, respectful manner.

Part 3, "The World Opens Up," outlines the conception, birth, and life cycle of the primordial human being (*Kuwái*), who is the son of an incestuous union between Made-from-Bone and his paternal aunt (*Ámaru*). The cycle of myths about *Kuwái* and *Ámaru* describes the origins of individual male and female humanness, the human life cycle, the passage of generational and historical time, and the ritual practices for controlling all these developmental and temporal processes. In addition, "The World Opens Up" includes several narratives about the origins of witchcraft, shamanic curing, the afterlife, and modernity.

Each grouping of narratives is introduced with an overview of major themes and short summaries of the narratives themselves. To make the narratives more readable and accessible, I have substituted English glosses for indigenous names of mythic characters throughout (for example, "Made-from-Bone" instead of *Iñápirríkuli*, "Grandfather Sleep" instead of *Dáinali*), and a glossary at the end provides a quick reference guide to the indigenous mythic characters and key cultural terms. Endnotes provide additional information to help contextualize everyday social or economic practices, historical events, or ritual and ceremonial activities that are mentioned or alluded to in the narratives. I have also written historical and ethnographic analyses in each of the book's three parts in order to illustrate some of the many ways in which Wakuénai mythic narratives enter into historical interpretation and social action.

After introducing and presenting narratives from part 1, "Words from the Primordial Times," I provide an ethnohistorical interlude that focuses on historical meanings discernible in the story of *Uliámaliéni*, an anaconda-child whose anger resulted in the origin of a type of sickness called "rawness." The narrative of Anaconda-Person marks the first moment when explicit reference is made to the historical arrival of white people (*yarináinai*). It may seem odd to find explicit reference to white people and colonial history implanted in a narrative set in primordial times when the creation of indigenous people and the surrounding world of forests and rivers was still in its infancy. However, the merging of historical and mythic time frames makes perfect sense if we understand Made-from-Bone not as some folkloristic remnant of a pristine indigenous past but as a dynamic symbolic practice of interpreting and engaging with the contemporary world we all share. The story about Made-from-Bone and Anaconda-Person shows how the Wakuénai understand their social world today as deeply rooted in the historical expansion of colonial and national states, along with an array of global forces, into the upper Río Negro and adjacent regions of South America. I will provide an overview of these historical forces of change in the next chapter and a detailed interpretation of the story of Made-from-Bone and Anaconda-Person in a later chapter (chapter 3, "Ethnohistorical Interlude").

The merging of history and myth speaks to the broader meaning of narratives about Made-from-Bone as cultural tools for navigating centuries of historical struggle by allowing the Wakuénai to create new interpretive and political spaces in contexts of traumatic changes driven by large-scale forces. Made-from-Bone, the mythic trickster-creator, is the key to understanding the persistence of indigenous cultural ways of life in the face of an array of outside agents that have struggled to annihilate them for nearly 300 years.

Part 2, "The World Begins," concludes with an ethnomusicological interlude providing an analysis of the social meanings of ceremonial musical performances at the time of my fieldwork in the upper Río Negro region in the early 1980s. As an ethnomusicologist who was studying indigenous music in the field in the 1980s, I became personally entangled in the special place of music in Wakuénai mythic history as a public vehicle for building relations of conviviality between different peoples. I carried a small acoustic guitar with me into the field and frequently sang American and Venezuelan folk songs for my Wakuénai hosts. I also learned how to make and play duets on long pairs of flutes (*máwi*, or *yapurutú*) that are played in *pudáli* ceremonies. I made handwritten transcriptions of these flute duets and learned how indigenous flute players used theme and variation as a method for improvising. After several months of living in Wakuénai villages along the Río Negro, I had learned how to improvise and compose new flute duets in collaboration with other men. A brief overview of *pudáli* ceremonies will be given in chapter 1, and I provide a more detailed account of these ceremonial musical performances and my experiences at learning them in chapter 5, "Ethnomusicological Interlude."

Part 3, "The World Opens Up," concludes with a narrative about a man who leaves his family and marries a white woman in a magical city made of gold. This city, called Temedawí, lies in the realm of disease-causing spirits of the forests and rivers. At one level, the story of Temedawí outlines a fairly simple, linear process of a man leaving his family to live in a supernaturalized version of the white people's city. However, the story also tells how this indigenous man transformed the white people's society into a giant healing machine based on shamanic curing practices. In the conclusion, "Ethnological Coda," I explore this narrative in relation to the political and historical changes that were unfolding in the Venezuelan Amazon in the 1990s.

Studying the narratives translated in this book is a project that has spanned most of my professional career and that has benefited from the generosity of many individuals and institutions. I am especially indebted to the late Horacio López Pequeira for his masterful tellings and explanations of "words from the primordial times" during my fieldwork in the 1980s. My thanks go also to Horacio's son, Félix López Oliveiros, who spent many long days in 1998 helping me to transcribe recordings of narrative speech and who wholeheartedly embraced the goals of recording and translating the entire cycle of mythic narratives about Made-from-Bone. I am grateful also to the extended family of Horacio and Félix as well as others living in Galito in the 1980s and Las Islettas in 1998 for their friendship and hospitality.

The late Hernán Camico, great-grandson of the legendary leader of messianic movements in the upper Río Negro region during the nineteenth century, cheerfully served as my guide and motorist while working with Curripaco speakers in Puerto Ayacucho and nearby communities in 1998. Hernán also let me rent his house in Maroa, which made an excellent jumping-off point for my travels on the Río Guainía. I will always treasure the memory of peaceful evenings spent with Hernán and his family while sitting under the little thatch-roofed *chiruata* behind their home in Puerto Ayacucho.

My sincerest thanks go to friend and fellow Arawak specialist Silvia Vidal, who helped me with applying for official government permission, opening a local bank account, buying field supplies, and all the nitty gritty practicalities of getting to and fro between Caracas and the Río Guainía. Other colleagues at the Department of Anthropology, Venezuelan Scientific Research Institute (IVIC), who provided moral, intellectual, and institutional support include Berta Perez, Dieter Heinen, Nelly Arvelo-Jímenez, Alberta Zucchi, Erika Wagner, Rafael Gasson, and Werner Wilbert.

Fieldwork in 1980–1981 during which I recorded sacred chanting and began to learn about Made-from-Bone was supported by dissertation grants from Fulbright-Hays, Social Science Research Council, and the American Council of Learned Societies. Fieldwork in 1984 and 1985 was funded by Fulbright-Hays Faculty Research Abroad and allowed me to continue studying sacred chants and begin recordings of "words from the primordial times." Travel to the Río Guainía in June through December 1998 afforded me the opportunity to place primary attention on narratives about Made-from-Bone and was supported by grants from the Office of Research and Development Administration at SIUC, National Endowment for the Humanities Summer

Research Stipends, and the Wenner-Gren Foundation for Anthropological Research. I am grateful to all these agencies for their support.

Two of my colleagues in the Department of Anthropology at SIUC, Prudence Rice and Andy Hofling, provided valuable comments on the initial proposal for this study, and a third, Anthony Webster, has generously shared his thoughts on Made-from-Bone from the perspective of a North Americanist who has grappled with the complexities of translating Navajo coyote poems. Two anonymous reviewers for the University of Illinois Press gave me a wealth of useful suggestions for improving the original version of the manuscript, and Norman Whitten Jr., editor of the *Interpretations of Culture in the New Millennium* series, did a helpful job of summarizing and interpreting the reviewers' comments. Finally, I am grateful to Joel Sherzer, Anthony Woodbury, and Heidi Johnson for inviting me to participate in their National Endowment for the Humanities project, "Archiving Significant Collections," at the Archives of Indigenous Languages of Latin America, University of Texas at Austin.

1

The Arawakan Wakuénai
of Venezuela

The Wakuénai, or Curripaco, live at the headwaters of the Río Negro, a region that is politically divided among the three countries of Venezuela, Colombia, and Brazil. From a modern perspective, the Wakuénai appear to be located in a marginal area that is far removed from major centers of power and commerce. However, when seen in the long run of history, Wakuénai ancestral lands are anything but marginal. Rather, they occupy the riverine territories that connect the central Amazon floodplains in the south to the Orinoco basin, grasslands, and Caribbean Sea to the north.

The Wakuénai language belongs to the Northern, or Maipuran, branch of the Arawak family. At the time of Columbus's first encounters with the Taíno and other indigenous peoples living in the Caribbean basin, Arawak was the most widespread language family in the Americas, extending for three thousand miles from the Taíno in the north all the way to the Chané and Terena in southern Brazil and for twenty-four hundred miles from the Yanesha in the west to the Palikur (Pa'ikwené) near the mouth of the Amazon River (see map 1). Linguistic reconstruction (Key 1979) shows that Arawak-speaking peoples occupied lands along a continuous, flowing network of rivers spreading like a gigantic handprint across South America and the Caribbean, with "fingers" radiating up to the headwaters of the main southern, southwestern, and northwestern tributaries of the Amazon River; across the Orinoco basin and its tributaries in the western grasslands of Venezuela; along the northeastern coast of South America; and up into the Caribbean basin. The Wakuénai view of their lands as the center of the world and as the place from which the world opened up through their ancestors' movements away

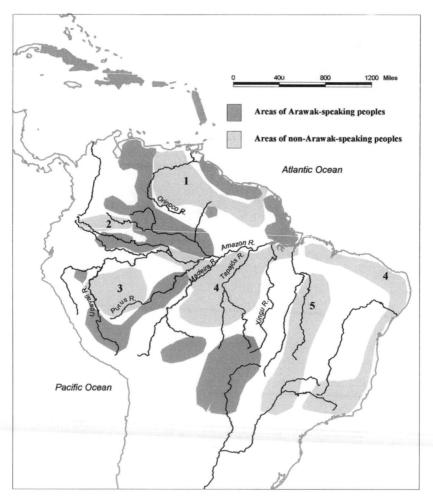

Map 1. Location of Arawakan language groups, fifteenth century

from and back to the mythic center makes perfect sense when understood in this broader historical and geographic perspective.

Five hundred years after Columbus's first encounters with the Taíno, the vast, continuous pattern of Arawak language groups across South America and the Caribbean has transformed into discrete pockets and clusters at the headwaters of major rivers, including the Orinoco, Negro, Purus, Ucayali, Madeira, and Xingu (see map 2).[1] Together with the lowlands of eastern Peru and westernmost Brazil, the upper Río Negro region of Venezuela, Colombia, and Brazil is one of the two areas where there is the greatest amount of linguistic, social, and cultural diversity among contemporary Arawak-speaking peoples.[2] The Wakuénai are the largest surviving group in the Northern, or Maipuran, branch of the Arawak language family.

The Wakuénai of Venezuela are located primarily in villages along the Guainía-Negro River from Victorino in the north to Cocuí in the south (see map 3). A smaller number of their villages are found along the lower Casiquiare River; the Río Atabapo and its tributaries, the Temi and Atacavi rivers; and neighborhoods and villages in and around Puerto Ayacucho. The number of Wakuénai speakers living in the Venezuelan Amazon has increased from 1,600 in the early 1980s (OCEI 1982 census) to 4,817 in 2002 (Programa Censal 2001).[3] Archaeological, linguistic, historical, and ethnographic evidence indicates that the Isana-Guainía drainage area of Venezuela, Colombia, and Brazil formed the core region of ancestral Wakuénai territories.

Wakuénai mythic narratives describe the creation of humanity as a process in which the trickster-creator, Made-from-Bone, raised the mythic ancestors

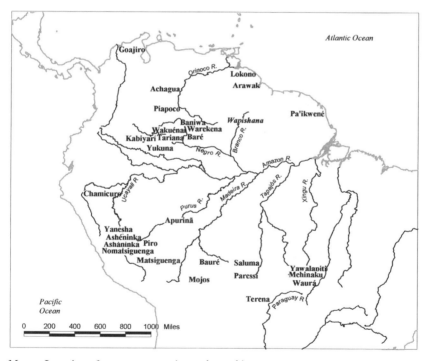

Map 2. Location of contemporary Arawak-speaking groups

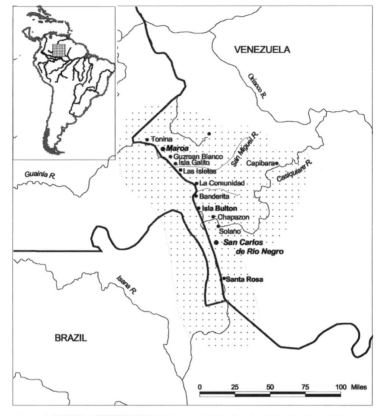

Map 3. Wakuénai (Curripaco) communities in the Río Guainía-Negro, Venezuelan Amazon, 1981

of Wakuénai phratries and patrisibs from a hole beneath the rapids at Hípana, a village on the Aiarí River in Brazil. In this myth, Made-from-Bone brought these ancestors to life by blowing tobacco smoke and giving each of them powerful spirit names. The narratives about mythic past times outline a process in which Made-from-Bone gradually shapes a world of primordial beginnings in which there is only one place into an expanding world of named, culturally and geographically distinct peoples and places. The contemporary world of fully human social groups and history unfolded as an opening up of the world through a series of movements away from and back to the mythic center, or place of emergence, at Hípana, during the cycle of mythic narratives about the birth, life, and "death" (or fiery transformation) of the primordial human being (*Kuwái*).

Wakuénai social organization is grounded in this understanding of mythic history as a series of outward expansions from and inward returns to the regional center at Hípana. The most dramatic social expressions of this process of mythic creation through opening up the world are the long series of *malikái* singing and chanting in male and female initiation rituals. These performances begin and end with singing that invokes First-Woman (*Ámaru*), her son (*Kuwái*), and their attachment to the world of living human beings via a celestial umbilical cord at Hípana, the place of ancestral emergence and "navel" of the world. Between the opening and closing songs, a series of chants lasting for several hours names all the places where Made-from-Bone traveled as he chased after First-Woman and tried to take back the sacred flutes and trumpets. In both male and female initiation rituals, sacred *malikái* singing and chanting aims to purify the sacred food, called *káridzámai*, that becomes the initiates' first meal as adult persons.

Place-naming in female initiation rituals moves down the Isana and Negro rivers and across the Casiquiare, Guainía, and Cuyarí rivers, musically mapping out the Isana-Guainía headwater region that forms the ancestral homeland of the Wakuénai (see map 4). In male initiation rituals, the chanting of place-names encompasses a much larger area of riverine territories extending from the Upper Río Negro downstream to the Lower Río Negro where it joins the Amazon River at Manaus and beyond, all the way to the mouth of the Amazon on the Atlantic Coast. Returning back upstream to the Upper Río Negro, the chanting of place-names continues north and east through the Atabapo and Middle Orinoco rivers until reaching the mouth of the Orinoco in the Caribbean Sea (see map 5). This enormous expanse of riverine territories is roughly equivalent to the geographic distribution of the northern branch of the Arawakan language family prior to the European colonization of South America in the sixteenth century. The chanting of place-names in initiation rituals is an episodic reopening of the world, an enchantment of the historical connections between the Wakuénai and their homeland in the Isana-Guainía headwater region, and a dynamic reconstruction of social networks that once extended across the two largest river systems in northern South America.

The basic unit of Wakuénai social organization is a group of brothers and their descendants who recognize shared identity by virtue of patrilineal descent from a common mythic ancestor. Anthropologists call such organization a "patrisib." Groups of four or five patrisibs are hierarchically organized into phratries on the basis of the order of mythic emergence of ancestral spirits. Patrisibs descending from firstborn, or "emerged," ancestors are the most

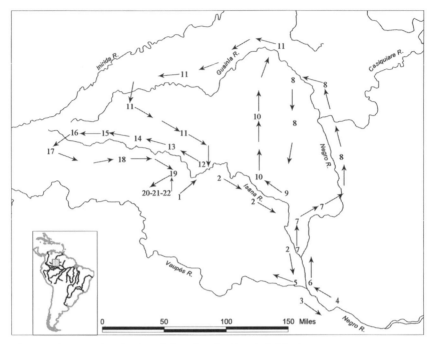

Map 4. Place-naming in ritual chanting for female initiation

highly ranked groups within each phratry and are referred to as "the older brothers." Lower-ranked sibs, or "younger brothers," are descended from mythic ancestors that were "born" or "emerged" later. Wakuénai phratries are internally ranked, but there is no evidence that there was ranking among the different phratries.

In spite of dislocations and migrations in the colonial and more recent periods, there are still strong associations between each phratry and specific riverine territories in the Isana-Guainía drainage area: the "Owners of the Jaguar" (*Dzáwinai*) phratry of Tonowí and the middle Isana River, the "Children of the Wild Chicken" (*Hohódeni*) phratry of the Aiarí River, the "Owners of the Duck" (*Kumadámnainai*) phratry of the upper Isana River, the "Grandchildren of the Pleiades" (*Waríperídakéna*) phratry of the Cuyarí River, the "Children of the Armadillo" (*Adzanéni*) phratry of the upper and middle Guainía River, and the "Owners of the Firefly" (*Tuirímnainai*) phratry of the middle and lower Guainía River (see map 6).

Most of the Wakuénai living along the Guainía-Negro River in Venezuela are members of the Adzanéni, *Dzáwinai, Waríperídakéna,* and *Tuirímnainai*

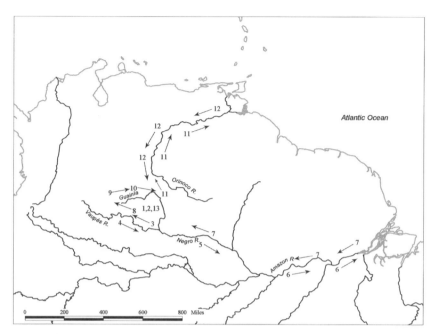

Map 5. Place-naming in ritual chanting for male initiation

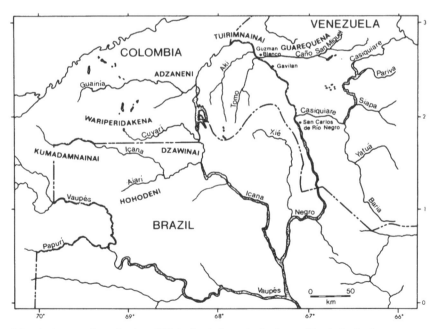

Map 6. Ancestral territories of Wakuénai phratries in Isana-Guainía drainage area

phratries. Since all the patrisibs within each phratry regard one another as brothers, they collectively form a single expanded mythic family that serves as the unit of marital exogamy. Postmarital residence is virilocal after a brief, one- to two-year period of bride service during which young men reside uxorilo- cally in their wives' families' villages and demonstrate their proficiencies at clearing forest plots for manioc gardening, fishing, and other basic economic activities. In addition, there is a direct linkage between marriage and rank, resulting in a pattern of "rank endogamy." Men from highest-ranked groups intermarry with women from comparably ranked groups, thereby ensuring that elite status and ritual hierarchy will persist across generations.

The ranking of patrisibs within phratries and its linkage to marriage prac- tices was still very much in evidence among the senior generation of men and women at the time of my fieldwork in the 1980s. Horacio and his brother, Herminio, were members of the second-highest ranked patrisib in the "Own- ers of the Jaguar" (*Dzáwinai*) phratry. Their wives, Antonia and Maria, were two sisters from the most highly ranked patrisib in the "Grandchildren of the Pleiades" (*Waríperídakéna*) phratry. This core group of highly ranked *Dzáwinai* men and their highly ranked *Waríperídakéna* wives formed the backbone of local social organization in the early 1980s.

However, rank endogamy and related practices, such as bride service and cross-cousin marriages, were giving way in the next generation of adults to marriages based on individual choice and other factors. For political and eco- nomic reasons, many young adults chose to marry members of other indig- enous groups who were more firmly established in the Venezuelan Amazon, such as the Baniwa, Guarequena, Baré, and Ye'kuana. Horacio's son Félix was married to his mother's brother's daughter, a highly ranked *Waríperídakéna* woman in 1980, but that marriage ended in divorce in 1982. By 1984, Félix had remarried a Baniwa woman from a prominent local family in Maroa. Félix's older sister Felicia had been married to a Ye'kuana man since the late 1960s. This trend toward interethnic marriage continued to accelerate in the 1990s and began to include an increasing number of marriages between Wakuénai women and nonindigenous (criollo) men from Puerto Ayacucho and other, more distant Venezuelan cities. When I returned to the Río Guainía in 1998, Felicia's oldest daughter, Ester, had married a criollo man and moved to Puerto Ayacucho with him in the early 1990s.

Wakuénai social organization is also grounded in language practices. There are different ways of saying "yes" (*áh-han, óh-hon, éh-hen*) or "no" (*cúrri, carrú, ñáme*), which have given names to the five major dialects of Wakuénai. There are strong associations between these different dialects and specific phratries. The Áh-han dialect is spoken mainly by the Adzanéni, Óh-hon by the Waríperídakéna, Óh-hon or Carrú by the Dzáwinai, Éh-hen by the Tuirímnainai, and Ñáme by the Hohódeni. In spite of significant lexical differences among these dialects, the Wakuénai regard all five dialects to be a single, mutually intelligible language rather than five distinct languages.[4] The term "Curripaco" most accurately describes the Áh-han-speaking Adzanéni and appears to have been adopted as the name for the entire set of dialect groups and phratries because Protestant missionaries chose to use the Áh-han, or Curripaco, dialect for their published translation of the New Testament. A more accurate ethnonym for all five dialect groups and associated phratries is "Wakuénai," or "People Who Speak Our Language," and that is the term I will use throughout this book.

The Wakuénai are masters of the headwater regions of the Guainía-Negro River, an area lying between 1 and 3 degrees north of the equator and forming a natural connection between rivers flowing northward into Venezuela (Orinoco and Atabapo) and southward into Brazil (Casiquiare and Guainía-Negro). The Atabapo, lower Casiquiare, and Guainía-Negro are blackwater rivers draining geologically ancient, nutrient-poor soils. Analysis of nutrient flows in forests near San Carlos de Río Negro have demonstrated that more than 98 percent of available nutrients are locked up in tightly closed recycling loops within the living components of the forest (Herrera et al. 1978). These white sand, blackwater ecosystems are so acidic (3 to 6 pH) that mosquitoes are unable to breed, and the region is relatively free of malaria, yellow fever, and other mosquito-borne diseases.

Producing or procuring sufficient food in the region's acidic rivers and sandy soils is difficult, and the Río Negro came to be known as "The River of Hunger" during the colonial period. Due to the region's proximity to the equator, rainfall is heavy throughout the year (3,600 mm average annual total). The slightly drier months of December through March allow people barely enough time to clear new gardens (*conucos*) and take advantage of more productive fishing and hunting conditions as the rivers fall to their lowest levels of the year. Burning of felled vegetation in February and March is crucial for successful gardening, since carbon and organic materials from burning and decaying vegetation is the main source of nutrients for garden soils and cultigens. Heavy rains in late March and April signal the start of a dramatic, seven-meter rise in river levels, resulting in the submersion of 65 percent of the region's forests. The long wet season from April through August is a period of scarcity when fishing and hunting productivity declines to a bare minimum. During the transition from dry to wet seasons in March and April (referred to as "The Mouth of the Pleiades," or *wáripérihnúme,* in Wakuénai), people experience a brief period of superabundance during the spawning migrations of bocachico (*Leporinus* spp.) fish. As the rivers and streams flood their banks, large schools of bocachico migrate into the newly flooded forests to spawn and are captured in weirs and traps as they return to the main channel of the river.

The Guainía-Negro River is characterized by a pronounced alternation between relative abundance of food in drier, low-water months and relatively severe scarcity in wetter, high-water months. Wakuénai economic activities are directly tied to this pattern of alternating abundance and scarcity. Looking broadly across the Isana-Guainía drainage area, the configuration of internally ranked phratric territories can be understood as a highly efficient human settlement pattern designed to take full advantage of the natural spawning migrations of various fish species into the headwater region and the annual felling and burning of forest vegetation to make gardens. A detailed study of nutritional status in four villages along the Guainía-Negro and lower Casiquiare rivers came to the surprising conclusion that the Wakuénai are generally well nourished, even at the height of the wet season (Holmes 1981). Another study demonstrated that bitter manioc production in *conucos* outside of San Carlos de Río Negro had an energy efficiency ratio of 10 calories output per 1 calorie of input, even in the sandy, nutrient-poor soils of the region (Uhl 1980).

Wakuénai socioecology cannot be reduced to purely material or technological factors alone but must be understood also in terms of social organization and related cultural practices. Ritual specialists known as chant owners (*malikái limínali*) and shamans (*malírri*) serve as community leaders in major rites of passage at childbirth and male and female puberty initiations as well as at times of individual or collective misfortune, illness, or death. As the intermediaries between mythic ancestors and their human descendants, both living and dead, chant owners and shamans have ritual powers that allow them to transform the relatively egalitarian relations of everyday social life into more hierarchical, exclusive, and tightly integrated forms of social organization. These special ritual powers become evident in any situation of danger, such as life-threatening illness or childbirth, but are most clearly manifested at times of collective misfortune, such as the measles epidemic that afflicted Wakuénai villages of the Guainía-Negro River in early 1981. Such epidemics are understood as a complete breakdown of relations between mythic ancestors and human descendants, analogous to a bolt of lightning that can strike and instantly kill an entire community. In this situation, chant owners must harvest the reddish-colored honey of the most powerful bee species, called *éenui* (*Trigona* sp.) and fumigate the village with smoke made by burning the resinous hive material. The entire village participates in the ritual drinking of *éenui* honey, and relations with other communities are suspended until illness and death have come to a halt. The ritual powers of chant owners and shamans provide an alternative, more hierarchical way of organizing local social relations in contexts of individual illnesses, collective epidemics, life-cycle transitions, and wet season deprivation.

The power of ritual leaders recedes into the background once the period of heightened ritual danger has ended, and people can return to a more egalitarian mode of organization. In conditions of relative abundance, Wakuénai social organization opens up and expands through daily sharing of cooked foods at communal meals, informal visiting between communities, and seasonal exchanges of smoked fish and game meat for processed manioc pulp in ceremonies called *pudáli*. These ceremonial exchanges can take place at any time of year whenever a local group has accumulated a large surplus of fish or game meat. However, the most common time to begin *pudáli* ceremonies is at the beginning of the long wet season in March and April when large quantities of bocachico fish have been captured in weirs after spawning in newly flooded forests.

In an opening, male-owned ceremony, a group travels by river with a gift of smoked fish and game meat and offers it to a group of potential affines in another community. As guests arrive with baskets of smoked meat, they form large ensembles of male flute and trumpet players accompanied by female dancers. Several pairs of *máwi* (or *yapurutú,* Yeral) flute players perform the standard, opening melody of *pudáli* and lead the procession in counterclockwise circles around the offering of food.

Behind the *máwi* flute players are men playing *kulirrína* trumpets, which are named after a species of large catfish (*kulírri,* or *surubím,* Yeral). The deep, rumbling bass sounds of these trumpets are said to reproduce the sound of streams and rivers filled to the brim with schools of migrating, spawning bocachico fish.

After these opening dances, which are named after different species of bocachico fish, the guests' headman formally offers the gift of smoked meat to the hosts for safekeeping during the night of drinking and singing. In the morning, the hosts' headman redistributes the food to guest and host families, beginning an entire day of feasting, dancing, making music, and socializing. At the end of this opening, male-owned *pudáli,* the guests give their *kulirrína* trumpets to their hosts as reminders of their obligation to hold a closing, female-owned *pudáli* several weeks later. Female-owned *pudáli* ceremonies are similar to male-owned ceremonies but differ in two important ways: the gift of food consists of processed manioc pulp rather than smoked meat, and dance-stamping tubes (*wáana*) are played instead of *kulirrína* trumpets.

Pudáli ceremonial cycles are complex cultural performances and multivocally evoke—through musical sounds, song texts, formal speeches, dancing, and mythic narratives—a variety of natural sounds and behaviors of fish, bird, and forest animal species from the Guainía-Negro region. The great German ethnographer Kurt Nimuendajú traveled among the Wakuénai living along the Isana River in the 1920s and asserted that the *surubím* (*kulirrína*) trumpets were the quintessential artifact of Wakuénai material culture (1950 [1927]). The making and playing of *kulirrína* trumpets brings the sounds and behaviors of rivers teeming with migrating, spawning fish into the realm of collective human social interaction, thereby making the natural processes of ecosystemic renewal into a metaphor for human social reproduction. In cultural terms, *pudáli* ceremonies are collective constructions of the mythic past, a precultural time before the distinctions between humans and animals, men and women, and the living and the dead had come into being. *Pudáli* ceremonies also embody the social processes of creating new relations of friendship, trade, and intermarriage through intercommunal exchanges of cooked and processed foods.

The Wakuénai have developed extensive networks of trade and intermarriage relations with other groups. Prior to European colonization, the Wakuénai were located at the center of a vast diaspora of Northern Arawak-speaking peoples: the Taíno of the greater Antilles, Lokono of coastal Guyana, Achagua of the western llanos, Maipure of the middle Orinoco, Manao of the lower Río Negro, and many neighboring groups in the Guainía-Negro and Casiquiare region (for example, Baré, Piapoco, and Guarequena).

The Wakuénai actively engage in interethnic trade and intermarriage not only with other Arawak-speaking peoples but also with Carib, Tukano, Saliba, Yeral, and other non-Arawakan groups. Prior to European colonization and as late as the eighteenth century, Wakuénai traders traveled to the middle Orinoco area during the January-to-March dry season to trade forest products for *quirípa* shell money, cotton cloth, salt, turtle eggs, smoked fish, and other goods that circulated through the vast trading networks of northern South America and the Caribbean (Morey and Morey 1975). In areas where trade and intermarriage have continued over several generations, the Wakuénai have formed transethnic relations with neighboring peoples such as the Yeral, Cubeo, and Uanano, resulting in "Arawakanized" Tukano speakers and

"Tukanoized" Arawak speakers along the Vaupés and Isana rivers in Brazil and Colombia.

The vast diaspora of northern Arawak-speaking peoples that had stretched from the Greater and Lesser Antilles in the north to the main floodplain of the Amazon River in the south in precontact times was sharply diminished by the ravages of disease, missionization, ethnic soldiering, and the slave trade during the colonial period. Larger, more sedentary agricultural peoples with strongly hierarchical forms of sociopolitical organization, such as the Taíno, Lokono, Achagua, and Maipure, had been reduced to mere remnants by the time of the Jesuit missions' expulsion from South America in 1767. Ancestors of the Wakuénai living in the headwater regions of the Guainía-Río Negro and adjacent Isana River were caught between two expanding, predatory colonial forces: Portuguese-Brazilian traders and missionaries from the south and east and Dutch-Carib slave traders from the north. Arawak-speaking groups living in the llanos and middle Orinoco initially profited from the lucrative trading of indigenous slaves from inland forests to the south, but eventually these middlemen themselves became objects of the slave trade. Between 1745 and 1755, Brazilian traders removed approximately twenty thousand indigenous peoples as slaves from the upper Río Negro region to plantations in coastal states of Pará and Maranhão (Wright 1981). After the official end of indigenous slavery in 1767, the Brazilian policy of forced relocations, or "descents" (*descimentos*), further weakened indigenous populations. Massive epidemics of influenza, smallpox, measles, and other exogenous diseases spread throughout the upper Río Negro region in the 1780s and 1790s, resulting in the total abandonment of nearly all communities along the Isana.

Spanish colonial presence in the Upper Orinoco, Casiquiare, and Guainía-Río Negro began with the military expedition of José Solano in 1758 and resulted in the founding of outposts at San Fernando de Atabapo, La Esmeralda, Solano, San Carlos de Río Negro, and Maroa. During the last half of the eighteenth century, the entire region had become a frontier "no-man's land." The Spanish military and missionary project of linking the Upper Orinoco at La Esmeralda to the Lower Orinoco at Angostura (Ciudad Bolívar) via a series of overland roads and forts was crushed by a Ye'kuana-led uprising in 1776 that mobilized support from Arawak-speaking groups in the Guainía-Río Negro (Baré, Guarequena, Baniwa, and Wakuénai) and other groups in the Middle and Upper Orinoco (Guss 1986).

Given the severity of political-economic, cultural, and biological forces that came together in the late colonial period, it is reasonable to wonder how the ancestors of today's Wakuénai even managed to survive into the modern period of nation-states. There are three general ways of answering this question. First, the collapse of colonial European governments and outbreak of revolutionary warfare in the llanos, Lower Orinoco, and other areas well removed from the Guainía-Río Negro resulted in a period of recovery when the Wakuénai and other Arawakan groups were relatively free from enslavement, missionization, and epidemics.

Second, written historical sources and indigenous oral histories both point to the importance of mobility as a key to local group survival. When diseases, slave traders, or other threatening forces came from downstream in Brazil, whole communities of people would pack up their belongings and migrate to safety in areas to the north or west that were beyond the Brazilian sphere of influence. Or they moved into smaller tributaries of the Isana and Guainía-Río Negro, such as the Aki, Tomo, or Caño San Miguel, where they could safely avoid colonial authorities. These movements, or "survival migrations," continue into the present as the Wakuénai in Colombia flee into Venezuela and Brazil to escape political violence. The association of movements from downstream to upstream with the escape from life-threatening illness, or witchcraft, to health remains strong in shamanic curing songs (Hill 1993, 2005).

A third way in which the Wakuénai's ancestors survived the atrocities and calamities of the late colonial period was through forming interethnic political confederacies in response to specific threats. The Ye'kuana-led rebellion against Spanish authorities in 1776 was the last in a series of such movements, which had an average duration of twenty years (Vidal 2002). Although these confederacies rose and fell in rapid succession, they played an important role in allowing indigenous peoples of the Orinoco and Guainía-Río Negro basin to organize themselves against colonial predation.

During the first half of the nineteenth century, the Wakuénai returned to their villages along the Guainía-Río Negro and Isana River in order to reconstitute their territorialized, internally ranked phratries centered around the place of mythic emergence at Hípana. However, by midcentury, many Wakuénai had become indebted to traders in San Carlos de Río Negro, Maroa, and other towns in the region, creating fertile conditions for social unrest. One such moment came on St. John's Day of 1858, when a Baniwa man named Venancio Camico prophesied the coming of a great fire that would destroy the white men's world and, along with it, the debt peonage in which the Wakuénai, Baré, and Baniwa had become ensnared. Although Venancio's movement was quelled by military authorities and missionaries, he escaped from captivity and continued to live at Makareo on the Caño Aki until his death in 1903

(Wright and Hill 1986). His teachings of resistance to the white's economy of indebtedness were absorbed into the ritual advice that Wakuénai elders and ritual specialists gave to their children in male and female initiation rituals (Matos Arvelo 1912). Through legends and oral histories, Venancio Camico continues to be regarded as a folk hero and saint-like figure by the Baniwa and Wakuénai of the Guainía-Río Negro region (Hill and Wright 1988).

The Amazon rubber boom (ca. 1860–1920) unleashed a new wave of violence and economic exploitation against the Wakuénai. The worst atrocities happened during the final years, when the boom was in rapid decline due to competition with newly created rubber plantations in southeast Asia. A rubber baron turned dictator named Tomas Funes raided indigenous peoples throughout the upper Orinoco, Casiquiare, and Guainía-Río Negro region, devastating entire villages of men, women, and children. Only the end of the rubber boom and Funes' execution by mutinous soldiers in San Fernando de Atabapo in 1923 brought an end to the violence, which was far worse even than the violence of the late colonial period. While the Baré and many other groups of the Guainía-Río Negro suffered tremendous losses of population during the rubber boom, the Wakuénai were able to survive in greater numbers by fleeing into remote areas away from major rivers and through survival migrations into Brazilian and Colombian territories beyond the reach of Funes and his soldiers. Many of the Wakuénai living in the Venezuelan Amazon in the late twentieth century claimed to have returned to locations where their grandparents had lived prior to Funes' reign of terror.

After the establishment in 1946 of a fundamentalist North American religious mission in Amazonas, the New Tribes, large numbers of Wakuénai converted to evangelical Christianity during the 1950s and '60s under the leadership of Sophia Muller. Sophia and her New Tribes colleagues labored to eradicate all of the most central elements of indigenous Wakuénai religious beliefs and practices. Indigenous people were taught to be ashamed of their social and religious practices, which were labeled in frankly denigrative terms as "evil" forms of "devil worship." Indigenous shamans and chant owners were especially targeted as agents of evil, and most of them were ostracized by their own kin groups. In their place, the missionaries constructed a neocolonial power structure of indigenous pastors. The missionaries also campaigned against Wakuénai social practices, including cross-cousin marriage, bride service, and rank endogamy. By the 1980s, an entire generation of Wakuénai-speakers had been born and raised into believing that their ancestors' way of life was an evil thing of the past. The minority who continued to practice indigenous rituals was ostracized by their evangelical kinsmen and took refuge by becoming affiliated with the Catholic Salesian mission that had worked in the Venezuelan Amazon since 1933. The number of Wakuénai-speakers remained high or even increased, since the missionaries translated the entire New Testament into Curripaco and conducted monthly "Semana Santa" services in that language. By the time of my fieldwork with the Wakuénai in the early 1980s, there were very few senior men who still actively practiced the singing and chanting of shamanic curing rituals and major rites of passage. A somewhat more tolerant attitude toward these ritual specialists had developed by the 1990s among many of the evangelical Wakuénai, who were frequent consumers of shamanic ritual healing.

The missionaries' ideology equated "good" with "Christianity," "modernity," and "capitalist prosperity." Much like the founding ideologies of the architects of independent nation-states in the early nineteenth century, the missionaries targeted indigenous traditions as an uncivilized, past, "evil," ignorant savagery that would over time be assimilated into a future state of civilized, enlightened modernity. It is not a coincidence that the missionaries' propagation of a staunchly nationalist trope of modernity in the 1950s through 1970s flourished in the context of Cold War ideological battles between good-Christian-capitalism and evil-atheistic-communism (see Hill 1994a). World War II and the ensuing Cold War brought an increased geopolitical awareness of the need for secure international borders in Venezuela, Brazil, and Colombia, so the Wakuénai found themselves divided by citizenship in three nation-states as well as by sectarian divisions between Salesian Catholicism and evangelical (Southern Baptist) Protestantism.

By the time of my fieldwork in the upper Río Negro region in 1998, it was clear that the shift to literacy as a way of preserving and transmitting cultural knowledge was part of a broader process of change. Compared to the 1980s, there was much less collective sharing of food and other goods. Instead of holding one or more communal meals each day like his father had done, Félix and his nuclear family ate in their own household. Collective rituals and ceremonies marking off passages in the life cycle or the forming of political alliances among kin groups were much less frequently practiced than they had been in the 1980s. Political and religious divisions within Wakuénai communities had the effect of undermining the cultural and economic practices that had allowed them to reconstitute their social world in the aftermath of colonial oppression and rubber boom terror.

The entire country of Venezuela was a beehive of political activity during the election year of 1998. In the national election, Hugo Chávez, who had been the leader of a failed coup d'etat in 1992, won a landslide victory as the new president and promised to make radical changes to the "corruptocracy." At local and regional levels, however, the established political parties held on to control over gubernatorial and legislative positions of power. Back in the early 1980s, such political changes would have had only sporadic effects on indigenous peoples living in remote areas such as the Upper Río Negro. By the late 1990s, the Wakuénai and other indigenous peoples of the Amazon region had become actively engaged in Venezuelan politics, in large part because Amazonas had gone from the status of federal territory with appointed leaders to statehood with elected leaders in 1991. This changing political landscape held out the promise of potential gains for indigenous peoples but also raised the possibility of increasing factionalism, individualism, cronyism, and corruption within indigenous communities. In local and regional elections, households and individuals became allied with one or another of a large number of gubernatorial candidates, resulting in political schisms that sharply divided supporters of the different candidates. At a more general, regional, and national level, the end of the Cold War and decentralization of national power structures had opened up new cultural and political spaces for indigenous peoples to recover or revitalize their cultural identities. Sadly, the campaigns of cultural transformation during the Cold War had resulted in a generation of young adults who were left with little of the cultural knowledge and competence of their parents' generation.

The 1990s was also a period when the various indigenous groups of Amazonas began to organize themselves into a pan-indigenous political group called *Organización Regional de Pueblos Indígenas de Amazonas* (ORPIA). In 1997, ORPIA won a major victory in the Venezuelan Supreme Court in a decision that nullified the 1994 Law of Political-Territorial Division. The Supreme Court supported ORPIA's argument that these divisions (called *municipios*) were based on urban criteria and had failed to consider "la especifidad indígena," the cosmovision and sociocultural organization of the ethnic groups. The regime of exception for indigenous communities meant that the new *municipios* must be adapted to the specific cultural, ecological, economic, geographic, and historical conditions of indigenous communities. Beyond this goal, the regime of exception, as it became elaborated and interpreted by the Supreme Court and in the indigenous organizations' subsequent "Project on the Law of Division" (November 19, 1997), was designed to allow indigenous peoples to participate in local and state government in ways that would harmonize the rights and interests of indigenous and nonindigenous populations in the region (Informe Annual 1998:57).

The 1997 Supreme Court decision in favor of ORPIA and the regime of exception for indigenous communities foreshadowed the profound legal and political changes that were to take place after Hugo Chávez's election as president of Venezuela in December 1998. As part of a more general restructuring of government, "The National Congress and Supreme Court were dismantled without signs of public affliction" (Coronil 2000, 38). The new national constitution that emerged from a year of constitutional assemblies in 1999 gave explicit recognition to the rights of indigenous peoples to "maintain and develop their ethnic and cultural identity, cosmovision, values, spirituality, and sacred places and rituals" (Constitución 1999: Capítulo 8, Artículo 121, my translation). Indigenous leaders such as Noeli Pocatierra were active participants in the 1999 assemblies that drew up the new constitution, which also included text guaranteeing "indigenous representation in the National Assembly and the deliberative bodies of the federal and local entities with indigenous populations" (Constitución 1999: Capítulo 8, Artículo 125, my translation). In a law passed in December 2000, the National Assembly gave clear definitions to the terms "indígenas," "hábitat indígena," "tierras indígenas," "pueblos indígenas," and "comunidades indígenas" and spelled out the policies and agencies that would govern the demarcation of indigenous lands (Asamblea Nacional 2000). These new laws and policies provide important opportunities for Venezuela's indigenous peoples, including the Wakuénai and other Arawak-speaking peoples of the upper Río Negro region. It remains to be seen whether and how the national government can effectively implement these new laws. However, it is clear that the new constitution of 1999 and subsequent laws have created a framework of legal rights and official recognition for indigenous cultural differences in ways that radically depart from previous national laws and that will continue to shape indigenous peoples' relations with the Venezuelan nation-state far into the twenty-first century.

Part 1

Words from the Primordial Times

Overview

The primordial times are explored in a cycle of narratives that focus on the invincibility of Made-from-Bone (*Iñápirríkuli*). These narratives are set in the distant past, before there were cultural distinctions between human and animal beings, men and women, old and young, day and night, here and there. What *is* present from the very beginning of primordial times is an irreducible principle of violence, deceit, and hostility between kin and affines. The story of how Made-from-Bone originally came into being starts with an act of violence in which a woman's husband kills her brother. Specifically, an evil animal-person whose name means "Great Sickness" (*Kunáhwerrim*) murders his wife's brother. The woman saves the bones of her slain brother's outer fingers, which then transform into two Cricket-Brothers. The narrative continues with a series of episodes in which Great Sickness tries in vain to kill the Cricket-Brothers. In this first story, the narrator does not yet use the name Made-from-Bone to refer to the Cricket-Brothers.[1] However, the story itself is called "The Origin of Made-from-Bone," and it is generally understood that the older of the two brothers is the forerunner of Made-from-Bone, the trickster-creator who goes on to become the central character in all three periods of mythic time. The Cricket-Brothers already possess the invincibility of Made-from-Bone because they always know in advance what Great Sickness is planning and manage to escape by transforming into different species of forest animals, insects, or birds. The story ends when the Cricket-Brothers trick their uncle, Great Sickness, into eating a pot of human flesh in which they had thrown poison.

The theme of violent interactions between kin and affines continues to develop through the next eight narratives. Like the more general organization of narratives into three cycles, or periods of time, the order of narratives making up the primordial times (*úupi pérri*) reflects collaborative decisions that Félix Oliveiros and I made during my fieldwork in 1998. The cycle begins and ends with a pair of stories that feature violent struggles between Made-from-Bone and his archenemy, Great Sickness. Between these beginning and ending stories are five narratives in which Made-from-Bone or members of his family fight against other kinds of dangerous animal spirits: a poison-bearing Owl-Monkey, a lecherous Anaconda-Person, bloodthirsty Bat-People, dangerous Fish-Spirits (*Yópinai*), and carrion-eating Vulture-People.

Immediately after the story about the origin of Made-from-Bone comes a narrative that explains the origin of death. In this second narrative, Great Sickness invites Made-from-Bone and his family to a *pudáli* ceremony and tries to kill them all by throwing poison into their drinks. Made-from-Bone's aunt (his father's sister) brings along medicine that saves everyone except the youngest brother, *Máwirríkuli,* who dies because the supply of medicine runs out. Made-from-Bone manages to bring his brother back to life by blowing tobacco smoke over his bones, but his magic is undone when the brother's wife violates the taboo against looking at her revived husband before Made-from-Bone can bring him the sacred food that would have completely restored him to life.

Having powers of clairvoyance, invincibility, and magical protection allows Made-from-Bone to thwart his enemies' attempts to kill him. However, such powers do not allow Made-from-Bone to stop the violence by cutting it off at its source or to completely block its effects on other members of his family, such as his youngest brother (*Máwirríkuli*). It is as if the original acts of killing with poison in the first two stories of the cycle have opened up a Pandora's box that can never again be closed. The limits of Made-from-Bone's ability to prevent outbreaks of violence become evident again in a narrative about Owl-Monkey, who has become the owner of poison. Made-from-Bone tries to put an end to the poison by secretly moving the monkeys' favorite fruit tree into the middle of a river late at night so that they will drown or be eaten by alligators. But the plan fails when Owl-Monkey transforms into a tiny ant and floats downstream in the husk of a dried-up fruit.

The myth of Anaconda-Person (*Uliámali*) offers a variation on the general theme of violence centered on relations between kin and affines. In this story, it is not a male affine (brother or father-in-law) but the wife who betrays Made-from-Bone and the wife's lover—Anaconda-Person—who becomes his principal adversary. Made-from-Bone learns of his wife's adulterous sexual relations with Anaconda-Person and kills him with poisoned darts and arrows. Made-from-Bone travels far downstream to cut off the snake-person's penis, brings the severed organ back upstream to his village, and tricks his wife into eating the penis by disguising it as a fish. The wife then becomes pregnant with an anaconda-child, who grows to enormous proportions inside his mother while stealing her food. With the help of her family, the woman manages to "give birth" to the snake-child by tricking it into climbing up a tall tree. In the end, however, both the woman and her snake-child are banished from the village of Made-from-Bone.

A narrative about the origin of bats continues the theme of bloodshed, violence, adultery, and revenge. Made-from-Bone and the other men are away from their village on a hunting expedition when the Bat-People show up and begin dancing and drinking with the local women. Late at night, when the women are drunk, the Bat-People begin taking them away in groups of three to kill them and eat their flesh. *Éeri*, one of Made-from-Bone's younger brothers, sees what is happening and follows the Bat-People to their village. When the hunters return home and learn of their wives' demise, *Éeri* leads them to the Bat-People's home to kill them.

A narrative about the origins of cooking with hot peppers returns to the theme of tension and violence between kin and affine. This time Made-from-Bone is not pitted against his archrival, Great Sickness, but an equally dangerous adversary known as *Yópinai*, a category of disease-causing spirits living in the forests and rivers. Made-from-Bone captures a *Yópinai* woman and takes her to live with him as his wife. When Made-from-Bone and his wife return to visit her family in the river, the *Yópinai* father-in-law is angry and wants to kill and eat Made-from-Bone and the bird-people who accompany him. Made-from-Bone uses hot red peppers and other means to thwart the *Yópinai*'s plans to kill him. The narrative provides one of the clearest demonstrations of the trickster-creator's powers of omniscience and invincibility. The *Yópinai* father-in-law sums it all up in two statements: "He knows in advance what I want to do" and "It is impossible to kill and eat Made-from-Bone."

Made-from-Bone is conspicuously absent from the lengthy narrative about the origin of vultures. The protagonist of the story is identified only as "a cousin of Made-from-Bone," and the action begins when this man finds a flock of Vulture-People stealing hot peppers from his mother's manioc garden. The man captures a young vulture-woman and takes her home to live with him as his wife. When the man and his vulture-wife go to visit her family, there is an initial, brief expression of potential violence between the man and his father-in-law/uncle. However, in this narrative, the father-in-law does not continue in an adversarial role but takes the young man hunting and fishing and even helps him by finding ways to accommodate the fact that he eats fresh meat, whereas Vulture-People eat only rotten meat. Violent opposition between kin and affines resurfaces in the figure of the wife's grandfather, who challenges the man to perform difficult tasks of making a canoe and weaving a hammock in an impossibly short time. In both cases, the man avoids the grandfather-vulture's threat to kill and eat him through help from a brother-in-law (the youngest of his wife's brothers). After overcoming these challenges, a son is born to the man and his wife, who eventually return with the boy to live with the man's mother. But the story ends with the failure of the man's marriage to the vulture-woman, who takes their son back to the Vulture-People's village and never returns.

The story of the Vulture-People thus explores many of the same themes of violence, or at least the potential for violence, between kin and affines found in so many other stories set in primordial times. However, it does so by inverting basic patterns of everyday social life. The man's marriage to a vulture-woman works only so long as the couple resides uxorilocally in the wife's family's village, thereby inverting the social practice of virilocal residence after a brief period of bride service in the wife's family's village. The fact that the man's father-in-law and brother-in-law help him adjust to their carrion-eating lifestyle and overcome dangerous challenges is in direct contrast to the usual pattern in which fathers- and brothers-in-law are depicted as potentially lethal adversaries of Made-from-Bone.

The cycle of narratives reaches a climax in the story of Great Sickness, or the origin of malaria. Like the story of the origin of Made-from-Bone, that of Great Sickness begins with an act of sheer violence against Made-from-Bone and his family. A younger brother of Made-from-Bone is married to the daughter of Great Sickness, and her brothers ruthlessly kill him while they are fishing in a stream with *barbasco* poison. Made-from-Bone takes his revenge against Great Sickness through a number of clever tricks and disguises. By cooking blood squeezed from his dead brother's heart and blowing tobacco smoke over it, Made-from-Bone creates a gigantic hawk that grabs Great Sickness and kills him by flying far away and dropping his body into the Orinoco River. As the body of Great Sickness rots beneath the river, it gives off poisons that make people sick with malaria when they drink from the river. With this victory over Great Sickness, Made-from-Bone decides to take pity on the children of Great Sickness by blowing tobacco smoke to help them overcome their sorrow at the loss of their father.

The narrative explaining the origin of evil omens brings the primordial times to a conclusion by demonstrating that Made-from-Bone has reached a new level of trickery. In this narrative, the trickster-creator does not just use his powers of omniscience and invincibility to thwart his enemies but creatively invents signs that produce an overwhelming, paralyzing fear. By attaching increasingly dire verbal interpretations to a variety of signs—bad dreams, strange sounds, a foul smell, a painful fall, and an unusual bird— Made-from-Bone develops a method of semiotic terror against the wife who had tried to kill him through complying with her brothers' plot of seduction and betrayal.

Looking at the overall set of narratives from the primordial times, there is a general change in the Made-from-Bone's way of using reflexive, interpretive distancing. In the opening narrative, the Cricket-Brothers use their powers of clairvoyance and self-transformation as defensive tools allowing them to anticipate and escape from the lethal traps set by Great Sickness. In later narratives, Made-from-Bone emerges as a fully active interpreter and creator of meanings who is able to use these powers as offensive weapons in order to mislead, frighten, or otherwise manipulate adversaries. In the narrative about the death of Great Sickness, Made-from-Bone creates an elaborate set of enticements and deceptions, rather like a police sting operation, to achieve final victory over his archenemy. And in the final narrative about evil omens, the trickster-creator goes from being a target, or potential victim, of a murderous scheme into a master of trickery whose powers of creating and interpreting signs terrorize and defeat all adversaries.

Narratives from the Primordial Times

The Cricket-Brothers; or, The Origin of Made-from-Bone

Great Sickness had a wife. That woman had a brother. Great Sickness killed his wife's brother. They gathered the bones. The wife of Great Sickness gathered the bones of her dead brother. She kept them in a hollow gourd and tied the top shut. She never left the gourd. Great Sickness said, "Why is it that she never leaves this gourd? Some day in the future she will leave it."

One day the woman left for her manioc garden. Great Sickness went to look for her, but he could see no sign of the gourd. They say that one day the woman said, "I am going for a few minutes to my manioc garden," and she left her house in a hurry. They say that she forgot her gourd. She left, arrived at her garden, and immediately began searching for her gourd. Then she said, "Now I am in trouble, for I have left my gourd behind. Now it is certain that they will kill the bones of my family."

Then Great Sickness said, "I'm going to see if she has left her gourd." When he went to look, there was the gourd. "Yes, now it is so. I am going to find out what it is that she has been hiding inside the gourd."

When Great Sickness opened the gourd to look inside, he saw two Cricket-Brothers. "Tse," he said, "Now I will kill them." He took them out of the gourd and threw them violently against the ground. He stepped on them and broke their stomachs, broke their stomachs until their guts came outside them. He picked them up and threw them on the trash heap.

Afterwards, one of the Cricket-Brothers said to his brother, "Let me put your guts back in place; later, you can do the same for me." Already he began to replace his brother's guts. He finished. He sewed up his brother's body.

"Let's go," said his brother, "Now you must let me replace your guts." He finished putting them inside his brother's body and sewed him up.

They say that the boys' aunt[1] hastily harvested some manioc tubers so that she could quickly return home to see her gourd. She returned, arrived in her house, and ran to look for her gourd, but it was not there. They say that she became very sad and that she cried for the bones of her family as she grated manioc.

Then one of the boys said, "Let's go to warn our aunt that we are fine and that she does not need to continue crying."

"Okay," said his brother, and he went and climbed on his aunt's shoulder and pinched her. The woman stopped crying and turned to see the boy. "You don't need to cry any longer; we are alive and well," he told her. The woman did not cry any longer; she was happy and resumed her work. On the next day, the two Cricket-Brothers already began to turn into people.

Then Great Sickness said to her, "Tell your nephews that they are going with me. We're going fishing together."

"Okay," she replied. Later she told the boys, "You are to go fishing with him, but be very careful because he wants to kill both of you."

"It is not so, Aunt, since nobody can kill us," they told her. "It is we who will kill him." Already they left with him to go fishing.

When they arrived at a lake, Great Sickness said to them, "You two are going to fish right here in this place while I will go to fish at another location."

Then the boys said, "Let's transform ourselves into hummingbirds; we must be careful so that he doesn't kill us." They flew up on a log and sat upon a knot in a tree. From up there, they fished in the lake below and killed many *viejitas*.

Great Sickness transformed himself into a jaguar. Meanwhile, the two brothers called upon jaguar-ants to come protect them. They saw that the jaguar was coming and that he went directly to the spot where Great Sickness had left them to fish. The jaguar went to look, but no one was there. "He walks about searching for us," said the brothers. The jaguar grew tired of searching for them and returned to his place.

The two brothers descended to the spot where Great Sickness had left them to fish. Great Sickness returned to the spot and said, "Eh, how many fish did you catch?"

"We were catching fish the entire time; and you, how many did you catch?"

"Nothing at all; where did you fish?" asked Great Sickness.

"We fished only in this one place," the boys answered. "He went looking to kill us, and that's why he didn't catch any fish," the boys said to themselves.

"Let's go back to the house," said Great Sickness.

They came across a beautiful stone as they were returning home. "Let me see your head lice," said Great Sickness.

"Okay," said the two brothers, and they sat down on the stone. As he grasped their heads, Great Sickness said, "Now I will squeeze until your heads break open." He grasped one boy's head and cleaned lice from one side, then the other. Then he did the same to the other boy's head.

Then the boys said, "Come here so that we can see your thorns and remove them from your feet."

"Okay," said Great Sickness, and he sat down next to them. When they looked at his feet, they saw many jaguar-ants. They laughed. Great Sickness grew angry at them. When they had finished, they returned to their aunt's house.

"How did it go?" the boys' aunt asked. They told her about everything that had happened. Great Sickness had cleared a large area of forest for a new manioc garden. "Tell them that they must accompany me while I burn the clearing," he said to the woman.

"Okay," she replied. Later she told her nephews, "Go with him to burn the new garden, but be careful not to let him burn you."

"No," they said to her, "don't even think about him killing us."

"Okay," she said, "go with him."

Already they went and arrived there at the new garden. Great Sickness made whistles out of *yagrumo* [*Cecropia* sp.] for the boys and said, "You two are going to dance for me in the middle of the clearing."

"Okay," the boys replied, "light the fire while the two of us are dancing." Great Sickness lit the fire and went rapidly around the edge of the garden until he had made a complete circle of fire. He looked at the two boys and saw that there was no way for them to escape. The boys remained in the middle of the garden and danced: "Hee, hee, hee [sound of their whistles]." The fire came close to where they were dancing. "Let's go," they said, before spitting into their whistles and throwing them on the ground. Already they left. They went under the ground and came up in the forest outside the garden. And that is the origin of leaf-cutter ants that we see today.

Great Sickness saw the fire arriving at the place where the boys were dancing. "Now it is certain that they are burning up. I will return home and tell their aunt, 'I warned them, but they did not listen to me.' That's what I'll tell her. 'That is how they burned,' I will say to her." Great Sickness stood up so that he could see the fire. They are burning up. "Now their guts are going to explode." Just then one of them broke open, and he heard "Too!" "Now it is certain. His guts already broke open; one more to go." After a minute he heard again, "Too." That was all. "Now I will return."

He returned near a stream and heard the boys playing. "Who could this be? People?" He went along little by little until he could see; it was the two boys themselves.

"Eh, you've returned," said the boys.

"Yes," he replied.

"We already returned before you, since it was getting very hot," they said. Great Sickness became very angry with them. They left and arrived at their house.

"How did things go with him?" asked their aunt.

"He tried to burn us up, but he could not kill us," they said. "We are the ones who are going to kill him."

A few days later, Great Sickness said to another woman, "It is impossible to kill them. Now you must try to kill them."

"Okay," she replied. "Let's go catch fish with *barbasco* poison," she said to the boys.

"Okay, let's go," said the boys. And they left.

They say that the boys transformed themselves into squirrels and climbed into a tree. The woman saw them and said, "What do these animals have?" She struck them on the hand with her *ataraya,* and blood poured out. They let the blood fall into a termite nest, and that is how the type of honey called *maapíwa,* or "the blood of *Duiménai,*" began. When the blood stopped flowing, they went until they arrived at a stream. Already they had transformed themselves back into people.

They arrived at the stream and began fishing with *barbasco* poison. They pushed the woman into the stream and struck her with a log. They killed the woman, quartered her body, and threw away her head. "Let's paint her with the markings of a paca," said one of the boys. "From now on she will be called paca," they said after painting her body. They butchered her. "Let's cook her in a pot." They plucked a hair from her head and sharpened it until it was very fine, then threw it into the pot of boiling meat. They returned to their aunt's house.

They cooked the pot of meat and left it sitting on the ground. Great Sickness returned. "Eh," he said, "you've come back?"

"Yes," they said, "we've arrived. We killed a paca. That's why we returned."

"And the woman?"

"She's still at the stream catching fish with *barbasco*," they said. Great Sickness opened the pot. "This is paca," they told him. "Go ahead and eat some if you like."

"Thank you, I will eat," said Great Sickness. He got a plate and took a bone out of the pot. He began to eat, the sharpened hair stuck in his throat. He tried to pull it out and coughed. He fell on the ground, already dead. "Good for you," the boys said, laughing at him. This is how the poison known as *camahái* began. Those two boys are known as *Duiménai*.

The Origin of Death

Great Sickness invited Made-from-Bone with his entire family to hold a *pudáli* festival so that he could kill him. Then he spoke to his wives, "Make some *yaraki* [a fermented, alcoholic drink] and throw poison [*camahái*] into it. Give it to Made-from-Bone and his people when they come to our village."

It is said that Made-from-Bone's people already knew that Great Sickness's people wanted to kill them. Then Made-from-Bone's people said, "You will prepare a medicine for us." They said this to his paternal aunt.

"Hoo, okay, I will prepare it for us," said the woman.

Already they arrived at Great Sickness's village. They drank. Their aunt was watching how they drank and saw that one of the men vomited. "This is poison," she said. She brought medicine for him and gave him some to drink. The same thing happened to all of them; they vomited, and she gave them medicine to drink.

After that the medicine was finished. The last brother, *Máwirríkuli*, vomited again. And with that he died, for there was no more medicine. Afterwards they carried him to their village, hid him, and buried him. They did not cry. When they knew for sure that all had rotted, they dug him up. They gathered up all his bones.

It is said that Made-from-Bone went to find tobacco with his grandfather. "Give me a cigar so that I can blow over his body," he said.

"Okay, here is a cigar," his grandfather said, "Blow over him."

Already Made-from-Bone went to blow tobacco smoke over the bones. He had left them in a house that had no owner. Immediately *Máwirríkuli* became a person, and Made-from-Bone raised him to his feet again. "Now it is so, I see my brother's body again," said Made-from-Bone. "And thus it will be for the new people in the next world."[2]

Made-from-Bone met with all the members of his family to speak to them about how they were to act toward their younger brother. "You, my little brother, I have already made your body stand up. You, all my family, none of you can look upon him. You women must not look at him, but you will see him at another time. We will hold a ceremony when I take him out so that he can be seen again."

"That's fine," the others replied. "We are happy because we will see him at another time."

Then Made-from-Bone said, "Today I am going to search for our sacred food;[3] tomorrow I will get it."

"Hoo, that's good," they replied. Made-from-Bone went out into the forest and searched for the sacred food.

"Can it really be true that my husband is going to return to life?" wondered *Máwirríkuli*'s wife. "I am going to look at him while hiding." All the people left to do their work, and *Máwirríkuli*'s wife was the only one left in the village. She went very slowly. "Where is he now?" she asked. He was sitting in the doorway of his house, looking at himself in a mirror and combing his hair.

As she entered little by little into the house, he turned to see her. "Daa," he exclaimed, and with that he fell to the ground, nothing but bones again. The woman was frightened and left immediately.

They say that rain fell on Made-from-Bone. He grabbed the rain in his hand. It fell into his hand. He saw blood fall into his hand. "Now we're in trouble," he said. "I know that they have seen my little brother." Quickly he returned.

He arrived in his village and went directly to the place where his brother had been. "Hoo," Made-from-Bone said, and arrived to see nothing other than bones. "Now it is certain," he said to the woman, the wife of *Máwirríkuli*. "You yourself went to see my brother, and that's why this has happened."

"It is not so; I did not look at him," said the woman.

"You yourself, you yourself, you yourself," said Made-from-Bone. "I am going to see him one more time." He blew tobacco smoke over *Máwirríkuli*, who rose only half way before falling to the ground again. He blew smoke again, but the same thing happened. A third time he blew over him, but it was the same again. It is for this reason that today we become very sick but we get medicine.

"Now we will cry," said Made-from-Bone. "That brother of mine, we will never again see his body. And thus it will be for the new people in the next world; they will die forever. If you had all heeded my warning, this would not be happening to us. We would die, and later we would return to wake up. That's how it would have been for the new people. But after what you've done,[4] now there is no remedy."

Owl-Monkey; or, Made-from-Bone Tries to End Poisoning

Owl-Monkey was the owner of poison [*camahái*]. "Now I am going to put an end to poisoning," Made-from-Bone thought. "Now I am going to gather up these animals that live in the trees." He left them a large tree[5] that was covered with many fruits.

"Come over to my place and eat some of the fruits I've planted."

"Okay," they said. They arrived at the place in the afternoon and saw an abundance of fruit. "Let's eat these fruits," they said.

"Go ahead and eat all the fruits that you collect," said Made-from-Bone.

"Okay," they said, eating until night fell. "Tomorrow we will eat again," said the monkeys—*kapárru* monkey, howler monkey, and all the others. They left.

"We will sleep here and will eat first thing in the morning before the others," he said to the *tsikota* monkeys.

"Okay," they replied, before going to sleep.

Owl-Monkey saw that the *tsikota* monkeys had fallen asleep. "Let's go. Now I can eat until the morning arrives here."

Made-from-Bone came to see, "Who are these animals in the tree?" He saw that the Owl-Monkey was eating. "Now it is so," he said. "This is what I was looking for." And he moved the tree out into the middle of the river.

Owl-Monkey ate calmly. He picked a fruit and let it slip from his hand; the fruit fell into the river. "Tee-phi [sound of the fruit splashing into water]," he heard, and then a piraña fish ate the fruit. "Ooo," he said, "what has happened to me?" Again he picked a fruit and threw it into the river. "Tee- phi," he heard and "Srooo," as a piraña fish ate the fruit. He threw another fruit to one side and heard the same sounds. "Now I am certainly in trouble," he said. "I don't know what to do to get myself out of here."

He picked another fruit and threw it straight down into the river. "Kooo," he heard, as a piraña fish ate it. Then he picked a dead, dried-up fruit and threw it into the river. He waited and listened, but the piraña fish did not eat it. "Aaa," he said, "This is how I will escape." Again he threw another dried-up fruit, and again the piraña fish did not eat it. He picked another dried-up fruit and transformed himself into a tiny ant. "This is how I am going to save myself." He went inside the fruit before letting it fall into the river. He waited to see what would happen, but again the piraña fish did not eat the fruit.

Early the next morning, the *tsikota* monkeys awoke and saw that they were above the river. They were frightened and began leaping through the branches. They fell into the river, where piraña fish and alligators ate them. Only one female monkey and her infant survived. She lived with her baby up in the *temári* tree.

A woodpecker came toward her. "Take me," she said. "Can you carry me over to the bank of the river?" she asked.

"Okay," said the woodpecker, "I can do it. Get up on my shoulder. Hold on tight and be careful not to fall." And he flew off with her. He went up-stream and downstream.

"I cannot get down," she said. "Take me back there again." The wood-pecker flew back to the tree.

"I cannot reach the river bank," he said. "I don't know what to do with you, so now I am leaving." And he left.

After that the alligator came over to her. "Eee," he said, "what happened to you?"

"Nothing," she replied. "I want to go to the other side of the river."

"Very well," said the alligator. "Come sit down on my shoulder."

"Okay," she said as she sat on his shoulder.

The alligator set off swimming with her. His stomach was swollen because he had eaten a whole family of *tsikota* monkeys. He belched. "Aaa," he thought, "I am going to eat her there on the river bank."

The *tsikota* monkey knew that alligator wanted to eat her. They were already getting close to the riverbank, and she calculated the remaining distance. Just at that moment she jumped and grabbed hold of a log. The alligator bit off part of her tail. This is why *tsikota* monkeys today have short tails. And she went on her way, that *tsikota* monkey and her infant.

That infant grew up and fathered other offspring until there were many of them. Today there are *tsikota* monkeys along all the rivers. Meanwhile, Owl-Monkey floated downstream until reaching the sea. He saved himself in this way, floating inside a dried-up fruit, and this is why poison did not come to an end and exists until today.

Made-from-Bone and Anaconda-Person

They say that in the distant past Made-from-Bone lived at the place where the world began and that he had a wife. They say that his wife lived with him there in Punta Loro.

They say that there was an Anaconda-Person named *Uliámali*. The wife of Made-from-Bone met with Anaconda-Person every time that she returned from her manioc garden. When returning to the village, she always passed by the port. They say that she carried a gourd dipper with which she hit the surface of the river, "To, Too!" Anaconda-Person came out of the river toward her, "Pow!" He took off his shirt [skin], which was just like the shirts we wear today. "Ee," he called, moving toward the woman and grasping her. After copulating with her, he departed for the bottom of the river. "Buliú [sound of submerging in the river]."

They say that Anaconda-Person paid the woman money. In those ancient days, there were women who fastened shells into necklaces that were called *koma*. Anaconda-Person put one of these necklaces on the woman after making love to her. This is how it worked all the time.

A long time passed with this happening, and the family of Made-from-Bone decided to speak to him about it. "What your wife is doing is not good," they told him. "The man gets on top of her. We have seen this with our own eyes, not just heard about it."

"Could this be true?" asked Made-from-Bone.

"Yes, it is certain," they told him and advised him to go and see for himself. "If you want to see, come along with us to watch her," they told him.

"Fine, let's go and see," Made-from-Bone answered.

In the early morning, the wife of Made-from-Bone went to her manioc garden. When she returned from the garden and arrived at her house, she finished peeling the manioc tubers and began grating them. Made-from-Bone was sitting nearby on a large rock overlooking the river-port with Bird-Person [*Dókutsiári*]. Made-from-Bone said, "Go and see how close she is to finishing her work of grating manioc."

"She has only a little bit left to finish grating," said Bird-Person.

"Go again to see how much she has left to finish."

This time Bird-Person reported that the woman had finished grating. "Here she comes," said Bird-Person. Just then she came from the village and descended to the port, carrying a large vat. "Look at her," Bird-Person said, "it is exactly as we told you."

The woman went and jumped into the river; Anaconda-Person came out of the water, "Too, too!" He came out! "There he is," Bird-Person exclaimed. From there Anaconda-Person came over to the woman and embraced her. "You are going to see what we were warning you."

"Damn, so be it, I don't care any longer," said Made-from-Bone. When Anaconda-Person had finished copulating with the woman, he gave her money.

Later Made-from-Bone went to his house. His wife finished bathing in the river and returned to the house. "I feel happy," she said while making cold manioc drinks [*yokúta*]. "Here is cold *yokúta*, Made-from-Bone, drink some with me," said his wife.

Later Made-from-Bone spoke with Bird-Person. "Let's kill this Anaconda-Person. We'll make a poisoned arrow and two darts." And together they made the arrow and darts. "Ta!" they finished. Made-from-Bone shouted for one of his younger brothers, *Éenuʰméeri*, to accompany him to the port. "One day we will kill him," he said.

The woman returned again from her manioc garden and began grating the tubers. She was happy. Then Made-from-Bone said, "Let's go up there on top of the rock to see how much grating she has left to do."

"She has already finished grating; here she comes," said Bird-Person. As she carried her large vat, the gourd dipper inside made sounds like "kla, kla, kla." She fell into the river, "Taa." "Pow!" "Ari-ari-ari-ta," shouted Bird-Person.

Anaconda-Person came out of the river again and swam toward the woman. When he reached her, he got on top of her and began to copulate.

Then Made-from-Bone's brother said, "There he is. Pierce him with the darts, then we will shoot arrows into him." Made-from-Bone placed a dart in the blowgun and raised the weapon to his lips, preparing to blow. "Don't do it that way; give me the blowgun," said Made-from-Bone's brother, who struck the mouth of the blowgun with his hand and forced the dart through the tube. The dart struck against the sky and returned directly on top of Anaconda-Person. It fell on his shoulder. Then they shot Anaconda-Person with an arrow. Anaconda-Person stood up in the river.

"Ooh," the woman sat up, then stood.

"'Ooh,' you say, you shameless woman; you survived even though our intention was to kill both of you," said Made-from-Bone.

Made-from-Bone returned to his house. When his wife returned to the house, she was ashamed of herself. She went about silently, without saying a word to Made-from-Bone. After five days, Made-from-Bone said, "I'm going to hunt for game. Make some manioc beer for us to drink, and later I'll catch some fish with nets. We will eat fish and drink beer later."

"Okay, Made-from-Bone, I will make beer for us to drink," said his wife.

Made-from-Bone went downstream, where he met a bird [*wanáli*]. "What's new?" Made-from-Bone asked.

"Nothing," said the bird.

"You haven't seen a person coming down the river?"

"Yes," said the bird.

"Okay, let's go search for him," said Made-from-Bone. Later he met a different bird [*dzáaliro*]. "What's happening? Have you seen anybody passing by here?" he asked.

"Yes, he passed by yesterday," said the bird.

"Okay, let's go search for him," said Made-from-Bone.

They found the body of Anaconda-Person in Éenutanhísre. They found him rotten, with many worms eating his body. These worms are known as the penis of Anaconda-Person, and it is said that they are the source of the white people of today. They also say that we indigenous people were born at Hípana [a village on the Aiarí River in Brazil]. Then Made-from-Bone got out a net and used it to pick up the penis of Anaconda-Person.

"Let's return home. We'll go fishing for white sardines," said Made-from-Bone. When Made-from-Bone arrived, his wife was preparing manioc breads. He carried a load of fish as he headed for his house.

"You've already returned?" his wife asked.

"Yes, I've returned, and I'd like to roast these fish on your manioc grill."

"Okay, Made-from-Bone, make your roasted fish so that I can eat with you," said his wife as she prepared manioc breads. "Pa, Made-from-Bone, give me some fish to eat." He took out two fish and gave them to her. She was happy, that poor woman. He gave her the penis of Anaconda-Person. She took out a piece of manioc bread and ate it with that fish.

While Made-from-Bone began to eat, she finished eating. Then Made-from-Bone said, "Thus it is that when one wants someone too much, you are destined to eat his whole body."

The woman heard what Made-from-Bone was saying and exclaimed, "Damn, now I'm in trouble."

She stopped her work and left for the port. There she grated a plant to make a potion, which she drank and vomited. A small crab came out of her stomach. She began to vomit again, and this time a fish called *molída* came out of her. When she had finished vomiting, she returned to her house. Made-from-Bone was through with her and sent her away. He never spoke with her again.

In one month's time, the woman's stomach had become large, and a baby anaconda was growing inside her womb. After eight months, the snake had grown much bigger but would not come out yet. After twenty months, the snake was enormous, but it still refused to come out of the womb. This caused the woman to suffer great pain, since she could not eat anything. Whenever she tried to eat, the snake would come part way out of her vagina and steal the food before she could get it into her mouth. She grew very thin because the snake would not let her eat anything.

Seeing the woman's plight, some of her kin gathered fruit from the rubber tree. When they gave some to her, the snake stuck out its head and asked for the fruit. The woman's kin told her where to find a tall rubber tree far away in the forest. They found a tall tree because the snake was very long and they wanted it to come all the way out of the woman's body as it tried to reach the fruits. The woman arrived at the rubber tree, which has fruits shaped like a small vase. She asked the snake to climb the tree to bring the fruits down to the ground, but the snake did not want to come out. Seeing the fruits, however, the snake came out to eat. He went a little way up the trunk of the rubber tree and stopped, fearing that his mother would leave him up in the tree if he went farther. The woman reassured him that she would stay. The snake was very long, almost ten meters. As he reached the fruits, he dropped them down to his mother. The woman took one of the vase-shaped fruits and spit inside it. Just as the snake's tail was leaving her womb, she stuck the tail into the fruit so that the snake would think it was still connected to her. Then she set the fruit on the ground, and the snake continued to collect fruits up in the tree. Whenever the snake called down to see if she was still there, its tail wiggled inside the fruit and made a sound like "Hoo," just as if his mother were answering him.

By the time the snake realized that his mother had left, she had been gone for a long time and had returned to her house. Upon arriving, her family asked, "How are you?"

"Good, I have already gotten rid of him," she replied.

"Come quickly. We are going to hide you from this shameful snake-child." They took her to a remote place in the forest, where they dug a hole in the ground and covered it with sticks, soil, and leaves. When the woman entered the hole, her family sealed it shut.

Anaconda-Child [*Uliámaliéni*] arrived in the village and asked, "How are you? Have you seen my mother?"

"No, we have not," they replied.

"It was you who hid my mother," said Anaconda-Child. He grew very angry and went searching through every house in the village. Then he went searching in the forest but could not find any trace of his mother. He finally gave up and told the women that he was going to his father's village below the river and that together they would return to find his mother.

After Anaconda-Child left, he never returned, since Made-from-Bone had long ago killed his father. The woman came out of her hiding place and was very thin. "You are not well; now you should follow your son," said her family. They grabbed her and threw her into the river, where she turned into a *bagre sapo* [type of small catfish that has an expandable belly].

The Origin of the Bat-People

In past times when bats were still people, a group of Bat-People arrived in a village of people. The Bat-People had brought *yuku* fruits and wanted to hold a drinking ceremony.[6] They arrived in the afternoon in a village where there were only women, for their husbands were all away hunting. The Bat-People said that they had brought *yuku* fruits with them. "Okay, but there are no men with us to drink manioc beer; they've all gone hunting," the women told them.

"Okay, it doesn't matter, we want to drink beer with you," the Bat-People answered. And they gave the *yuku* fruits to the women.

Later on as night fell, the Bat-People began to dance with the women, who brought out a large vat of manioc beer. They danced until midnight, and the women became drunk. It was then that the Bat-People began to eat.

While they were dancing with the Bat-People, the women left their children in the care of their mother. One of the Bat-People went to light a cigar in the old woman's fire, and she saw that he had a claw on his wrist. So she pinched one of the children to make him cry, and one of the women returned from dancing. "These men are not people," the old woman said. "Just now one of them came here to light a cigar in my fire, and I saw that he had a claw on his wrist. Go back out there with them," she told the woman.

"Nonsense," the woman answered, "They are people, and we are dancing with them." In the very early morning, the Bat-People began to eat.

A younger brother of Made-from-Bone named *Éeri*[7] was watching what the Bat-People were doing and noticed when they had begun to take the women to a small field nearby. *Éeri* saw them leave; there were three women. Soon they left again with another woman and returned to the village. Again they left with three women. None of the women who left returned with the Bat-People.

Éeri went to look in the field and saw only skins, bones, and blood. He returned and went to warn the old woman. "They've already eaten the women; I just saw their bones, their skins."

"I warned them, but they didn't listen to me. Now there's nothing we can do because the men are not here with us," she said to *Éeri*.

At dawn, the Bat-People returned to the village before leaving. The old woman said to *Éeri*, "Follow them and find out where they came from, these bastards."

"Okay," he said, "I'll go after them."

And he went, following the Bat-People into the forest. He made a trail behind them by painting the trees with black, red, yellow, green, purple, and brown clay. He went behind them to their village. When he arrived there, he saw that they lived in a tree called *móri*. He saw that they were bats and returned to his own village.

He told his people that he had seen where the Bat-People live. The men were happy when they returned from hunting, thinking about drinking manioc beer. But they arrived to hear the bad news. "What?"

"The Bat-People ate the women," *Éeri* told them.

"Have you seen them?" they asked.

"Yes, I saw them where they live," *Éeri* said.

"Okay, go and show us so that we can kill them."

"Let's go," said *Éeri*. And they all left.

They carried many *seje* palm leaves with them and arrived there. "Here it is," *Éeri* told them. They heard a sound where the Bat-People lived in the tree and lit a fire. They used the *seje* palm leaves to block the hole where the bat-people lived. Only two bats escaped, one male and one female. Only these two survived, but they produced many offspring, and those are the bats that live here today.

The Origin of Cooking with Hot Peppers

There was a *yuku* tree bearing fruit. Made-from-Bone went to harvest the *yuku* fruit and heard people beneath the tree. "Who could they be?" he said and went to look for them. He saw them and greeted them, "Eee."

"Eee," the people answered. They were gathering *yuku* fruit. Then they jumped into the river.

"How can it be that these people jumped into the river?" said Made-from-Bone.

Made-from-Bone returned to his house. He told everyone that he had seen people gathering *yuku* fruit. Another day he went back to the *yuku* tree and gathered fruit. Right there he saw the people. He approached them, but they jumped into the river. Afterwards Made-from-Bone said, "I am going to put sawgrass in front of them to catch them." When he finished placing the sawgrass, he returned to his house.

On the following day he went to the *yuku* tree again and saw the people gathering fruit. He went toward them. "Eee," he said. They turned and saw him, and again they jumped into the river. They went right through the place where Made-from-Bone had placed the sawgrass to catch them. Made-from-Bone went to look, but there was nothing. "This is not right," he said. "Now I am going to set out *kamáwa* [a type of sticky vine], and with this I will succeed in catching them."

He went and found some *kamáwa* vine and set it out in front of the people. When he finished, he returned to his house. On the following day he went back to look. He saw the people again and approached them. "Eee," he said. They turned to see him and jumped into the river again. One woman jumped directly into the *kamáwa* vine. It caught in her hair, hard, and she was stuck there.

Made-from-Bone ran quickly toward the woman to catch her. "Don't touch me; let me go," she said to him.

"No," he replied, "I am not going to let you go. Now I will take you to my house." Later he took her to his village. "You are going to live here with me," he told her.

"No," she said. "I am not a person like you. We are *Yópinai*."[8]

"That doesn't matter," he said. "Over time you will become accustomed to living with us." From then on the *Yópinai*-woman lived with Made-from-Bone and his family.

The *Yópinai*-woman said to Made-from-Bone, "Let me go to see my family."

"Okay," he said to her. "Now we are going to gather leaf-cutter ants to bring to your family." And they gathered many ants of different kinds [*kúhwe, máaki, kéetu, píti*]. "Let's go," said Made-from-Bone.

"I am going along with you," said a *guaco* bird [*únuli*].

"Me, too," said *golondrina* [*tirrípi*].

"Me, too," said a *gaviota* [*kákue*].

"Me, too," said a *wánawanári* bird.

"Okay, let's go then," said Made-from-Bone. And they left.

When they were close to the woman's village, she said to Made-from-Bone, "I believe that my family is already here. Now you will see them." She took out a gourd dipper filled with leaf-cutter ants and threw them into the river. The fish ate up the ants, "Ko, ko, ko, ko, ko." "I will advise them," she said to Made-from-Bone. "Look at how my family is; they are fish."

But before they could leave, Made-from-Bone said, "It doesn't matter, let's go." And they arrived in her family's village.

They went over to the house of the *Yópinai*-woman's father. He greeted her. He was very angry. "What happened to you; it's been a long time since you were lost from here," her father said.

"Some people captured me," she said. "He [Made-from-Bone] took me to his house, and I lived with him. He treated me very well," she said to her father.

"Okay," he said, "It doesn't matter. I thought that they had killed you." Just then he greeted Made-from-Bone. Three times he greeted him, but Made-from-Bone did not respond to him. On the fourth time, yes, this time he answered the man's greeting. "Tse," said the woman's father, "He knows in advance what I want to do, and for this reason I will not eat him. If he had responded to me when I first greeted him, I would already have eaten him."

Made-from-Bone spoke to him, "I took your daughter to be my wife. It was not a bad thing, and I treated her well. I did not make her work."

"Okay," he said, "This is how I wanted it to be with you. Bring some food so that we can drink *yokúta* [cold manioc drink]."

"Hoh," said the old man's wife, and she brought a large bowl to him. The bowl was full of water, and there were fish living in the water, live fish. "Yes, Made-from-Bone," he said, "Here is some food that you can eat together with your family."

"Thank you," said Made-from-Bone, "Come to eat."

"Okay," said the *guaco* bird, "Let's go eat now." He jumped into the bowl and bit into a small catfish [*bagre choro*, or *dzóri*]. Already the *guaco* bird had swallowed the fish, but the sharp "horn" [bony fin] broke the bird's throat, "Ta, ta, ta," until it came out through his neck. "Mmmm, oooo," said the catfish's "horn."

Made-from-Bone turned to look at the *guaco* bird. "Daa," he said, "What happened to you? This is not right. We must wait to see how this is to be done."

Made-from-Bone took out a hot red pepper, broke it open, and threw it into the bowl. In a little while the water began to boil. He left it to boil.

"Let's go," he said. "Now, yes, we can eat." And just then they started eating. The *guaco* bird was not eating. Already Made-from-Bone had started the way we kill the rawness in our food today. They finished eating and gave the bowl back to its owner. "Here is your bowl; we have eaten," said Made-from-Bone.

"Tse," said the old man, "It is impossible to destroy this Made-from-Bone."

"Let's go find your things." They went and got them, returned to the house, finished. "Hang up your hammocks so that you can rest," the man said to them.

"Okay," said Made-from-Bone. They hung up their hammocks and talked.

In the afternoon, Made-from-Bone said to them, "Let's go where it would be good to bathe."

"We don't know. Go and find out for us," they said to Made-from-Bone. So he left in the direction of the village headman.

"Where would it be good to bathe? We'd like to bathe now," he said.

"Okay," he replied, "Over there in front of that rock."

"Thanks. We're going to bathe," said Made-from-Bone.

"Let's go," said the headman, "Now we must wait in the river so that we can eat them when they are bathing."

"Okay," they [the *Yópinai*-people of the village] said. Already they left and transformed themselves into *cajaro* [large catfishes]. They went to the river beside the rock and waited for Made-from-Bone. Made-from-Bone ate some coca leaves. He was divining to know how they could bathe. He foresaw bad things.

"Let's go bathe up higher," he said. "I believe that they are waiting for us here in the river," he told them.

"Okay," they said. Already he went with them and gave shirts to each one. They dressed in the shirts and started to bathe, running across the top of the river. They ran with their wings, their backs. When they finished, they returned to the rock. They undressed again and gave their shirts back to Made-from-Bone for safekeeping.

"Let's go back to the house."

"You've already bathed, Made-from-Bone?" asked the headman.

"Yes, we bathed," said Made-from-Bone. Then the *Yópinai*-people, the ones who had wanted to eat Made-from-Bone, returned.

"What's up?" they said. "It is impossible to kill and eat Made-from-Bone. They went to bathe far away in the middle of the river. They didn't even enter into the river but bathed up high, on top of the water. It was impossible; not even the slightest chance." This is the end of this story from the past.

The Origin of the Vulture-People

There was a cousin of Made-from-Bone whose mother had a large number of hot pepper plants in her manioc garden. Those pepper plants were filled with many peppers. One day she said, "I'm going to gather my peppers, my son."

"Okay, go and harvest them," he replied. She left. When she arrived at her garden, she saw that her pepper plants had no peppers. "Now who could be gathering my peppers?" she said. Another day, the same thing happened again.

The woman said, "My son, go to see what is eating my peppers."

"Okay," he said, "tomorrow I will go early in the morning." The next morning, he left before dawn and arrived very early. He hid himself behind a log. He stood there and waited to see. He heard them coming, conversing, laughing. "Could these be people?" he said.

They came and arrived very near to him. As they arrived, they sat down on a log. "Let's gather peppers," they said. They took off their shirts and left them lying on top of a log. They were vultures, and they gathered peppers.

"I am going to hide one of their shirts," the man said [to himself]. He hid one of the vultures' shirts and went toward them. "Hee," he said. Quickly they put on their shirts, and soon they were flying.

But there was one woman who was searching for her shirt. She went around in circles right there. Then the man jumped out of hiding and grabbed the woman by the arm. "Don't grab me," she said, "Let me go and give me back my shirt. You are the one who hid it."

"I am not going to let you go, not even for a minute," said the man.

"No, let me go. I am not a person. Look at them—my family," she said.

"It doesn't matter," he told her, "You have the form of a person. Now I will take you back to my house." She did not want to go with him. He pulled her behind him little by little until they reach his mother's house.

"Mama," he said to her, "Here is a woman. She is the one who was gathering your peppers."

"Aaaa. Good. Take her to our family, my son," she said. "Now, my niece, you are going to live with my son, the poor little bachelor. You are going to work for him when he works in his manioc garden."

"So be it, but we are not people like you," the young woman said. "We do not eat the way you do. We eat differently."

"It doesn't matter. You will become accustomed after spending time living with us," said the older woman. The young woman agreed and lived with the man as his wife.

Later the woman said to her husband, "Now I want you to come with me. I want to see my family, my father, my mother."

"Okay," he said, "I will wait for you while you see them. Mother, she wants to see her family. I am going to take her to see them."

"Good," his mother said, "Go ahead and let her see her family." And they left. They arrived there in the village of the Vulture-People.

"My father is very angry. Be careful that he doesn't eat you," the woman said to her husband. "The first two times that he speaks to you, do not answer him. The third time that he speaks, then you can answer."

"Okay," he said.

They saw that they were arriving at the Vulture-People's place. "Oooo," they said, "Where do you come from? It's been a long time since you've been lost. Where have you been living?"

"Some people took me away, but they treated me well," she said.

"Good," said her father, who went over to the woman's husband. "How are you, my nephew?" he asked [in a falsetto voice]. The man did not answer him. He [the vulture] asked again; no answer. On the third time that he asked, this time the man answered him.

"No, my uncle, I came here with your daughter. I love her," he said.

"Okay," said the woman's father, "The only bad thing is that we do not eat the same way you eat. You will live with us." The man agreed and lived for a time with them.

After a while the man's father-in-law said to him, "Let's go hunting for deer with arrows. The deer are eating a lot of *káma* flowers."

"Hoo, very well," the man said. A few days later he went to make a platform and sat down on it to wait for a deer to come. He finished making the platform and returned to his house. "Tomorrow I will go to kill a deer first thing in the morning," he said to his wife.

Very early in the morning he went to his platform and sat down. He saw a deer approaching, eating *káma* flowers below him. Quickly he shot it with an arrow. The deer jumped, then fell, already dead from the *curare* poison. Afterwards he climbed down to the ground and went to see the dead deer. "I will return," he said. "I am going to invite my companion. We will come to look for you. Very heavy," he said. He left and arrived at his house.

"How did it go?" his wife asked. "Did you kill a deer?"

"Yes," he said, "I managed to hit one with an arrow, but I'm not sure if it died. Go tell your father that I shot it so that we can go look for it."

The woman spoke to her father, "He shot a deer but does not know if he killed it."

"Okay, we'll go have a look," said her father. They left and arrived at the place.

"Where exactly were you when you shot it?" he asked.

"I was standing right here. I shot it, and it jumped over there."

"Okay," said the father-in-law, "let's go look for it. I'll go over here, while you go over there. Let's go." The old man left; his son-in-law left, too. The old man went and saw the deer lying down, dead. He was careful to hide the deer. His son-in-law stood up and looked toward him from a distance. He saw that his father-in-law was picking *macanilla* leaves to cover up the deer. He finished and called to his son-in-law. "Eeh," he said, "have you seen it over there?"

"I don't see anything. Maybe it already left. And you?" he asked in return.

"I don't see anything," said the father-in-law. "Maybe it already left, or maybe you didn't hit it with your arrow. Let's go back; maybe it has already gone." Already they went back and arrived at their house.

"Eee, you've returned," said the woman. "And the deer?"

"Your father has hidden it," he said to her in a very low voice.

"He, hee," she laughed, "I warned you that we do not eat like you people. We don't eat fresh meat like you. Instead, we eat rotten meat."

Three days passed. The father-in-law spoke to his family, "Let's go fishing with *barbasco* poison in Deer Creek." There were plenty of fish. No sooner had they begun fishing with *barbasco* than many fish were dying. They gathered the fish with *ataraya* nets. Each one of them had a basket for collecting the fish. They caught a lot of fish; all kinds, little tiny ones and big ones, too. They finished fishing with *barbasco* and returned, arriving at their house in the afternoon.

They became happy about eating. The son-in-law went to see how many fish they had caught and saw that there were many worms inside their carrying baskets. "How do these people eat?" the father-in-law asked his daughter.

"These people eat differently," she explained, "They eat fresh food."

"Okay," said the old man, "From now on whenever I kill large game animals, tell him that he should take a piece of fresh meat. Then the rest will be left to rot for us."

"My father says that from now on, if you kill a large game animal, you should take a portion for yourself and then leave the rest for us," [the woman told her husband].

The old man told his daughter, "Put these drops of our medicine into his eyes."

"Hoo," she said. "Come here so that I can give you this medicine."

"Okay, that's fine," said her husband.

The woman put drops in his eyes, finished and told him, "You have to keep your eyes closed for a while."

"Okay," he said. He closed his eyes for a few minutes.

"Let's go, open your eyes," his wife said, and he opened his eyes. "Let's go. Come with me to the port to help us clean fish to cook and eat."

"Okay," he said, "Let's go." And he went with her to the port. He saw that the worms had turned into all kinds of fish: small catfish, painted eels, *cascaradora, guabina*, sardines, and so on. Already he began eating with the others.

Later the father of the man's father-in-law said, "My son, go tell the husband of my granddaughter that I want a canoe from him. He must finish making it this same day."

"Okay," said the father-in-law, "I will tell him to make it for you."

"My nephew, go and make a canoe for the old man. You must finish it today."

"I don't know," said the son-in-law, "I am going to see if I can make it in a single day." He chopped down a tall *amarillo* tree and hollowed it out rapidly. He finished. Then he burned the wood and opened it. He finished, then put small benches inside. He finished. That was all. He finished and returned to the old man in the afternoon.

"I have finished making the canoe," he said to his father-in-law. "There it is in the port." Then he said to the old man (his father-in-law's father), "There is your canoe. Go and see if you like it."

"Hoo," he said, leaving. He jumped and landed on the prow of the canoe. Oooo, it split into two halves. The old man became very angry with him [his son's son-in-law]. "I don't like this," he said, and left for his house. "This canoe is worthless," [the old man said to his son.] "I want a canoe like the ones we make for ourselves. Tell him that he must make a canoe for me again, one more time. If he doesn't finish it today, I am going to eat him."

"Again you must make a canoe for the old man, and you must finish it for him today," said the father-in-law.

"It's impossible to make it the way he wants," the man said to his wife. "Your grandfather is going to eat me."

All the people had already left for their work, and the man remained all by himself in the village. He thought. His brother-in-law, the youngest of his wife's brothers, came back to the village. "Let's go," he said, and they left.

"How are you?" his brother-in-law asked. "What are you thinking about?"

"Yes, I am thinking that your grandfather is going to eat me."

"It's not so," the brother-in-law said to him, "what he wants from you is right there in front of us. Make a cigar for us, and let's go over there to see." Hooh, the man made a cigar. He finished. "Now let's get going." They left and arrived at a place where they saw a large stone. "What size canoe did he ask you for?" asked the brother-in-law.

"Small," the man replied.

"Okay, so be it," said the brother-in-law. "Light the cigar." The man lit the cigar and gave it to his brother-in-law. Already he was blowing smoke. He blew smoke over the rock. Three times he blew tobacco smoke over the rock, which formed itself into a small canoe. He put a bench inside it. Ready. "Let's go carry it over to the port," he said. They hauled it over to the port.

"Now you must go find *macanilla* leaves to polish the inside of the canoe. We are going to break the old man's head. But don't tell anyone else that I accompanied you."

In the afternoon, he returned and arrived at the old man's house. "There is the canoe in the port, go and see," he told him. The old man was extremely angry and didn't even answer him. He left in silence and arrived to see the canoe. He jumped and landed in the bow of the canoe, then fell over to one side. He stood up again and stepped again on the bow; and the same thing happened. Three times, no more.

He left for his house. "Now I am happy," said the old man. "That's how I wanted things to be.

"Now I want him to do something for me one more time just as I like. When he has finished this, then he can take my granddaughter as his wife. What I want him to do now is to roll *moriche* fibers into string. I want him to finish making it today," the old man said.

"Go and roll up *moriche* fibers into string for the old man," the father-in-law told the man. "He wants you to finish it today."

"I don't know; I've worked with this type of fiber before but very slowly," said the man.

"Let's go to the manioc garden," his wife told him.

"Okay," he said, "I cannot finish weaving this *moriche* in a single day. Your grandfather is going to eat me." And they left to go do their work.

The man sat down and thought. "How am I going to get out of this place?" Meanwhile, he saw his brother-in-law coming toward him.

"Ee," said his brother-in-law, "What are you thinking about, my brother-in-law?"

"I am thinking that your grandfather is going to eat me. I cannot finish this work that he wants from me," he replied.

"It isn't so. Don't think like that. I am going to help you," said his brother-in-law.

"Thank you," he said.

"Bring that *moriche* fiber over here," said the brother-in-law. The man brought the *moriche* fiber over to him. Already he burned it. When he finished, he took a large gourd dipper and placed all the ashes inside it. He poured water in the dipper and mixed it with the ashes. Then the brother-in-law drank the mixture of ash and water. He waited a few minutes, then sneezed. A long string or twine came out of his nose. "Here it is. Now you can ravel it up." Already the man began balling up the *moriche* twine. He finished. "That is all. Now we are finished, and I am going away again," said the brother-in-law. He left a small piece of the *moriche* twine unravelled. "This is the remainder that you will work with. I am leaving."

"Okay," the man said, and his brother-in-law left.

In the afternoon, he went back to see his father-in-law. His wife arrived, came over to him, and asked, "Have you finished rolling the *moriche* fibers?"

"Yes," he said, "I have finished. Tell your grandfather so that he can come to look for his *moriche* twine."

"My grandfather, come and find your *moriche*," he said.

"Okay," said the grandfather. The old man was very happy.

"Here is your *moriche*; I've already finished rolling it," said the man.

"Hooh, thank you," said the old man. "Now you can live together with my granddaughter, since you have learned how to do things like we do." Thus it is that until this day among all people it is the youngest brother-in-law who treats one the best.

The man lived with them for a while and had a son. "Now let's go back to see my mother," the man said to his wife. "Afterwards we will come back here again. Tell your father that we will return here."

His wife said to her father, "We will return; we'll be back."

"Okay," he said, "Go with him." And they left; they went back to his village.

His mother saw him, "Aaa, my son, you've come back."

"Yes," he said.

"How have you been?" she asked him.

"Nothing happened, it's okay," he said. "I already have a son."

"Good," she said. She was happy to see her grandson. She lived with her grandson for a little while.

"I am going to fish," said the man. "Make some manioc breads for us."

"Hooh," said his wife. She pressed manioc pulp in a *sebucán*. Then she put feathers on her son's arms. The baby shouted out in pain, "Aaaa."

"What happened?" said his grandmother.

"Nothing happened," said the boy's mother. "He is crying because I am taking out his *anigua* worms." She lied to the old woman. She finished.

"Let's go. You go in front, and I'll go behind," the woman said to her son. She threw him, and he began to fly, little by little. Already the boy was up high. His mother took off flying, too. There was a sound when she flew.

The old woman came outside to see. "What happened? Why are you leaving?" she asked. "Why are you taking my grandson, who I love so much?" Already they left. The old woman stood up and saw them up in the clouds.

The man returned in the afternoon. He was happy in the village of his mother. She spoke to him, "Now we are in bad times."

"What?" he said.

"Your wife just left," she told him, "and she took your son with her."

The man began to cry. He thought of his son. He thought of his wife. Already she had returned to her family's village. And her husband lived in his own village. Thus it ends.

Great Sickness; or, The Origin of Malaria

They say that Made-from-Bone had a younger brother, who took the daughter of Great Sickness as his wife. They say that his brothers-in-law did not like him and that they did not want him for their brother. The man lived with his brothers-in-law, but they looked at him with malice. It is still just the same today. If a man takes a woman as his wife, her family looks badly upon him. Thus it was when the world began, and that is still how it is among us today. There are few good people.

The man spent a long time living in the village of his brothers-in-law.

"Let's kill him," said the brothers-in-law. "Let's go to close off a stream, brother-in-law," they said to him. But it was to kill him.

"Let's go," he said, "Let's go right away." And they left, arrived at the mouth of the stream. They planted sticks. "Go and put the sticks at the bottom of the stream," they said. They sharpened one of the sticks. "Let's dive into the water," they told him. "When you arrive at the bottom, grab the stick and leave the point by your shoulder," they said. "Then put the point into the river bottom."

"Okay," he said. They say that he dove until he reached the bottom. He said to himself, "This is not right; I am not going to put the point of the stick on my shoulder." So he left the point of the stick in the ground. He shook the stick, and his brothers-in-law pushed on it until it entered into the ground.

"Well done," they said, as bubbles came to the surface. "We've already killed him. Made-from-Bone is not going to know." Just then the man came out of the water. The brothers-in-law turned to look at him. "Tsee, he survived, that bastard," they said. The man came out of the river and went back home. "Let's go home," they said. When they arrived at their house, they saw that their brother-in-law was with his wife.

During the night, they went to close off the stream. When they finished, they returned to their house. In the early morning, they went to see the *kakúri* trap in the stream. "Lots of fish. Now we will kill him for sure," they said. And they went to pick *macanilla* palm leaves, which they ground up and used to make the log very smooth. Already they finished. "Let's go find some *barbasco* leaves to go fishing in the stream, brother-in-law," they said.

"Okay, let's go, then," he replied. And they went. They arrived at the stream and began fishing with *barbasco* poison. Already the fish were beginning to leave the water [that is, float to the surface of the stream]. They say that one fish came up to the surface beneath the log.

They said to the man, "There is a fish, brother-in-law, go and shoot it with an arrow. Go across the log."

"Hooh," he said. He ran on top of the log. His foot slipped to one side, and he fell into the water. They say that they shot him with arrows, those brothers-in-law. "Uum," said the man.

"You will become a *raiao* catfish," they told him, "so that they can eat you, those people who will arrive in the future world." They were there at Hípana at a sandy beach called Kulirriána.[9]

Made-from-Bone was clearing a new manioc garden when a fine rain began to fall. Blood fell in his hand. "Could it be that they have killed my younger brother?" he asked. "I will leave my work and go to see," he said to himself. Already he left and arrived there. He arrived and saw that they were cutting and quartering his brother. "Okay," he said to himself, "They killed my brother. But it doesn't matter; all I want is his heart so that I can seek revenge."[10] Already Made-from-Bone had turned himself into a wasp called *awarána*. He flew from there towards them.

"We must watch out for Made-from-Bone," they said.

"Not so; nobody is going to tell him; Made-from-Bone doesn't know anything," said one of them.

"But Made-from-Bone is very strong, one cannot defeat him."

Made-from-Bone arrived as a wasp, bit into the corpse of his brother, and took away his heart. Already he was gone, and he had taken away the heart. "Oooo," they said, "That wasp has taken away the heart." They threw clods of dirt at the wasp. "Now we're in bad shape," they said. "That Made-from-Bone," they said, "Now he will finish us off, he will kill us all." Then one of them said to the others, "It is not so. This is only a wasp, not Made-from-Bone."

Made-from-Bone returned to his house. "I am going to go see where my brother is," he said. And he went away. Made-from-Bone arrived in the village of Great Sickness. "Eh, what's happening?" he said.

"Nothing," they said, "Enter."

"Okay," said Made-from-Bone, and he entered the house. "And my brother, where is he?" asked Made-from-Bone.

"He is coming from that direction," a woman answered him.

"Okay," said Made-from-Bone, "I will leave. Later I will come back again. If I do not come back in a few minutes, then I will arrive early tomorrow morning." He came back early the next morning. "What's happening?" he said, "Has my brother arrived yet?"

"No. He has been catching a lot of fish," said the woman. "He is still smoking them," she said.

"Okay. I am leaving. I will come again." He left. Made-from-Bone came back again, and again he asked, "Has my brother arrived?"

"No," the woman said, "They are over there, still smoking fish, they say."

"Could it be that they are going to kill my brother?" he said. "If they have killed my brother, things are going to be very bad for them. Later I will come back again to see if my brother has arrived." And he went back to his house.

Made-from-Bone returned home, furious. Already he worked with his brother's heart. He lit a fire in the clay manioc griddle and carried the heart over to it. He squeezed the heart over the manioc griddle, and a small bird came out. It was a small hawk called *péeri*. Then Made-from-Bone blew tobacco smoke over the bird. He flew off and sat down. He sang, "Fwia, fwia, fwia." Then Made-from-Bone said to him, "Open your wings so that I can see them." The bird spread its wings, but they were small. "No," said Made-from-Bone, "These are not any good." "Go away," he said, "Go look for your food, butterflies, little bird." And the bird flew away.

Made-from-Bone squeezed the heart again, and again a small hawk [*péeri*] appeared. He sent it away. He squeezed the heart again, and this time he took out a different bird. He blew tobacco smoke over the bird, which was a medium-sized hawk called *háwa*. "Spread your wings so I can see them," said Made-from-Bone. He spread his wings, and they were larger. "This is not good for anything," said Made-from-Bone, "Go and look for your food, whatever that may be." Then Made-from-Bone said, "Could it be that I am not going to succeed in getting revenge for my brother? I will try one more time to see what happens."

Then Made-from-Bone grasped his brother's heart and squeezed it with great force. He took out a bird, which sang, "Fwia, fwiaa, fwiaaa." "Spread your wings so that I can see them." He opened his wings. "Tan!" They say that it was like a huge airplane. The bird went and picked up a log, a large, heavy log. Made-from-Bone said to him, "Grab it and lift it in the air so that I can see; carry it and throw it over there."

"Okay," said the bird. And just like that he grasped and lifted the heavy log. He flew into the air with the log. He went and threw it far away, flew back, and arrived. "Tsa!"

"Aaa, now it is certain that I will succeed in getting revenge for my brother," he said. "Now I will take you with me so that we can kill them, my brother's revenge; we are going to finish them off."

Then he said to the bird, "Fold your wings back." He became a small bird. Made-from-Bone made a small vase and put the bird inside it. "Let's go and see." They arrived there. "What's new? Has my brother arrived yet?" he asked.

"No," the woman said, "He was here earlier, but he must have left again." Made-from-Bone became furious. He had heard that she was laughing about his brother.

"Yes, perhaps he did," he said. Then he threw some fruits. He picked *matapalo* [*kómakhé*] fruits, grasped them, and stuck them into the soles of his feet. This is why today we have *aniguas* in our feet.

"Made-from-Bone, what is this you have brought?" the woman asked.

"It's my pet," he replied.

"What kind is it?" she asked.

"It's a baby bird [*awádu*]," he replied.

"Why do you have it?" she asked.

"It eats *aniguas*," he replied. "If you want to see, come look for *aniguas* with me so that you can give it some to eat," he said to her.

"Bring it over here so that I can see your foot," she said. She dug into Made-from-Bone's foot and took out an *anigua*.

"Give it to him to eat," he said to her.

"Okay," she said, and gave the *anigua* to the bird to eat. She took out another *anigua* and again gave it to the bird to eat. "Paa, Made-from-Bone, this pet of yours is really good. Why don't you give it to me so that it can eat my father's *aniguas*," she said.

"Okay, here it is," said Made-from-Bone. And he gave her the bird.

She picked up the bird. "Papa, here is the pet that Made-from-Bone gave to me. It will eat your *aniguas*," she said to her father. "He eats them very well."

"It's good, my daughter, that he eats *aniguas*," he answered. "I have many *aniguas*." She picked up the bird and set it down on her father's shoulder.

It was the time when leaf-cutter ants were flying. The *matapalo* fruits had turned into flying ants. "Made-from-Bone, what are these things flying?" she asked.

"Hee? These are leaf-cutter ants," he said. She caught some of the ants and brought them over to the bird, and gave him some to eat. The ants were flying farther away. "Go and catch a lot of them for the bird," said Made-from-Bone.

"I will go catch them," she said to him.

"Go catch them, go catch them," he said.

While she went off to catch ants, Made-from-Bone went inside her house. He blocked the blowgun and made cuts in the bow and arrows. "Let's go; grab him," said Made-from-Bone, and he winked at the bird.

That hawk opened his wings to grab Great Sickness.

"Aaa, your pet is killing me." Already it flew away with him and carried him away.

"Made-from-Bone, it carried my father away. Come quickly to shoot it with an arrow," the woman said.

"Okay," he said, "bring me the arrow."

She ran back to him. "Here is the arrow," she said.

Made-from-Bone grabbed the arrow and tried to place it on the bowstring. "Toko!" the bow broke. "Hooh," said Made-from-Bone, "It's broken."

"What?"

"Bring the blowgun," he said.

The woman went to find the blowgun and brought it to Made-from-Bone. "Pierce him, Made-from-Bone, quickly. He is killing my father."

Made-from-Bone put a dart inside, then blew into the blowgun. "Pft." The blowgun was blocked. A wasp-person, *Kálimátu*,[11] had stopped up the "belly" of the blowgun. "Hooh, the blowgun is blocked. It's impossible to pierce him." Already the bird had left with him and taken him far away.

The giant bird went away with him, going down the Isana River until he reached a place called "Fish Trap of the Jaguar" [*Dzáwi Iupíte*]. He let him drink some water, then flew off with him again. Then he flew away with him, "Toam!"—he threw him into the Orinoco River. Great Sickness turned into a rock that is still there today. He died, and his body rotted, rotted beneath the river. People who drink water from the Orinoco get sick with malaria. That is how malaria began.

The woman and her brothers cried for the loss of their father. When they cried, the children of Great Sickness died. They say that is how they were finished off. "This is not right," said Made-from-Bone, "I will blow tobacco smoke for their spirits." He picked a *kuwáida* fruit and blew tobacco smoke over it. When he was finished blowing smoke, he gave the fruit to the family of Great Sickness. He went to see. They were crying. He carried the *kuwáida* fruit and threw it to them.

The children turned to look at it. "Ooo," they said, *"danholi!* Hee, *danholi, danholi!"* [a nonsensical expression of laughter.]

The woman turned to look. "Hee," she began to laugh. They went to bathe, returned, and came out of their house. They made manioc drinks [*yokúta*] and drank them. And they were happy. Thus it would be in the future for the "new people" in the other world. And so it is today. When someone in our family dies, our mother, our father, we cry a lot. Then we blow tobacco smoke for ourselves. Made-from-Bone himself started this in ancient times. He saved them.

Made-from-Bone Creates Evil Omens

"There are the others, the family of Great Sickness," he said, "we must finish them off." Then Made-from-Bone went to them. "I want a wife," he said.

"Okay." And they gave him a woman, who lived for a short time with him in Hípana.

One day she said, "Now I want you to take me to see my family."

"Okay," he said, "Let's go." They left and arrived in her family's village. Made-from-Bone was staying with them.

"Now we are going to kill him, in revenge of our father," they said. Made-from-Bone knew that they wanted to kill him.

Later Made-from-Bone said, "Let's return home again."

"Okay, let's go," said the woman. Then she said to her family, "Now we are going away from here." Made-from-Bone was there, some distance away.

"Go with him and sleep at the halfway point of the trail. We are going to kill him," they said to her.

"Okay," she said. And Made-from-Bone and the woman left.

"It's already afternoon. Let's sleep here. Tomorrow we can start again," she said.

Made-from-Bone cut down a log and implanted it. "Hang your hammock," he told her. Made-from-Bone had a blowgun. He cut a plantain leaf and lay down on it. He gathered some kindling that made white ashes. He had many poisoned darts, and his quiver was very full. The woman picked up one of the darts and started to weave with the pointed end. Made-from-Bone stole two of the darts from the quiver; it was still early. The woman did not know that he stole the two darts. He put them inside the blowgun. He lit a fire and lay down next to the flame. His wife lay down in her hammock.

Then she said, "Made-from-Bone, come here to lie down with me."

"No, I cannot lie down with you. I am a person who does not lie down in a hammock with a woman," said Made-from-Bone.

"It's alright, lie down. Come and lie down with me," she said, "come and hold me."

"No, I am a person who does not like to do this." Made-from-Bone blew tobacco smoke; he blew smoke over her. She slept like a dead person, like a drunkard.

Later Made-from-Bone blew over the fire, and white ashes fell over him. It was getting very close to dawn. He heard them coming, "To-ro!" "Here they come, those bastards," he said. Made-from-Bone jumped up and grabbed his blowgun. He went to wait for them, "To-ro!"

They arrived above him and took out their poison. "Here comes blood, Made-from-Bone," they said. He jumped to one side. They began to throw poison again. "Here comes blood, Made-from-Bone," they said. He leapt to one side.

Made-from-Bone looked and saw dark shapes against the moon. "For you the blood is coming," he said. Made-from-Bone shot one of them with a dart, "Tsa!" Again he loaded a dart, "Tsa!" He shot the other one with a dart. And he went back.

He returned and lit a cigar. He blew smoke over the woman to wake her up. Then Made-from-Bone jumped and lay down next to the fire. He blew over the fire, and white ashes fell on top of him. His wife woke up. Her two brothers fell from the trees to the ground. She heard "Ti!," then the other one, "Ti!" She tried to wake up Made-from-Bone. "Made-from-Bone! Made-from-Bone!" He was sound asleep, snoring. "Made-from-Bone! Made-from-Bone!"

"He, hee," said Made-from-Bone, "What happened to you?"

"I was frightened by what I heard," she said.

"Paa," said Made-from-Bone, "I was sleeping like a man dying of old age. Just now I woke up because you woke me. What did you hear?"

"What I heard was frightening. Right here I heard something fall close to us. What I heard falling was heavy. Ti!"

Then she said, "Made-from-Bone, you didn't kill my two brothers?"

"Not at all. Why would I kill your brothers?" he said.

"Okay. I am going to look at the darts," she said.

"Go ahead and look at them," he said. The woman counted[12] all the darts. They were all there.

"What you heard was nothing important; let's go to sleep," said Made-from-Bone. She went and lay down again in her hammock. Already she was asleep again. Made-from-Bone lit a cigar and blew tobacco smoke over her.

She slept like a dead person. Already Made-from-Bone was standing up. He lit up a torch so that he could see his way. He saw a *cuchicuchi* monkey lying on the ground and lifted up its arm. He plucked and bent in half the hairs from the monkey's armpit. That is how it would be for the new people in the future world. This was the beginning of poison in the world of people. He cut off the monkey's head and stomped on it until it entered the ground. He went and found the other monkey, cut off its head, and stepped on it until it went under the ground. This would become food for the new people in the future world. It is a tree called *dzapúra*. Made-from-Bone went back. He lit a cigar again and blew tobacco smoke over the woman.

She woke up early in the morning. They were conversing when Made-from-Bone said, "Paa, I had a terrible dream. I think that your family has fallen ill."

"Is it possible that this happened?" she asked.

"Yes, it is so," he said.

"Okay. Wait for me while I go back and find out," she said. "Okay, let's go." And they went off on the path, back towards the village of the family of Great Sickness.

She had an evil omen. She went ahead of Made-from-Bone, who carried the blowgun in his hand. He placed the blowgun in front of her at a curve in the path. Her foot tripped over the blowgun, and she nearly fell down. "Paa, Made-from-Bone. Just now I stubbed my foot. What does this mean?" she asked.

"Hmm. You are having an evil omen. To stub one's foot, this is an evil omen," he said. "This is not a good sign for your family. You, you have an evil omen. Let's go and see what's happening with your family." And they set off again.

He found some *guambé* [*palúwaa*] vine. He took the knots off the *guambé* vine and threw them in front of the woman. She found the knots as she went along the path. They spoke, "Tse, tse, tse."

"What could this be, Made-from-Bone?" she asked.

"It's a little bird, called *hádzee*. These are *hádzee,* and they are an evil omen; very bad for your family. You, you have an evil omen," he said. And they set off again. They were getting close to where they had started.

He ran across some worm shit, which he took and put under his loincloth along the side of his torso. "Yaa!" he shouted in pain.

"What happened to you?" she asked.

"Something bad just happened; my glands are swollen," he said. "Ayaa, I cannot go on. Go and see your family."

"Okay, you stay here. I will go to see my family." And she left. When she was still close by, Made-from-Bone stood up. He took the worm shit from his body and threw it away. Thus it was to be [this inflamation of the glands] for the new people in the future world.

The woman arrived at their place. "Hoh, it is serious," they told her.

"What happened to you?" she asked.

"We are sick," they said. "Made-from-Bone, where is Made-from-Bone?"

"Made-from-Bone is right over there. He fell ill, too," she said. "I think he already died there."

Made-from-Bone had already returned to his house. "I have killed them. I have finished off all of them, the revenge for my younger brother," he said.

3

Ethnohistorical Interlude: Historical Themes in the Myth of Made-from-Bone and Anaconda-Person

This chapter arises from a specific connection between the mythic narrative about Made-from-Bone and the Anaconda-Person (*Uliámali*) and the widespread practice of using necklaces made of shells and beads as a form of currency during the colonial period. Taken in isolation, the occurrence of a single mythic episode about the use of necklaces as "money" in the upper Río Negro provides little more than an interesting footnote on the likelihood that such necklaces were in use and circulating among indigenous groups at least as far south as the northern Brazil–southern Venezuela frontier. However, when this mythic episode is understood within the regional ethnographic and historical context in which it occurs, a broader pattern of economic and social exchange becomes evident. Moreover, historical sources from the colonial period support the view that Arawakan societies of the Upper Río Negro region were connected to the colonial exchange of shell necklaces that had spread across northern South America and that had come to be centered on the middle Orinoco basin by the seventeenth century (Gasson 2000).

Elsewhere in South America, the practice of making necklaces out of coins is still practiced among the contemporary Emberá and Wounaan living in the Darién Peninsula of eastern Panama, where women keep small baskets in which they store coin necklaces. These coins come from Venezuela, Colombia, Chile, Ecuador, the United States, and other countries and date back to the nineteenth century or even earlier (Velásquez Runk 2005:166–67). "Gathered from many foreign systems of exchange, the coins have been inserted, refashioned, and kept in this indigenous culture"; the coin necklaces are passed down from mother to daughter over many generations, and "some coins are so old that they are smooth from wear" (Kane 1994:131). Similar coin necklaces and bracelets made of pierced silver coins were observed in the early years of the twentieth century among the Ye'kuana, Piaroa, Mako, and other groups of the Upper Orinoco (Matos Arvelo 1912:32; Gasson 2000:597). These coin necklaces and bracelets are historical descendants of a long and widespread tradition of interethnic trade in body ornaments made from strings of *quirípa* (shell "money"), glass or ceramic beads, or bone (Gasson 2000). In addition to their importance as a form of currency during the colonial period, these body ornaments served as symbols of rank and prestige within the more hierarchical societies of the Orinoco basin, such as the Otomac. "Similar to many other groups of the llanos, the Otomac esteemed the quirípa as a symbol of wealth and power. Tavacaré, the powerful Otomac chief, wore many strings of quirípa on his neck and forearms; his sister was also dressed in a similar fashion" (Gasson 2000:595).

Regional Networks and Colonial Transformations in the Middle Orinoco Basin

Anthropological and historical research on indigenous groups of the northern lowlands of South America has emphasized the importance of mobility and horizontal ties of warfare, trade, and alliance extending over the entire llanos and Guiana Shield regions (Morey and Morey 1975; Morales Mendez and Arvelo-Jimenez 1981; Biord Castillo 1985; Butt Colson 1973; Thomas 1972; Rausch 1984; Whitehead 1988; Hill 1999; Gasson 2000). The central core of this vast interregional network was the middle Orinoco basin, where the abundance of turtle eggs and fish during the dry season brought together indigenous peoples from llanos areas to the north and west as well as from forested zones to the south and east. Maipure, Achagua, and other Arawak-speaking peoples were the most numerous inhabitants of the upper Orinoco basin, and various Carib-speaking peoples predominated along the lower Orinoco. The middle Orinoco was a transitional zone in which Arawak- and Carib-speaking peoples overlapped and exchanged subsistence items for various trade goods. Carib and Arawakan peoples accounted for approximately 70 percent of the linguistic diversity in the middle Orinoco region, with the remaining 30 percent Saliba-speaking peoples, such as the Piaroa, and speakers of various unclassified languages (Biord Castillo 1985:91). Although the distribution of language groups demonstrated clear concentrations of Arawakan speakers in upstream areas along the lower Orinoco and its tributaries, there was no clear-cut boundary dividing the two language families, and there were frequent instances of intermarriage between them (Gilij 1965 [1782]).

Radiating outwards from the core region along the middle Orinoco were three major chains of trade. To the north and east, Carib-speaking peoples traded such forest and coastal products as blowguns, arrows, baskets, poison, pigment, and pearls in exchange for *quirípa*, turtle oil, smoked fish, gold, and salt (Morey and Morey 1975:18). These trade networks channeled products from the llanos and middle Orinoco basin throughout coastal areas of Venezuela, the interior forests and coastal plains of Guiana, and up into the Antilles. To the west, the Achagua and other Arawak-speaking peoples traded products of the llanos and forests with the Muisca and other Chibcha-speaking peoples of the northern Andes (Rausch 1984:11). Gold, salt, and cotton cloth were the principal trade goods obtained from Andean peoples (Morey and Morey 1975:18–19). To the south, Saliba- and Arawak-speaking peoples of the Upper Orinoco and Río Negro traded forest products, such as curare poison and resins, in exchange for turtle oil, smoked fish, and *quirípa*. Trade networks crisscrossing the northern lowlands centered around the production of surplus fish and turtle oil in the middle Orinoco basin, but there is no evidence of powerful chiefdoms dominating this central region. Instead, the middle Orinoco, at least as it is known through early historical documents of European explorers (Federmann 1945 [1530]; Humboldt 1818) and missionaries (Gilij 1965 [1782]; Rivero 1956 [1733]), had developed into a zone of intercultural trade and contact among a variety of linguistically different people. "The Andean Cordillera, the Upper Orinoco (tropical forest; Amazonia) and Guyana interconnected themselves with the llanos by means of trade. . . . The commercial relations with the Andes, the upper Orinoco and Guyana appear to have passed *across* the llanos but not *toward* the llanos" (Morey and Morey 1975:27–28, translation and emphasis mine). Political relations among various indigenous peoples in the middle Orinoco basin consisted of horizontal ties "in which no one group dominated the others" (Biord Castillo 1985:96, my translation).

Relations with European explorers and missionaries during the colonial period disrupted indigenous trade and political linkages in the northern lowlands. The introduction of steel tools, firearms, and other European trade goods tipped the balance of power in favor of Carib-speaking groups living along the lower Orinoco who enjoyed the most direct access to centers of colonial wealth and power. Aside from the spread of contagious diseases, the most devastating effects of the early colonial period were internecine wars aimed at capturing slaves to sell or barter with the Europeans. The enslavement of enemies captured in warfare had almost certainly formed part of the horizontal political ties among neighboring indigenous peoples prior to the arrival of Europeans, yet "neither the subsistence base nor [the level of] sociocultural complexity promoted the development of slavery among the indigenous groups" (Morey and Morey 1975:25, translation mine). During the seventeenth century, Dutch traders formed alliances with Carib-speaking peoples in Guiana and the lower Orinoco region against the Spanish and their allies, the Arawak-speaking Lokono (Whitehead 1990:363). This process of ethnic soldiering favored the more numerous Carib-speaking peoples, who also controlled interior trade routes in contraband goods between Spanish settlements and the Essequibo Dutch.

The Dutch-Carib alliance had profound effects through the northern lowlands in the seventeenth century, as the trade in indigenous slaves spread not only across more accessible areas of the llanos but into the Upper Orinoco, Casiquiare, and Río Negro regions. In the early seventeenth century, Arawak-speaking groups of the middle and upper Orinoco acted as middlemen in the Dutch-Carib slave trade as well as the Portuguese slave trade emanating from the Río Negro region (Morey and Morey 1975:20). The Achagua of the Río Meta, for example, traded animal skins, feathers, and *quirípa* in exchange for captives from other indigenous groups, who were then sold to Carib traders in return for steel tools and other European trade goods. The extremely high values placed upon such trade goods and the exponential rate of inflation between central and peripheral regions were evident in the rates of exchange: "for one axe, one machete, and four strings of pearls, it was possible to buy one child. From the Dutch, they [Carib traders] received for each slave ten axes, ten machetes, ten knives, ten bands of glass pearls, one piece of cloth for a *guayuco,* one mirror, one scissors, and sometimes a rifle, powder and lead molds, a bottle of rum, and some needles, tweezers, and fishhooks" (Morey and Morey 1975:12, translation mine). Later in the seventeenth century, Arawakan groups such as the Maipure and Achagua suffered major losses as they became objects of the Dutch-Carib slave trade, and by the mid-eighteenth century the Achagua had become badly decimated from the combined effects of the slave trade and diseases.

Seventeenth-century trade partnerships between the Arawakan Achagua and Dutch-Caribs are an important example of the more general socioeconomic processes of change unfolding in northern South America during the colonial period as well as the profound importance played by *quirípa* shell money within the colonial economy. Written accounts from the period portray the Achagua as a complex, strongly hierarchical society with hereditary chiefs and specialists who produced *quirípa* for trade (Gasson 2000:593). When the Dutch-Carib slave trade spread across the llanos in the mid-seventeenth century, the Achagua used *quirípa* "to obtain Western commodities, particularly iron tools and firearms from the Carib" (Gasson 2000:593). Due to the scarcity of precious metals in colonial Venezuela, a shortage of metal coins led European and indigenous peoples alike to engage in the widespread adoption of *quirípa* as a form of generalized money. "Everyday exchange was carried out by using *quirípa,* not money; . . . *Quirípa* strings were also used to pay debts and taxes under a fixed rate. . . . For these reasons the shell beads became synonymous with money and certainly acquired the characteristic of contemporary currencies (e.g., they had value standards, were kept as savings, and were used to pay taxes and debts)" (Gasson 2000:594). Thus, the colonial economy of the middle Orinoco region emerged through a process of hybridization in which indigenous forms of exchange became a standard of value for interethnic trade relations as well as everyday transactions.

Northwestern Amazonia in the Late Colonial Period

In a previous analysis of ethnogenesis in northwestern Amazonia (Hill 1996), I set forth and explored several hypotheses about how the contemporary regional pattern of northern Arawakan and eastern Tukanoan fishing and horticultural societies arose during the late colonial period through the intertwining of indigenous forms of ritual-political power with alien forms of power introduced into the region by colonial missionaries and traders. The colonial period brought massive social, demographic, and economic changes to northwestern Amazonia. Recently, Vidal (1993, 2000, 2002) has documented the emergence of a series of chiefdoms and political confederations among the Manao, Baré, Piapoco, and other Arawak-speaking peoples during the eighteenth century. These hierarchical political formations rose and fell apart in rapid succession throughout a vast region of riverine territories stretching from the lower Río Negro to the headwaters of the Negro (Guainía) River and, via the Casiquiare and Atabapo rivers, on into the upper and middle Orinoco basins.

These political transformations unfolded during a period when the Achagua alliance with the Dutch-Caribs in the llanos to the north was in steep decline but when the Portuguese slave trade emanating from the south and east was reaching its zenith. Researchers have estimated that Portuguese traders enslaved approximately 20,000 indigenous people from northwestern Amazonia between 1745 and 1755 (Wright 1981; Chernela 1993). Alarmed at the overwhelming superiority of Portuguese colonial power in the Upper Orinoco and Negro rivers, the Spanish colonial government launched a belated effort to establish mission settlements and forts at San Carlos de Río Negro, Maroa, La Esmeralda, and San Fernando de Atabapo in the late 1750s and 1760s (Hill 1999; Guss 1986). After the expulsion of Jesuit missionaries in 1767, the Portuguese government launched a campaign of forced relocations to downstream sites that greatly reduced Arawakan and Tukanoan peoples living along the lower Isana and Vaupés (Chernela 1988; Wright 1981; Wright and Hill 1986). Compounding the impact of these forced descents, or *descimentos,* was the arrival of successive waves of epidemics of flu, measles, smallpox, and other exogenous diseases in the 1780s. The survivors fled to remote, inaccessible areas at the headwaters of the Isana and Río Negro (Guainía). Large permanent settlements along the lower Vaupés, Isana, and Negro rivers were left totally abandoned for several years.

The pattern of interethnic relations found among northern Arawakan and eastern Tukanoan peoples of northwestern Amazonia in the modern (post-rubber boom) period originated during the traumatic changes of the colonial period. By the mid-seventeenth century, Arawak-speaking groups of the upper Río Negro region were trading indigenous slaves for *quirípa,* steel tools, and firearms with the Achagua and their Dutch-Carib allies in the middle Orinoco basin (Morey and Morey 1975:20). In all likelihood, eastern Tukanoan peoples living along the Vaupés River and its tributaries were among the primary targets of the Dutch-Carib slave trade during this early period. Later, as the colonial period came to an end, the Arawak-speaking middlemen themselves became the primary objects of the Portuguese slave trade, the expansion of late Spanish colonial power into the region, and the Portuguese policy of *descimentos.* Sometime during this shift, northern Arawakan and eastern Tukanoan peoples formed the complex regional ties that have formed the subject of recent ethnographic studies (for example, Goldman 1963; Reichel-Dolmatoff 1971, 1975; C. Hugh-Jones 1979; S. Hugh-Jones 1979; Jackson 1983; Chernela 1993; Wright 1981; Hill 1983; Journet 1995).

The Myth of Made-from-Bone
and the Anaconda-Person

The first time I heard the myth of the Anaconda-Person was in the context of a prolonged curing ritual in 1981 in the community on the lower Guainía River where I was doing research for my doctoral dissertation (Hill 1983). Robin Wright recorded a slightly different version of the narrative among the Hohódeni living on the Aiarí River in Brazil (1981:571–575). The version provided here is based on a 1998 transcription of the 1981 recording.

The anaconda is considered one of the primary life-forms in Wakuénai cosmology, and in ritually powerful songs and chants (*malikái*) the anaconda is invoked as a categorical term encompassing all aquatic animals: reptiles, fish, amphibians, and mammals. However, the life-giving powers of the anaconda as prototypic water-animal spirit are accompanied by more negative associations with the hunger and diseases people experience during the long wet seasons. It is primarily the latter, more negative meanings that are explored in the myth of the Anaconda-Person.

Since the full text of the narrative is provided above (see "Made-from-Bone and the Anaconda-Person" in chapter 2), I will reproduce here only those passages that refer explicitly to the origin of the white people (*yarináinai*) and the practice of making and exchanging shell necklaces as "money" (*paráta*).

> They say that Anaconda-Person paid the woman money. In those ancient days, there were women who fastened shells into necklaces that were called *koma*. Anaconda-Person put one of these necklaces on the woman after making love to her. This is how it worked all the time.

At the end of the next episode, there is a second reference to "money" (*paráta*) as a form of payment:

> When Anaconda-Person had finished copulating with the woman, he gave her money.

And several episodes later, when Made-from-Bone has found the rotting body of the Anaconda-Person:

> They found the body of Anaconda-Person in Éenutanhísre. They found him rotten, with many worms eating his body. These worms are known as the penis of Anaconda-Person, and it is said that they are the source of the white people of today. They also say that we indigenous people were born at Hípana [a village on the Aiarí River in Brazil]. Then Made-from-Bone got out a net and used it to pick up the penis of Anaconda-Person.

Interpreting the Myth of Made-from-Bone and the Anaconda-Person

The myth of the Anaconda-Person is a highly multivocalic narrative that forms part of a larger set of narratives about the trickster-creator, Made-from-Bone, and his ongoing struggles to deal with a series of adversaries. In these narratives, the trickster is portrayed as an omniscient, powerful being who uses his superior knowledge to turn the tables on his enemies. In addition, the myth of the Anaconda-Person touches upon many of the key elements in the cycle of myths about the primordial human being *Kuwái*, who is the son born of incestuous sexual relations between Made-from-Bone and First-Woman (*Ámaru*).[1] However, the myth of the Anaconda-Person inverts the symbolic processes surrounding the birth of *Kuwái* and the subsequent creation of human and natural worlds.

In the myth of *Kuwái*'s birth, the unborn child is unable to escape from his mother's womb until Made-from-Bone creates a birth canal. After birth, *Kuwái* is taken away from his mother and the rest of his family and placed in a remote house in "the corner of the sky." *Kuwái* escapes from his place of confinement and flies about the skies, creating the species and objects of nature by humming and singing their names. The remainder of the myth cycle tells how Made-from-Bone and his brother, the first chant owner (*Dzúli*), lured *Kuwái* down to the ground at the mythic center of the world and place of ancestral emergence (Hípana) and harnessed his musical naming power by learning the ritually powerful ways of singing, chanting, and speaking (*malikái*).

Bodily and cosmic processes of birth and creation are turned upside-down in the myth of the Anaconda-Person. The conception of *Kuwái* is genital and incestuous, whereas the Anaconda-Child (*Uliámaliéni*) is conceived through a morbid, adulterous, and gastronomic intercourse. And whereas *Kuwái* was stuck inside his mother's womb until Made-from-Bone's intervention, the Anaconda-Child refuses to leave its mother's womb except to steal her food, making her sick. Moreover, movements of *Kuwái* about the sky, his musical naming power, and its establishment as the basis of ritual power in human social life outline a process of creation in which ritual specialists, called *malikái limínali* (chant owner) and shamans (*malírri*), control the developmental stages of the human life cycle as well as the reproduction of social groups over time. In contrast, the Anaconda-Child's growth within its mother's womb is destructive, sickening, and life-threatening—an antidevelopmental process that foreshadows the mother's expulsion from human social life and transformation into a species of catfish that eats fish larger than itself and vomits up the bones after digesting the flesh. The cycle of myths about *Kuwái* explains the creation of a humanly fashioned social world through successfully mediating the supernaturalized powers of mythic beings, whereas the myth of the Anaconda-Person demonstrates the disintegration of human social life that occurs when individuals fail to control their sexual desires and open the door to violent acts of revenge.

Although the myth of the Anaconda-Person does not explain the origins of exchange in positive terms, it does assert the capacity of local groups to defend themselves against outsiders whose predatory sexual actions threaten to weaken or violate prescribed patterns of exchange between groups. Through killing the Anaconda-Person and tricking his unfaithful wife into eating the dead anaconda's penis, Made-from-Bone expels the source of danger and restores proper social relations. Moreover, the ex-wife's transformation into an anomalous species of catfish serves as a living reminder of the fate awaiting anyone who would dare to undermine proper relations of exchange.

The Anaconda as Historical Metaphor

In addition to its multiple resonances with the cycles of mythic narratives about Made-from-Bone, First-Woman, and the primordial human being (*Kuwái*), the myth of Anaconda-Person explicitly links the anaconda's destructive powers to colonial history in the upper Río Negro region through asserting that the worms eating Anaconda-Person's decomposing body are the source of white people. It is highly significant that Anaconda-Person's rotting body is found several days' journey *downstream,* since the expansion of Portuguese colonialism came up the Río Negro from downstream areas to the south and east. The association of downstream, southeastern regions with colonial history is established in several important mythic narratives and ritual performances (Hill 2002) that explain the origins of steel tools, contagious diseases (witchcraft), and the colonial trade language known as *lingua geral.* The overwhelmingly negative imagery of Anaconda-Person's worm-infested body as the origin of white people is part of this larger set of mythic and ritual symbolism that links downstream, southeastern regions with the traumatic losses of indigenous life, land, and autonomy that accompanied Portuguese expansion up the Río Negro during the colonial period.

Conversely, the movement *back upstream* to the mythic center of the world and into remote headwater areas is associated with the restoration of life and shamanic reversals of death and disease. This process of recovery through moving back upstream is clearly present in the myth of Anaconda-Person, where Made-from-Bone's movement upstream sets the stage for his expulsion of Anaconda-Person's antisocial progeny. The fact that Made-from-Bone brings the mythic source of white people, or Anaconda-Person's penis (*Uliámali íshi*), back to the center of mythic space gives acknowledgment to the profound changes that Portuguese colonialism brought to the very core of indigenous societies in the Upper Río Negro. For it is only through deliberately bringing Anaconda-Person's destructive power back to the mythic center that its lethal effects can be reversed. Moreover, the image of the Anaconda-Child (*Uliámaliéni*) stealing his mother's food so that she becomes weak and emaciated even as her belly swells up to enormous proportions also makes an appropriate metaphor for the predatory economic expansion of colonial trade goods, *quirípa,* and indigenous slaves across the northern lowlands of South America.

The myth of the Anaconda-Person also speaks to the increased importance of interethnic relations between the Arawakan phratries of the Upper Río Negro and the eastern Tukanoan language groups living along the Vaupés River and its tributaries to the south and west. That the anaconda of Wakuénai myth can also be interpreted as a historical metaphor for the eastern Tukanoan peoples is supported by several lines of evidence.[2]

First, the anaconda is the most central figure in the mythologies of eastern Tukanoan language groups (S. Hugh-Jones 1979; C. Hugh-Jones 1979; Jackson 1983; Reichel-Dolmatoff 1996; Chernela 1993). For the Desana, Wanano, Cubeo, Barasana, and other eastern Tukanoan language groups, the anaconda is not merely a prototypic aquatic life-form subsumed by a more generalized mythic being but is the very source of humanity. The eastern Tukanoans explain their mythic origins in terms of descent from ancestral anacondas that took the form of immense canoes that came up the rivers, dropping off the first peoples in the riverine territories now inhabited by their descendants.[3]

Secondly, written historical records demonstrate that both Arawak- and Tukano-speaking peoples of northwestern Amazonia retreated into remote headwater areas of the Río Negro basin in response to Portuguese slave trade, diseases, and forced relocations (*descimentos,* or "descents") during the last half of the eighteenth century. By this time, downstream areas that had been major points of intersection in the vast network of northern Arawakan peoples stretching from Manaus to the Middle Orinoco had become centers of colonial control, epidemics of contagious disease, and economic exploitation of indigenous labor. Arawakan peoples of the headwater regions survived the colonial period by moving further upstream to more protected, remote locations, and this movement brought them into increasingly permanent contact with eastern Tukanoans of the Vaupés and its tributaries. The initial movement of Arawakan peoples into Tukanoan areas was almost certainly a period of interethnic competition and warfare. With the decline of colonial governments in the region, competitive pressures eased as many Wakuénai sibs returned to downstream areas along the Isana and Negro rivers. Not all Wakuénai sibs returned to downstream areas; some remained in the Vaupés basin where they became Tukanoans.[4]

Beyond these various indirect lines of evidence, the plausibility of reading the myth of the Anaconda-Person as a historical metaphor for relations between Arawakan and Tukanoan peoples is directly supported by the fact that the Arapaço, an eastern Tukanoan group living on the Vaupés River in Brazil, tell a version of the same mythic narrative in which the anaconda lover is explicitly identified as "our ancestor" (Chernela 1988:41–43). In the Arapaço version of the myth, the Anaconda-Person (called *Unurato*) is said to transform itself each day into a young man whose striking beauty and shiny gold ear ornaments enchanted the wife of *Iapo* (a clear reference to Made-from-Bone, the trickster-creator of Wakuénai myth). As in the Arawakan version of the myth, *Iapo*'s wife had sexual intercourse with the Anaconda-Person every day upon returning from her manioc garden. But the entire story, which unfolds in nearly identical terms, is narrated from the Anaconda-Person's (*Unurato*'s) perspective rather than that of *Iapo* (Made-from-Bone): "We are grandchildren of the Anacondas, we are the Arapaço snake-children. He was our grandfather. *Unurato* is our oldest and most cherished brother. He will come back to us; we are waiting for him" (Chernela 1988:41). Later, after the anaconda has been hit by *Iapo*'s poisoned dart, the narrator states, "Our grandfather, the snake, had been poisoned. We are the family of that snake; he is the grandfather of the Arapaço" (Chernela 1988:41).

In sharp contrast with the Wakuénai myth of Made-from-Bone and the Anaconda-Person, the protagonist of the Arapaço myth (*Unurato*) does not die after being poisoned by *Iapo*'s dart. Instead, *Unurato*'s body rolled downstream for two days, where *Iapo* caught up with him, cut off his penis, and mixed it with small fishes that his wife later ate. The Arapaço myth also ends with the wife's tranformation into a fish but continues with two more sections in which *Unurato* travels downstream to Manaus and Brasilia, eventually returning to the Vaupés River in the form of an enormous submarine filled with boxes of trade goods (Chernela 1988:43). The return of *Unurato* as a submarine symbolically recapitulates, albeit in technologically modern form, the story of eastern Tukanoan origins through ascending the Vaupés in anaconda-canoes that dropped off the first ancestors. Only in the myth of *Unurato*, it is the story of a people struggling to return to life after suffering through horrendous losses during the rubber boom (ca. 1860–1920) and the colonial period. The myth of *Unurato* ends with a prophecy of social renewal: "Now we are few, but he will give us back our prosperity, and our numbers" (Chernela 1988:43).

Conclusion

The Arapaço myth of *Unurato*, when taken together with current ethnographic and historical research on northwestern Amazonia, makes it plausible to interpret the Wakuénai myth of Made-from-Bone and the Anaconda-Person as a historical metaphor for the initially hostile interethnic relations between Arawakan and Tukanoan peoples during the colonial period. The myth of Made-from-Bone and the Anaconda-Person establishes the practice of making shell necklaces (*koma*) for trade as an ancient tradition among Arawak-speaking peoples of the upper Río Negro region: "In those ancient days, there were women who fastened shells into necklaces that were called *koma*." The myth thus corroborates historical evidence that *quirípa* shells were traded into the Río Negro from the middle Orinoco basin during precolonial times (Morey and Morey 1975). The use of shell necklaces in the Río Negro was also consistent with their importance as markers of elite social status among hierarchically organized, Arawak-speaking societies, such as the Achagua, of the llanos and middle Orinoco basin.

At the same time, the myth of Made-from-Bone and Anaconda-Person makes it clear that by the time of heightened Arawakan-Tukanoan interrelations, the meaning of shell necklaces was shifting from its prior significance as a marker of social status to a form of money for mercantile exchange: "They say that the Anaconda-Person paid the woman money," and "When the Anaconda-Person had finished copulating with the woman, he gave her money." Although it is impossible to pinpoint the exact time when this economic shift developed in the upper Río Negro region, it is comparable to the process of economic hybridization through which *quirípa* had become a form of general purpose money among the Achagua and other groups of the middle Orinoco basin by the mid-seventeenth century (Gasson 2000:599–600). The memory of this colonial historical process persists today among the Wakuénai phratries of the Upper Río Negro through the condensed yet multivocalic imagery of the myth of Made-from-Bone and Anaconda-Person.

Part 2

The World Begins

Overview

In the narratives set in the times called "The World Begins" (*Hekuápi Ikéeñuakawa*), the trickster-creator uses his skills of trickery to get things from various animal-persons and mythic beings. Made-from-Bone obtains nighttime and sleep from Grandfather Sleep (*Dáinali*), fire from a spirit being named *Yáwali,* and peach-palm fruits from an anaconda-person named *Malíhwerri.* Unlike the life-and-death struggles of Made-from-Bone against Great Sickness and other adversaries during the primordial times, the confrontations between Made-from-Bone and others during "The World Begins" are more like puzzles or games in which the trickster-creator must outsmart his interlocutors in order to take away their goods.

Violence and bloodshed are almost entirely absent from these interactions. One way of measuring the qualitative difference in levels of violence between the two mythic periods is by counting the frequency of the verb "kill," excluding cases where animals or fish are specifically mentioned as objects. In the nine narratives from the primordial times (*Úupi Pérri*), the verb "kill" is used against Made-from-Bone or his enemies a total of forty-three times, whereas the same verb appears only five times in the six narratives from "The World Begins." And the rationale for the trickster-creator's actions is no longer to inflict violent revenge but is now much more directly focused on the need to create things that are necessary to pave the way for "the new people of the future world."

The theme of "the new people of the future world," or fully human beings living in the world in present and recent past times, is found in several of the narratives set in the primordial times. However, the theme does not emerge organically as a motivating factor in those narratives as it does in the ones set in "The World Begins."

The status of Made-from-Bone is now a well-established social fact known among powerful mythic beings throughout the cosmos. Grandfather Sleep (*Dáinali*) greets Made-from-Bone as "my famous grandson who knows everything" and notes that "people speak about you." Later, Made-from-Bone and Grandfather Sleep blow tobacco smoke together before going to sleep, and Made-from-Bone impresses Grandfather Sleep again by knowing how to use the special word *alíra* that allows him to continue on in his quest to get nighttime and sleep.

After experiencing his first night of sleeping and dreaming, Made-from-Bone must choose between two kinds of sleep, "sleep of the eyelid" or "sleep of the heel." As always, Made-from-Bone makes the correct choice, or sleep of the heel, avoiding the fate of Grandfather Sleep, whose eyelids had grown to enormous proportions as he had aged. "Okay, you must know already, my grandson. No one can pull one over on you. The one you want is the better one because the heel has nowhere to grow bigger," says Grandfather Sleep. Because Made-from-Bone made the right choice, "the new people living in the future world" would have eyelids that stopped growing when they reached adulthood.

Bringing the night, or sleep of the heel, back to his village presents Made-from-Bone with additional challenges. The bag containing small pieces chopped from the heels of Grandfather Sleep is so heavy that it takes several people to lift and carry. In spite of Grandfather Sleep's explicit warnings not to open the bag until reaching their village, Made-from-Bone and his companions decide to open it just enough to peek inside and find out why it is so heavy. A large *gallineta* bird (wild chicken) flies out of the bag and disappears over the western horizon, taking the sun along with it. They become frightened as night falls because they "don't even know how morning will come." When some birds begin singing, they become hopeful that morning is finally coming.

Made-from-Bone sends a sloth up a tall tree to look for any sign of light, but the sloth tricks everyone by opening and closing his anus to create light and darkness. Finally the sloth points to where the sun is rising from downstream (that is, the eastern horizon), surprising everyone because they were expecting the sun to come up in the west where they had seen it go down. When they reach their village at Hípana, Made-from-Bone and his family settle into a regular pattern of sleeping at night, working and sharing food together during the day. If they had not opened the bag and let the large *gallineta* bird escape at the midpoint of their journey home, all the fish and game at Hípana would have turned into manioc, and "the new people living in the future world" would have nothing but manioc to eat.

In a second narrative in "The World Begins," Made-from-Bone gets cooking fire from *Yáwali,* the master of fire. Made-from-Bone invites two companions, Squirrel and Alligator, to accompany him to the village of *Yáwali.* Made-from-Bone begs *Yáwali* to give him fire so that he can use it to cook fish and warm manioc drinks. Finally, *Yáwali* agrees to send the fire to Made-from-Bone's village: "Go, Made-from-Bone. When you arrive there [in your village], I will order that it be sent behind you." But before Made-from-Bone and his two companions could reach their homes, they heard and saw an enormous fire approaching along the path. Squirrel captures smoke from the fire in his urn, but it is Alligator who swallows the burning coals and becomes the source of cooking fire.

Two other narratives in "The World Begins" focus on a younger brother of Made-from-Bone named *Káali,* who is the mythic creator of manioc and other cultivated plants. In one narrative, Manioc-Man (*Káali*) punishes people for spying on his magical techniques for clearing and planting manioc gardens. A man who grows curious about how Manioc-Man can make his garden so quickly discovers that he has an enormous cord that allows him to pull down whole sections of the forest. But when the man spies on Manioc-Man, the cord breaks. "From now on it will be like this for the new people in the future world. They will have to work very hard to make new manioc gardens." Similarly, Manioc-Man's magical basket would plant manioc sticks by itself until a woman spied on Manioc-Man, and the basket tied its cord around her head. "Now you will have to carry it," Manioc-Man said to her. "You want to work . . . and this is how it will be for all the new people in the future world."

The second narrative about Manioc-Man and his children (*Kaaliéni*) tells how ceremonial dance music (*mádzerukái*) originated as a way of asking for drinks at social gatherings. There are two distinct parts to this narrative. In the first part, Manioc-Man's wife leaves him for another man, and Manioc-Man uses magic to destroy her manioc garden by turning all her plants into useless weeds. When this action causes his children, a son and a daughter, to suffer from hunger, Manioc-Man uses his magical powers to make manioc starch from frog eggs so that his children can eat. In the second part of the narrative, Manioc-Man remarries, becomes a father to four sons, and teaches them how to sing and dance ceremonial dance music (*mádzerukái*) as a way of politely asking him for drinks. Manioc-Man hides most of the fermented drinks inside his house as a way of testing his sons' social skills. While Manioc-Man is lying down, he hears the boys singing his name as they dance and sing outside. "I am happy. . . . They have learned *mádzerukái* as I had hoped."

Manioc-Man's invention of ceremonial dance music (*mádzerukái*) as a way of teaching his sons how to ask their hosts for drinks marks a key transition in mythic history. Coming against the background of Made-from-Bone's earlier battles with Great Sickness and other dangerous adversaries, the invention of ceremonial dance music can be understood as a process of socializing the distance between groups of people, transforming fear and hostility into relations based on respect and reciprocity.

Another narrative set in "The World Begins" tells the fate of a man who journeys to a village of fish-people beneath the river to participate in a *pudáli* ceremony. While playing *yapurutú*, or *máwi*, flutes with the fish-people, the man chokes on water that has entered his flute. The *guabina* fish who is headman of the community hosting the *pudáli* ceremony announces that he suspects the presence of a human being, but the man's musical dancing partners help him conceal his identity until the ceremony ends. The man and his dancing partners drink beer and other fermented beverages for two days and nights. Before returning to the surface world of human beings, the man is told by his friends that he must not tell anyone about his experiences with the fish-people. But his wife and family learn that the man has been drinking when he vomits up beer, and they get him drunk again to get him to talk about his experiences. After the man has broken the fish-people's command by telling everyone about the underwater *pudáli* ceremony, he goes outside to urinate and dies after being bitten by a poisonous snake.

"The World Begins" concludes with the story of how Made-from-Bone takes peach-palm (*pípirri*) fruits from their owner, Grandfather Anaconda (*Malíhwerri*), who lives beneath the river. Although the theme of violence and killing resurfaces in the narrative about peach-palm fruits, the violence between Made-from-Bone and Grandfather Anaconda is relatively lighthearted and inconsequential when compared to the much more serious, sustained violence between Made-from-Bone and his adversaries during primordial times.

When Grandfather Anaconda refuses to give Made-from-Bone the peach-palm fruits, Made-from-Bone slices up his body from head to tail. But another being, *Éenuʰméeri*, comes to Grandfather Anaconda's support, gives him water to drink, "and immediately the pieces of his body became reconnected." When Made-from-Bone returns to ask again for the source of the fruits, Grandfather Anaconda gives in. "I will get it for you. You cannot be denied, Made-from-Bone; you are famous," says Grandfather Anaconda. After opening up the river with a sacred vine (*kadápu*) and traveling to his village, the anaconda-person sets a trap for Made-from-Bone by telling him to sit down over a hole in the ground where he is to plant the peach-palm seed. Made-from-Bone knows that Grandfather Anaconda is lying and sits near the hole rather than directly above it. "At the very moment when the seed fell, it burst forth like lightning and struck against the sky." Although the tree trunk grazes Made-from-Bone's body and makes a vertical groove along the center of his back, it does not have the intended lethal effect.

Narratives from "The World Begins"

Grandfather Sleep; or, The Origin of Night

Long ago Made-from-Bone lived at Hípana, the place where the world began. There was no night, no night for them. The sun was stuck in a single place; it never moved.

Made-from-Bone went to work, grew tired, and returned home all the time. He went again, returned, drank *patsiáka,* and finished; he was tired. He went again; it was like this all the time. He did not know how to rest. "It's not good how we are living," said Made-from-Bone.

Then some people told him that they lived well elsewhere. "The night falls, then the morning arrives. They work during the day, then they rest at night. They live well," they said to Made-from-Bone. "They drink *patsiáka* in the afternoon, and when they're finished they sleep. Early in the morning they bathe."

"Okay, let's go and find this for ourselves," said Made-from-Bone.

"Let's go," they said. Already they left. They walked, "taa," very close to the place where they were going. Afternoon began. "The night has already begun to arrive," they said to Made-from-Bone. "We're already arriving." They reached the village of *Dáinali,* who is called Grandfather Sleep. "Ee, my grandfather."

"Ee, my grandson, who are you?" said Grandfather Sleep. "What is your name?"

"I, I am the one who has the name Made-from-Bone."

"Aaa, so it is, my grandson; I have heard about you, my grandson," he said. "My famous grandson who knows everything. People speak about you.

Now I know you in person. How did you come? Why did you come here?"
he said to him.

"I came to get night. I have no night. I go to work, return, and the sun is
stuck in a single place. It is not good how we are living," said Made-from-
Bone.

"Aaa, I live well, my grandson. Spend the night here and drink some *patsiáka*.
Eat your fill, sleep, and rest," he said to Made-from-Bone. "We'll get up in
the morning, make some *patsiáka*, drink until we're finished, and then go to
work. In the afternoon we'll return and arrive again. Thus we live."

"I came here because that's what I heard. That's why I came to your village, so that you would give it to me," said Made-from-Bone.

"Yes, it will be so, my grandson, but it's bad. Look at how I am," he said
[he had enormous eyelids]. "In order to look at you, I have to hold my
eyelids up to see. When they fall down, I don't see a thing. Tso, it's bad,"
he said.

Then Made-from-Bone said, "Bad it may be, but I still want it."

"Okay," said Grandfather Sleep, "tomorrow we will see how it goes. Either
you get it or you do not." They talked.

Grandfather Sleep made a cigar, lit it, and smoked. He blew tobacco smoke.
Then he passed the cigar to Made-from-Bone. "Yes, my grandson, smoke
the cigar," he said.

"Good, my grandfather." Made-from-Bone smoked the cigar, blew, finished, and gave it back to Grandfather Sleep. "Yes, grandfather, tobacco."

"Good, my grandson."

"*Alíra* tobacco, my grandfather," he said.

"*Alíra* tobacco, my grandson. You already know, it seems, that this is the
word." Thus it will be for the new people living in the future world. "I used
to be young, now I am old. I have the sleep of old age," he said. "Let's sleep,
my grandson, until tomorrow."

Made-from-Bone did not sleep; he thought. How was he to get this sleep?
Morning came. Made-from-Bone divined whether it would be better to have
sleep of the eyelid or sleep of the heel of the foot. He divined that it was the
sleep of the heel that was good. Made-from-Bone said, "If it is the sleep of
the eyelid, this would not be good for the new people, for they would have
eyelids like this old man, Grandfather Sleep." Then he divined that it was to
be the sleep of the heel, and he felt good. This would work, since the heel
of the foot has no place to grow and fall down.

They stepped on the ground and went to bathe early in the morning.

"Good day, my grandson." "Good morning, grandfather." "How did you sleep?" "Nothing. I slept well," said Made-from-Bone.

"So it goes. Every now and then, my grandson, one has bad dreams that indicate what is to come. At other times one has good dreams, but it's only a lie that seems to be true. At other times, my grandson, one dreams with certainty. Come, let's drink *patsiáka,* my grandson. Hoo, it's good," Grandfather Sleep said. "Good." And they drank.

When they finished the sun was high in the sky. "Now, grandfather, I am leaving you," said Made-from-Bone.

"So be it, my grandson, you came here and got to meet with me. Now I know you," he said.

"Now I want what I came for. Give it to me," Made-from-Bone said. "Give it to me. That's why I came here."

"Okay, my grandson," he said to Made-from-Bone, "I will give it to you. It was for this very thing that you came here, just as you said. Here now is what you want." Grandfather Sleep took out a *cortadera* fruit. He opened it up and said, "Which kind of sleep do you want, my grandson, sleep of the eyelid or of the heel?"

"I want the sleep of the heel, grandfather," said Made-from-Bone.

"Aaa," said Grandfather Sleep, "Okay, you must know already, my grandson. No one can pull one over on you. The one you want is the better one because the heel has nowhere to grow bigger. When you grow older, your eyelids will not grow larger. If you had asked for the sleep of the eyelids, this would not have been good for you. Then your eyelids would grow large. The older you'd get, the larger your eyelids would become. That is how it will be for the new ones. When they reach middle age, their eyelids are complete and will not grow larger."

Grandfather Sleep took out a knife and cut off a piece of his heel. Then he cut off a piece from the other side of his heel. He put the pieces inside the *cortadera* fruit and placed the fruit inside a small bag.[1] He tied it tightly shut. Then he said to Made-from-Bone, "My grandson, here is what you want. Now, grandson," said Grandfather Sleep, "you must take this until you reach your home. There you may open it. You untie the bag, take the string off it, and when you finish the night will already arrive for you. Do not untie the bag while you are still on the way home. It's very heavy, this bag. You must lift it up together. The sleep of old age is very heavy, and no one can endure it."

"Let's go, young men," said Made-from-Bone. "Hold it up and let's go."

"Okay," they said. And they went away carrying the bag together. "Very heavy, this thing, Made-from-Bone," they said. "It doesn't matter. Let's take it." Already they had left. After going a little ways, they stopped to rest. Thus they went and rested. The sun was stuck in a single place. They set off and arrived at Point Sleep, halfway along the path. They rested there.

"How can it be that this bag is so heavy?" asked Made-from-Bone.

"We don't know," said his family. "Nobody knows."

"Okay, untie it and let's see what could be so heavy. Let's open it just a tiny bit."

"Okay, let's do it," they said. They untied the bag very slowly. They finished and opened it to look inside. "What could be so heavy here?" As soon as they opened the bag, a large wild chicken flew out. It came out of there. They closed the bag up, but it was too late. The bird had already left. That wild chicken flew away to where the sun falls. The sun ran off together with the wild chicken.

Night fell, and they became afraid. "Okay, now we don't even know how morning will come." In the village of First-Woman [Ámaru],[2] Mutʰípani, the afternoon had already started. "Well, what is happening to us now? Night is arriving among us; it's dark," she said. She went outside and met with the others. "I think that he did this to us, Made-from-Bone himself," said First-Woman. "He went and touched some part of the world that no one is supposed to touch." She plucked out one of her pubic hairs and blew in the direction of Made-from-Bone. *Sancudos* [biting black flies] arrived on top of Made-from-Bone; lots of them.

Made-from-Bone swatted the black flies against his body. "Hoo, enough *sancudos*," Made-from-Bone said. He divined toward First-Woman and discovered that she was the one doing this to him. "Aaa, it's First-Woman who did this to us," he said. He lit a cigar and blew in the direction where the *sancudos* had come from. "Good." Already the *sancudos* had left. They sat there the rest of the night and waited for morning to come.

They were singing, those *pauhwí pedrera* birds: "itchirri, itchirri, itchirri."

"What does it mean now that these *pauhwí pedrera* are singing?"

"Ooo, could it be that the morning is coming? Let's wait and see." The birds stopped singing. They waited to see, but there was nothing. They waited again, hoping to see.

Already the dawn was near. Then some yellow *pauhwí* began to sing. "Those are yellow *pauhwí* singing," said Made-from-Bone. "Soon the dawn will come."

"Climb up that tree to see if there is any light," Made-from-Bone said to the sloth.

"Okay, I'll go up to look." The sloth climbed up a tall tree. He arrived and sat down on the very tip of the tree. "What do you see?"

"Nothing; everything's dark."

"I lied to Made-from-Bone," said the sloth. He opened up his anus, and immediately there was light for Made-from-Bone.

"Ooo, good, already the dawn is starting."

The sloth began laughing and closed his anus. Darkness fell again. One family member said to Made-from-Bone, "The sloth did it; he opened his anus."

"Eee, Made-from-Bone, dawn is here. There comes the sun," said the sloth.

"Where is it?"

"There it comes from downstream," said the sloth.

"Wee, that's strange.[3] But that is how it is going to be for the new people in the future world," said Made-from-Bone.

Because Made-from-Bone opened the bag in the middle of the journey, that is how it is for us today. When we travel to distant places where we think about going, there we spend the night. Made-from-Bone opened it up, and this is why nowadays we spend the night wherever we are in our journey. We sleep, and the next day we arrive in the place where we are thinking of going. It was Made-from-Bone who made it so.

They got up in the morning and left again. The bag was no longer heavy. The sun traveled across the sky, and they arrived at Hípana. "How are you? How was your journey?" the people there asked.

"It went well," said Made-from-Bone, "I got what I went to find. But things didn't go too well for me. You will see when it gets dark."

"We know that it was you who did this," First-Woman said to Made-from-Bone.

"They gave it to me and told me to bring it all the way here. But then I went ahead and opened it in the middle of the path. It was very heavy, and that's why I opened it. Here is what he gave to us, but its owner has left. Okay, let's have a look. There's nothing inside," Made-from-Bone said to First-Woman. They opened the bag, and a small wild chicken came out. It flew away. "It's a good thing that we opened it earlier and that the large wild chicken already left," said Made-from-Bone. "If we hadn't opened it, things would be very bad for us," he said.

The large wild chicken fell far away in the Río Sipapo. There are no fish and no animals there. Actually, there are animals and fish, but their bodies are made of bitter manioc. People eat only manioc breads there. Here we eat well; animals, fish, everything. We have manioc to make *casabe* breads, but only a little, just enough for ourselves.

Night fell. "Good night, let's go to sleep. See you in the morning," said Made-from-Bone.

Morning came and they bathed and went outside. "Good morning," they said.

Made-from-Bone said, "They make *patsiáka*, drink, and finish. Already they go to do their work and see how the sun travels. In the afternoon, they return home, arrive, finish, meet, drink *patsiáka*, and eat fish. After eating, they converse until they reach the hour for sleeping. Thus it is all the time until today."

The Origin of Fire

This is how fire started in the past. The owner was *Yáwali*, the master of fire. It is said that Made-from-Bone did not have fire. "This is no good, the way we're living," he said. "To leave things this way for the new people would not be good. There is no way to eat fish. Okay, I'm going to get fire for us. People say that *Yáwali* has fire."

"Let's go. I want some companions."

"Okay," said Squirrel, "I'll go with you."

"Me, too," said the Alligator.

"Let's go now," Made-from-Bone said to them. And they set off along a path.

They went until reaching the village of *Yáwali*. "Ee, what are you doing," said *Yáwali*.

"I am walking this way and have come to see your village," said Made-from-Bone.

"Okay," said *Yáwali*. Made-from-Bone saw how he lived. He cooked so that he could eat fish. And early each morning he made hot *patsiáka* to drink. "He lives well," Made-from-Bone said to his companions.

Yáwali invited them to drink *patsiáka*. When they had finished, Made-from-Bone said, "I have come now to your village to get fire. Over there where we live, we don't have fire. We live poorly. There is no way for us to eat fish the way you do here."

"Yes, that may be so, but it is very dangerous that you will be burned," said *Yáwali*.

"But I want it, I want it, I want it," said Made-from-Bone.

"Let's see. I am still thinking about it. I will let you know," said *Yáwali*.

"Okay," said Made-from-Bone. "Now I want to know your decision, and I want you to give it to me."

"Paa," said *Yáwali*, "It's impossible to deny you, Made-from-Bone. So be it. If you really want fire, then I will give it to you tomorrow."

"Okay," said Made-from-Bone, who was happy.

Then Made-from-Bone said to his companions, "How is he going to give it to us?"

"We don't know," they replied.

"We'll have to wait and see," said Made-from-Bone. *Yáwali* was relaxing in his house. "I'm going to ask him for it again," said Made-from-Bone. "It looks as though he doesn't want to give it to us." So he went and asked again.

"What?" said *Yáwali*.

"I want you to give it to me now so that I can leave."

"Go, Made-from-Bone. When you arrive there, I will order that it be sent behind you," said *Yáwali*.

"Okay," said Made-from-Bone, and they left.

They left and sat down along the path. "What to do now?" they said.

"I don't know; let's wait and see," said Made-from-Bone. They heard the fire coming toward them, "ti, ti, ti, ti, ti." They were frightened. "Listen, here it comes," he said to them. They saw an enormous fire coming their way. It was rolling as it came.

"How are we going to take it?" asked Made-from-Bone.

"I will get it for us," said Squirrel. It is said that the squirrel opened his urn and put smoke inside it.

"What happened?" asked Made-from-Bone.

"I got it," said Squirrel.

"Okay," said Made-from-Bone. The fire was still lit. Since then it has been called Squirrel's fire.

Alligator stood up to look inside the urn where this fire was coming from. He saw something that looked like a burning rock. "Aaa, there it is," said Alligator. He jumped and bit it, then dove into the river.

Already the fire went out. "Okay," said Made-from-Bone, "The fire has died out."

"Tse," said *Yáwali*. "You can't mess with Made-from-Bone. Who took it?" he asked.

"I did," said Squirrel.

"Bring it here to show me," said *Yáwali*. Squirrel opened his urn, "tura." "Betee," then some smoke came out. Nowadays it is called Squirrel's fire. "It isn't so. You didn't take anything. Where is Alligator?"

"I don't know, he's not around," said Squirrel.

"Okay, let's go," said *Yáwali*. They went until they had reached Squirrel's village. "What happened?" they asked.

"He gave it to us, but it looks like alligator took it. We are waiting to hear," said Made-from-Bone. They heard that Alligator already had the fire. "Now I will go to him. What's happening?" Made-from-Bone asked as he arrived in Alligator's village.

"Um, um, um," said Alligator. He could not speak because the fire had burned his tongue. Already he had been given the fire, and that is the fire that we have today.

The Origin of Working in Manioc Gardens

This is how manioc began in the distant past. There was a man named *Káali,* or Manioc-Man, who had an enormously long cord. With this cord he made manioc gardens rapidly and without any effort. "How can it be that he makes his garden so quickly? Now I am going to go see how he does it," said another man. Just then Manioc-Man went to make a new manioc garden with his cord. The other man followed behind him to see how he worked. Manioc-Man pulled his cord over the trees. The man was there watching him. When Manioc-Man pulled on the cord, it broke.

"What's this?" he said. "Now we're in bad shape. Now we will have to work with great force in our manioc gardens. I had wanted this cord to be for all of us and for the new people, but then you broke it in half. From now on it will be like this for the new people in the future world. They will have to work very hard to make new manioc gardens. But that is not how it used to be," said Manioc-Man.

Manioc-Man had a newly burned clearing and was breaking manioc sticks for planting. He put the sticks into large carrying baskets, which he left lying on the ground. He left them there and went home. The carrying baskets went by themselves until they arrived at the newly burned garden. "How can it be that these baskets carry themselves?" asked a woman. "I am going to hide myself and watch how they are walking along the path." She hid herself at the edge of the path and could hear that the baskets were coming. She saw one of the baskets and suddenly felt one of them tie a cord around her head from behind.

"Now you will have to carry it," Manioc-Man said to her. "You want to work," he said to her, "and this is how it will be for all the new people in the future world. You did wrong to us and for those new people."

The Origin of Ceremonial Music

In the past Manioc-Man had a wife. There were two children, one son and one daughter. They lived for many years with him. But then his wife left him. She looked badly upon him. She wanted to marry another man.

Manioc-Man became furious. He had a very large manioc garden. His wife went to the garden, and Manioc-Man followed her there and sat down on a dead log. He transformed himself into a tiny woodpecker. She looked at him and said, "Tse, Manioc-Man is here, that bastard."

"Now I will definitely destroy her manioc garden. Then she will have to find some other place to get manioc breads for herself," said Manioc-Man. His wife came back another time to her garden and arrived to find that those manioc plants had turned into *kapuíru* [an unidentified wild plant with leaves that resemble manioc]. She became very sad and returned to her house. But she did not bring any manioc.

She wept. "Where are we going to get manioc breads to eat?" she asked.

"Because you threw out our father," her children said to her. She lived with them for a while. Hunger was killing them.

Then Manioc-Man came to his children's village. "How are you?" he asked. "How are you living?" he said to them.

"Bad," they told him, "We're always hungry."

Then Manioc-Man said to them, "I am going to bring food for you." He heard a large frog singing. "Go and collect this foam. Put it into an urn and tie the lid on tight. In the early morning, open it up. But don't let your mother eat."

"Okay," they said. And early the next morning they opened the urn. It was full of manioc starch, pure starch. They were happy, drank *patsiáka,* ate starch, and began to feel better. They hid the starch from their mother.

After a while their mother lost all her strength because she was growing thin from hunger. Those children, they were fine. "I believe that you are eating with your father," she said to them.

"No," they said, "We haven't eaten anything. Earlier you argued and our father left us."

"Today I am going to hang your hammocks above mine," she told them. In the afternoon she hung their hammocks above her own. At night the children were eating manioc starch in their hammocks and allowed a piece of starch to fall on top of their mother. "What are you eating?" she asked.

"We're not eating anything," they said.

She picked up a piece of the starch and ate it. She felt good after this one piece of starch. "This is not right," she said to them, "that you eat more than me. I got one little piece in my hammock. Now give me your food." And they gave food to their mother.

Later Manioc-Man met another woman and married her. He lived in her village with her. They had four children, who were called *Káaliéni*. He arranged a ceremony for them to teach them how to dance *mádzerukái*. All the dances of *yapurutú*, whip dances, dances with stamping tubes, the catfish trumpets, *déetu* flutes, *yapurutú* flute, everything. He prepared drinks: beer, liquor, rum. He put all the drinks in a canoe and began drinking with his children. Already he had taught them how to dance and sing *mádzerukái*. "These whip dances are done this way," he said to them. "They say that this is how to ask for a drink," he said. He finished, then started another dance. Then another dance. And so on.

"I am going to hide the drinks from them," said Manioc-Man, "to see if they know how to ask for drinks." Then Manioc-Man took the drinks away to another place. He left a little bit in the canoe. "Go and find drinks for us," he told them, and one of his children went to look for drinks.

He arrived at the canoe. "Tii," very little. He returned and said, "There is no more. It must be all gone."

"It's already gone?" said Manioc-Man. "Let's go to sleep. See you tomorrow," he said. "The drinks are already finished off." He returned and entered inside his house.

"Let's dance. We can sleep after a little while," they said.

They sat down on a bench and began to converse. "Maybe our father threw away our drinks," said one of them.

"It was all there," he said. "This can't be."

Then one of the others said, "It's not so. The drinks are already finished off."

"Can it be so?" he replied.

"Yes, it's true," said the other. "He hid the drinks."

"Okay, let's dance with whips to ask him for more drinks," he said. The youngest brother among them began to dance with them.

Manioc-Man was lying down and heard them singing his name. "I am happy," he said. "They know *mádzerukái* as I was hoping. Now I will go out to them to drink and dance together and to teach them well. Everything." And he went out to them. "Eee," he said, "My children, it is just as you are saying in the song, you already know. Now we are going to drink. There is our drink." And he brought it to them, throwing it back into the canoe.

Thus it is today that the youngest of our sons is the one who best learns *mádzerukái, malikái,* or whatever else. They drank again. Manioc-Man taught them to dance until the sun rose. Thus it is for men, and thus it is also for women until today.

The Origin of Bocachico-Fish Dances

In the past there was a different people. It was winter when the heavy rains fall and there were leaf-cutter ants making holes. They say that a man had a bench where he caught leaf-cutter ants. "I'm going to catch ants," he told his wife. He went and sat on the bench, catching leaf-cutter ants.

A group of people came toward him from downstream. "Eh, what are you doing?"

"Nothing, just catching leaf-cutter ants," he replied. "And where are you all headed?" he asked.

"We're going to hold a *pudáli* ceremony at the mouth of Caño Tigre, but we're missing a companion. Why don't you go with us?" they asked.

"I don't know. I have my ants," he said.

"Leave them there beside you," they said. "We'll return the day after tomorrow. We'll come back to this very place and leave you here."

"Okay, I'll go with you," said the man.

And they left. They were close to the place where they were going to dance. All the people were arriving for this gathering. "Who are we missing?" asked the headman.

"The people from the Río Casiquiare aren't here yet," they said, "And those from the Cayarí [Vaupés], too." Later everyone else arrived, and they began to dance.

"Everyone must dance well," said the headman, a *guabina* fish. "I believe that there is a living person among you," he said.

"It isn't so; there are only fish-people among us," they answered. "Not so; there is a person there," said the headman. "I don't know where he is among you, and I don't want to eat the revenge of his sons."

They began dancing with *yapurutú* flutes, making great turns around the headman's house. When they were passing the corner of his house, water entered into the flutes and got into the man's mouth. He coughed. "Hee, listen, there he is, but where?" said the *guabina*. They kept dancing but did not answer him. "I don't know where he is," said the headman.

There was a *kakúri* fish trap that they had put in front of the fish. They played with the *kakúri* and threw feathers in it. They were happy looking at it. This *kakúri,* they say, was very "delicate." They drank liquor and beer all night long. Thus they passed the next day and night. On the second morning, they said, "Now we've finished. Let's return."

They returned with him. They went back again to the same place where they had met him earlier. And they left him there. "We're leaving you. Do not speak about us," they told him. "If you do not speak to anyone about us, then we will take you to dance with us every year."

"Okay," he said. And they left him.

The man went to find leaf-cutter ants. These were good ones, these ants. He was still drunk when he arrived again at his house.

"You're back again," said his wife.

"Yes," he said. He didn't bring anything. The woman went to look inside his canoe, but there was nothing. She returned and said, "What work were you doing? Your family caught more fish than you did."

"It doesn't matter that they caught fish," he said. He fell asleep, then vomited up liquor and beer.

His wife said to him, "Ooo, where did you drink liquor?"

"Nowhere," he said. "I think I'm sick."

"It's not so, you are drunk," she said.

Afterwards the man's family came over to him and asked, "Where were you?"

"I didn't go anywhere," he replied.

"He's joking. He went to drink beer," his wife said to them.

Just then he vomited a lot of beer. "Where have you been drinking?" they asked him.

"Nowhere, I got lost," he answered.

"It's not true," they said to him, "You have seen something; tell us what it was."

He did not want to tell them. "Let's go make some beer and give him some. Once he's drunk, we'll ask him again," they said.

Already the man began to speak about how he had traveled. "Hoo, thank you," they said. When they had finished making beer, they gave some to the man, who quickly got drunk again. They began to ask him, but he still refused to tell them. They continued giving him beer, and he became even more drunk.

Again they asked him to speak. This time he told them everything about how he had traveled with the fish-people. "It is true that I have seen something," he told his kinsmen, "but they did not want me to tell anyone about them. If I tell you, they will kill me."

"It's not so," said his family, "tell it to us."

"Okay," he said to them, "perhaps I should tell you. Perhaps you do not want me to continue living in this world." He told them about how the fish-people live, what are their customs. He told them everything. He finished. "Now I must go to urinate," he said. He went outside, and a snake bit him. "Aaa," he said, "just now a snake bit me, but I told you everything and now I will die." And he died. Thus it ends.

Pípirri; or, The Origin of Peach-Palm Fruits

This is how peach-palm fruits began a long time ago. The first owner was *Éenuʰméeri;* later it was Grandfather Anaconda [*Malíhwerri*]. *Éenuʰméeri* worked in his manioc garden and lit a fire. He put the peach-palm fruits into the fire.

Made-from-Bone stood up to watch from a hiding place. Then he came out and went toward *Éenuʰméeri.* "Eee, *Éenuʰmée,*" he said, "What are you doing?"

"It's my work. Don't come over here. My work is very dangerous, and you'll get burned," said *Éenuʰméeri.*

"It's not so," said Made-from-Bone, "I am going to work with you. I'm an old man who knows how to work."

"I warn you again not to work with me. It's very dangerous here."

Made-from-Bone approached him. "I'll work with you," he said.

"No, no, no. Get out of here," said *Éenuʰméeri.* Made-from-Bone had arrived directly over the fire and was already working with *Éenuʰméeri.* "You're going to burn up, but this won't cause me any harm," said *Éenuʰméeri.*

"No, I know how to work," said Made-from-Bone.

Made-from-Bone pushed a stick into the fire and saw some of the fruits come out. "*Éenuʰméeri,* what are these?" he asked.

"These are called 'head-splitters.' Don't touch them."

Made-from-Bone grabbed one of the fruits, broke it open, and smelled it. It smelled delicious. "Very tasty, *Éenuʰméeri,*" he said, "I am going to eat a little."

"No, Made-from-Bone," said *Éenuᵇméeri,* "Don't eat it. If you eat it, you will have a terrible headache."

Made-from-Bone ate a little of the fruit. The moment he ate it, his head began to ache. Made-from-Bone shouted out in pain, "Aaaa, already my head hurts, *Éenuᵇméeri,*" he said. "Come here to help me."

"I warned you not to eat it. I don't know what kind of person you are to completely ignore my warning." Just then *Éenuᵇméeri* grasped his head to heal him. "Now you can eat as much as you want," said *Éenuᵇméeri.*

After a few days Made-from-Bone said, "Where did you get these fruits that you were eating so that you can give them to me and I might own some?"

"They're not mine," said *Éenuᵇméeri.* "Grandfather Anaconda [*Malíh-werri*] is the true owner."

"Okay," said Made-from-Bone. "I will go take some from him so that I can have it."

Made-from-Bone went to the village of Grandfather Anaconda. "Eee, my grandfather, *Malíhwerri.*"

"Eee, my grandson, what are you up to?" said Grandfather Anaconda.

"I have come to get your fruit tree," said Made-from-Bone.

"I don't have any," said Grandfather Anaconda.

"Yes you do," replied Made-from-Bone.

"Who told you that I have it?"

"*Éenuᵇméeri* told me that you have it," said Made-from-Bone.

"It isn't so," he said, "he was tricking you, I don't have any."

"Yes you do," said Made-from-Bone. "If you don't give it to me I am going to slice you from your tail all the way up to your head."

"Go ahead and cut," said Grandfather Anaconda, "It doesn't matter to me. Cut me."

"You won't give me the fruit," said Made-from-Bone.

"I won't give it to you and I don't have it." Made-from-Bone began cutting him. "Daka, daka, daka," close to his stomach. "Ayaa," he shouted, "Made-from-Bone has already killed me." Made-from-Bone ran to hide himself.

"*Eenuᵇmeeee,* come over to me. Made-from-Bone is killing me because of what you did," Grandfather Anaconda shouted to *Éenuᵇméeri. Éenuᵇméeri* went over to the village of Grandfather Anaconda. "Bring me water," said Grandfather Anaconda. He brought him a gourd dipper and gave him water to drink. Grandfather Anaconda drank the water, and immediately the pieces of his body became reconnected. *Éenuᵇméeri* went back to his village.

Made-from-Bone went again to the village of Grandfather Anaconda, who was lying on a sandy beach. "Now it's time for you to give it to me," said Made-from-Bone. "If you don't give it to me, I'm going to cut you up again all the way to your head."

"Okay, so be it," said Grandfather Anaconda, "I will get it for you. You cannot be denied, Made-from-Bone; you are famous. Now I know you in person. What you are looking for is in the river. Let's go look for it," said Grandfather Anaconda. "Bring along a *kadápu* vine."

Made-from-Bone brought some *kadápu* vine with him as he arrived at the edge of the river. "Strike the *kadápu* vine hard against the river," Grandfather Anaconda said to Made-from-Bone, who then lashed the river. The river opened up just like the door of a house. He saw a village of people, the village of Grandfather Anaconda. "There it is. What you want from me lives there," said Grandfather Anaconda. "Let's go find it for you."

They went searching for it. Grandfather Anaconda gave it to him. "Here is what you wanted from me," said Grandfather Anaconda. He gave him a ration of the fruits. They were green, yellow, and red. Only three fruits had seeds inside them. "Go sit down at the edge of the river," said Grandfather Anaconda to him. Break open the fruit like this to take out the seeds."

"Okay," said Made-from-Bone. Then he left.

He went and sat beside the river. He broke open a fruit. He tried to grab the seed, but it jumped into the river. Already the seed had transformed into a fish, called *pipíshi*. "Hoo, now there are only two seeds left. How is it possible to grab hold of it?" wondered Made-from-Bone. He broke open another seed, and again it jumped into the river. "Hoo, only one left now." He brought an *ataraya* fishing net and broke open the fruit while holding it inside the net. Made-from-Bone grabbed it; it was stuck in the fish net. "This time it's certain. I have one of the seeds."

He went back to the village of Grandfather Anaconda. "How do you plant this?" Made-from-Bone asked him.

"You have to make a hole in the ground. Sit down over this hole and drop the seed into the hole," said Grandfather Anaconda.

Made-from-Bone used his powers of divination and saw that Grandfather Anaconda was lying, that he really wanted to kill him. Made-from-Bone sat down near the hole and dropped the seed inside it. At the very moment when the seed fell, it burst forth like lightning and struck against the sky. The trunk of the tree passed by, scratching Made-from-Bone across his back. Thus it is that people today have a groove in the center of their backs. "Grandfather Anaconda almost succeeded in killing me," said Made-from-Bone, "but I escaped his trap."

A few days later Made-from-Bone went to look and saw that the tree was already bearing fruit. He reached the ground beneath the tree and saw red fruit, yellow fruit, and green fruit. It was already ripe and beginning to fall to the ground. Made-from-Bone began to gather it up in a ceramic bowl. He started to prepare and clean the fruits.

When he had finished preparing the fruits he called his family. "Come over here to try this new fruit that we have," said Made-from-Bone.

"Okay," they said. They came over and entered the house, which was an enormous house. He let them all sit group by group among themselves. "Let's go," said Made-from-Bone, "Let's begin with our cousins over here. Try them to see how they are, my cousins."

"Good," they said.

He gave them a gourd dipper, and they passed it from one to the other until they had finished drinking. He waited for a few minutes, then asked, "How does our new fruit make you feel?"

"Aaa, it's terrible. This is not right."

"Now let's see how it turns out when we put it in the fire," said Made-from-Bone. He gathered some more fruits in the large bowl and lit a fire. He cooked and prepared it. When he was finished, he invited his family to eat again. "Let's go, try it to see how it is," he said to a different group.

"Okay," they said. He gave them some, and all of them drank it. After waiting a few minutes he asked, "How do you feel?"

"It's good," they said, "Good, good."

"So it will be for us to eat our fruits," said Made-from-Bone.

"Now we still don't know what to call it," he said. "We must wait until we hear the name," he said. In the early morning a *wíripippi* bird [small yellow bird] began to sing: "Wi-pi-di."

"Aaa, what did you hear?" asked Made-from-Bone.

"We don't know," they said.

"Listen again. Wait so that you hear it well," said Made-from-Bone. The bird sang again, "pí-pi-ri." "What did you hear?" he asked one of them.

"I heard him say 'pípirri,'" the man replied.

"And you, what did you hear?" he asked another man.

"I heard him say 'pípirri,'" said the other man.

"And you?" he asked another.

"I heard exactly the same thing." Everyone heard it the same way.

"Aaa, pípirri will be your name," said Made-from-Bone. And thus it will also be for the new people who live in the future world.

Then another bird came along and sang for them, "Irrai-ka-wa-pipe, tsu, tsu, tsu."

"What did you hear?" asked Made-from-Bone.

"Red says the peach-palm tree," they answered.

"Paa, so be it," said Made-from-Bone, "pípirri will be your name." They went outside to see the peach-palm tree. They looked at it, "tsss," its fruits were red. Thus it ends.

Ethnomusicological Interlude: The Catfish Trumpet Festival of 1981, or How to Ask for a Drink in Curripaco

There are a group of musical performances, dances, and other activities that make up *pudáli*, a tradition of ceremonial exchange that originated in the time of "The World Begins." The origin of *pudáli* and the accompanying subgenre of ceremonial dance music, called *mádzerukái*, marked a crucial transition between the earlier period of Made-from-Bone's violent struggles against his adversaries and the more recent, fully human world created during the lifetime of the first human being (*Kuwái*). In "The World Begins," Made-from-Bone's invincibility and his ability to survive life-threatening challenges are less prominent than his omniscience and capacity for getting things for people by asking various mythic owners. Made-from-Bone knows what to ask for and how to get what he wants. His power to ask for and get things is transferred to the human social world in the story about Manioc-Man, who taught his sons how to ask for drinks from other people through the collective singing, dancing, and instrumental music of *pudáli* exchange ceremonies.

At the time of my first fieldwork in 1980–81, *pudáli* ceremonial exchanges were in a state of flux, reflecting major changes in social organization and subsistence economics happening throughout the Venezuelan Amazon Territory. In those villages where the musical dances of *pudáli* were still being performed, the context had changed from the exchange of food gifts between affines to small social gatherings for the purposes of dancing and drinking together. Nevertheless, my inquiries in various Wakuénai communities along the lower Guainía River indicated that ceremonial exchanges of surplus foods had been commonly practiced until the recent past.

The mythic meanings of collective singing, dancing, and music making persisted in the changing conditions of life along the Upper Río Negro during the early 1980s. These performances continued to serve as ways of creating conviviality and solidarity between communities of people through asking for and receiving drinks. What was different in the 1980s was the extent to which collective dancing had become a means for creating new social ties between the Wakuénai and other indigenous peoples, such as the Baniwa, Guarequena, and Yeral. *Pudáli* was still at its base a process of building relations of friendship and alliance, but it was more focused on neighborly relations between the Wakuénai and other ethnic groups living along the Río Negro.[1]

In July through November 1981, I devoted much of my time to recording, photographing, and studying the collective musical performances of *pudáli*. In the process of learning about these performances, I became increasingly identified with the music I was studying and learning to perform. It is not surprising that anthropologists working in the field become identified with the topic(s) that they are studying. The traditions of performing *máwi* (or *yapurutú*) flute duets with Curripaco men and women placed me in a sphere of more inclusive, egalitarian relations that provided some much-needed balance to my association with masculine ritual power. Unlike the ritual chanting and singing I had been studying for several months and that continued to form a central focus of my field research, the ceremonial music was lighthearted and playful and required direct physical interaction between male flute players and female dancers.

After recording several hours of ceremonial music played on pairs of flutes, called *máwi*, I became aware of a basic contrast between standardized duets played on two or more pairs of *máwi* flutes during the opening stages of *pudáli* ceremonies and improvisatory duets played on a single pair of flutes in the closing stages of *pudáli*. I learned to play several of these improvisatory pieces with Horacio, Félix, and other men in the village. Performing and improvising *máwi* flute music was an enjoyable activity that required close physical collaboration with my Wakuénai hosts. *Máwi* duets are played in a hocket style in which higher and lower notes from longer and shorter, or "male" and "female," flutes are interwoven to create single melodic lines. In addition to this intimate collaboration between pairs of male flute players, *máwi* flute duets require that each male flute player be accompanied by a female dance partner who holds his upper arm. By learning to participate in *máwi* flute dances, I became much more aware of the physical, nonverbal dimensions of the indigenous experience of musical artistry (photos 4, 5, and 6).

As I became more competent as a *máwi* flute player and dancer, I was rapidly becoming more knowledgeable of the broader range of instrumental and vocal music that formed the basic ingredients of *pudáli* exchange ceremonies. Although nearly all the men in the village knew how to play *máwi* flutes, Horacio was the only person who could fully explain how *pudáli* originated in the times when the world began and how all the different styles of instrumental music, singing, and formal speeches were arranged into cycles of male- and female-owned ceremonies. A synergy developed between our shared enjoyment from performing *máwi* flute dances with men and women in the community and the more intellectual process of fleshing out the meanings and orderings of ceremonial dance music.[2]

Photo 4. Pairs of "male" (longer) and "female" (shorter) máwi *flutes. Photo taken by Jonathan D. Hill.*

Photo 5. (top left) Author learning to perform máwi *flute dances with local man, 1981. Photo taken by Jonathan D. Hill.*

Photo 6. Pairs of máwi *flute players and women dancers, 1981. Photo taken by Jonathan D. Hill.*

In part as a response to my questions about these ceremonial musical activities, Horacio and his family decided to make a set of trumpets, called *kulirrína,* named after a species of large catfish. The making and playing of these instruments developed into a multicommunity event that I refer to as the "Catfish Trumpet Festival of 1981."

The Catfish Trumpet Festival of 1981

Life on the Río Guainía has its own rhythm and tempo, dependent largely upon the amount of rainfall and the rising and falling of the river level. By mid-August 1981, the heavy rains of the long, April-through-July wet season had given way to bright sunny days and ferocious thunderstorms in the late afternoon, evening, and nighttime hours. The river level had reached its peak in early August, and fishing and hunting were starting to yield better results as the waters receded. People were beginning to make plans for the drier months of September and October, which is the best time of year to select new garden sites and cut down trees and other vegetation.

Horacio's house was the gathering place for daily communal meals and special events, such as drinking and performing *máwi* flute dances. The packed clay floor of Horacio's house was sacred ground, the place where he and Herminio had recently sung, chanted, and blown tobacco smoke over the sacred food for one of their granddaughters' passage into adulthood. By 1981, the thatched roof had begun to wear out, allowing small beams of sunlight and trickles of rainfall to enter inside. Horacio sent Félix and a group of young men to a site upstream where they could harvest sufficient quantities of palm fronds to replace the old roof.

Life grew quieter in the village during the week of Félix's absence. There were no new performances of *máwi* flute dances or other musical events to record, so I spent considerable time typing up notes I had written during various recent activities and interviews. Reviewing my typed notes with Horacio each day stimulated new inquiries and stories. It was during these conversations that Horacio first told me about Manioc-Man (*Káali*), the mythic owner of manioc, and his invention of ceremonial dance music as a way of teaching his sons how to ask their hosts for drinks. In response to my questions about offering food gifts between guests and hosts, Horacio demonstrated the formal, ceremonial speeches of offering and receiving food gifts in *pudáli.* We also discussed the catfish trumpets (*kúlirrína*) of male-owned *pudáli* ceremonies, dance-stamping tubes (*wáana*) of female-owned ceremonies, and men's and women's drinking songs (*pákamarántakan*) performed in both male- and female-owned ceremonies.

It was ironic that our collaborative explorations of *pudáli* exchange ceremonies flourished in the conditions of relative scarcity at the end of the long wet season. After all, *pudáli* ceremonial cycles celebrated the abundance of food, ideally during the *Leporinus* fish spawning runs at the very beginning of the wet season. The temporary departure of Félix and other young men to harvest palm fronds for Horacio's new roof had only exacerbated the problem, since they were the most active and productive fishermen-hunters in the village. So while I recorded Horacio's renditions of formal speeches meant to accompany exchanges of surplus fish and game meat, we survived mostly on canned food and dry goods that I had bought in San Carlos de Río Negro or Maroa.

When Félix and his coworkers arrived in the port with an enormous quantity of bundled palm fronds, plans for thatching the new roof in September and October converged with the idea of making dance-stamping tubes and catfish trumpets (photos 7 and 8). Building a new roof on Horacio's house would renovate the public, ceremonial center of local social life and provide a more suitable setting for greeting visitors with fermented drinks and inviting them to participate in *máwi* flute dances. At the same time, making a set of catfish trumpets would serve not only to teach Félix and other young men in the village how to construct and play these instruments but also pique the curiosity of people living in neighboring communities along the Río Guainía. Coordinating the roof building with the making of musical instruments would pose no serious problems, since September is when men begin clearing forest vegetation for new manioc gardens, providing them with ample opportunities for harvesting bundles of straight *máwi* palms and other plant materials for making *máwi* flutes, catfish trumpets, and dance-stamping tubes.

But before any of these plans could be acted upon, we had to have better hunting and fishing conditions so people would not feel hungry. I had been in the field for about three months and had nearly exhausted my supply of fishing and hunting materials by distributing them as gifts to men in the village. So when Félix and Horacio began planning a trip for hunting and fishing far up in the Caño San Miguel, I offered to support the trip by purchasing two tanks of gasoline for the community's outboard motor. Loaded up with about a dozen people, three hunting dogs, small canoes, hunting and fishing gear, and personal belongings, the little motor was barely able to move us upstream to the mouth of the Caño San Miguel (photo 9). After two full

Photo 7. Canoe filled with palm fronds for thatching Horacio's roof, 1981. Photo taken by Jonathan D. Hill.

Photo 8. Bundles of máwi palm tubes for making flutes, blowguns, and fish traps. Photo taken by Jonathan D. Hill.

days on the river, we reached a place called Punto Sapo (Frog Point) just as darkness was falling and less than a minute ahead of a torrential rainstorm.

Somewhere near the middle of a vast flooded forest encompassed on three sides by the upper Orinoco, Casiquiare, and Guainía rivers, we rose the next morning to the sounds and sights of macaws, parrots, and herons making their daily rounds. Each evening, the rush hour of avian traffic went in the

Photo 9. Hunting dog in small fishing canoe traveling up the Caño San Miguel in search of fish and game, 1981. Photo taken by Jonathan D. Hill.

opposite direction. It was the first time I had seen such large flocks of birds in the Río Negro. Fishing and hunting were more productive in the Caño San Miguel than they had been along the Río Guainía, but not so much that they would allow us to bring more than a few kilos of smoked meat back to Horacio's village in a few days' time.

I had spent most of my last money on the two tanks of gasoline for the fishing and hunting expedition, and the men had used up most of their hunting and fishing supplies. Clearly, if there was to be an adequate supply of food for celebrating the simultaneous completion of Horacio's new roof and the catfish trumpets, I would need to replenish the men's hunting and fishing supplies so that they could take advantage of improving conditions as the river level began falling in September and October. To do that, I would have to make the long journey downstream to San Carlos de Río Negro and by air to Puerto Ayacucho and Caracas. After packing my essential belongings for the trip, I left my tape recorders and other field equipment with Horacio and Félix for safekeeping. On August 31, the day before my departure, I met with Horacio and all the adults in the village to compile a list of trade goods—shotgun detonators, lead shot, fishhooks, nylon fishing lines, flashlights, batteries, cloth, and jewelry—that I promised to buy in Caracas.

It took me two-and-a-half weeks to make the trip all the way to Caracas and back to the Río Guainía. I arrived tired from traveling and searching for

trade goods all over Caracas and Puerto Ayacucho but happy to settle back
into the daily routines of life on the Río Guainía. The thatching of Horacio's
new roof was well underway, and the supply of palm fronds was sufficient to
extend the old roof an extra two meters across the entire front of the house
to make a covered porch and front entrance (photo 10). The river level had
fallen by three meters and was continuing to fall at a rapid pace, so fishing
and hunting conditions were improving as well. After giving presents of
cloth, soap, and other goods to Antonia and other women in the village, I
wasted no time in distributing the men's hunting and fishing supplies that I
had bought in Caracas and Puerto Ayacucho. A steady flow of fish and game
meat began to appear over the weeks ahead (photo 11). Even *I* was successful
at catching several fish using a hook and line. Fishing in the afternoons with
Félix and other men in the village became an almost daily routine, and by
early October I had become skillful enough to make regular contributions
to the evening communal meals held on the floor of Horacio's house.

*Photo 10. Building a roof, 1981. Photo
taken by Jonathan D. Hill.*

Photo 11. Félix holding pavón *and* pavón
grande *fish, October 1981. Photo taken by
Jonathan D. Hill.*

In late September, Herminio's son Julio began making a set of stamping tubes (*wáana*) out of *cecropia* trees harvested from an old manioc garden. These percussive instruments are made by hollowing out a three-foot-long log about five inches in diameter. A handle is carved at the top end of the log, which is then thumped against the ground in unison with the down step of men's right feet as they dance and sing the stamping-tube dances (*waanápani*). After Julio had carved and decorated several of the stamping tubes, Horacio began leading and teaching the various songs making up the repertoire of stamping-tube dances. During the days, I worked on transcribing and translating these song texts with Horacio, and in the evenings I recorded the men's collective singing and continued to participate in *máwi* flute dances.

Preparations for the catfish trumpet festival were by now visible in the new roof on Horacio's house and could be heard in the strength of men's voices as they sang the stamping-tube dances. There was great anticipation and much curiosity about the catfish trumpets when Horacio initiated their construction by cutting and carving a balsa wood log to use as a mold for weaving the trumpet's resonators. Weaving the tubular resonators was a slow process that lasted for nearly two weeks, even with other men joining in to help. Visitors from nearby villages and people passing by from places far upstream or downstream stopped to talk with Horacio and complimented him on his new roof. Seeing the woven resonators in various stages of completion inevitably led to questions: What are those things? How do they look when they're finished? What sounds do they make? Why are you making them? One elderly woman from a village downstream remembered catfish trumpets from her childhood and was clearly excited about seeing them again after so many years. The Catfish Trumpet Festival of 1981 emerged from this outpouring of interest during the early stages of the trumpets' construction. After estimating how much longer it would take to finish making the trumpets and teaching other men how to play them, Horacio set the date of the festival for October 24.

News of the festival spread across the region, and soon there were not only Wakuénai visitors but Yeral speakers from the Casiquiare, Guarequena from Guzman Blanco, and Baniwa from Maroa who were all interested in seeing and hearing the catfish trumpets. The roof-building project was nearing completion by mid-October, and Horacio organized an evening of singing, music making, and dancing to celebrate his new roof and to rehearse *máwi* flute dances and stamping-tube dances prior to the festival. Several Guarequena families traveled from their village to attend Horacio's housewarming party. As I recorded the evening's flute duets and singing, I could not help but notice that the spatial organization of people within the house was exactly as Horacio had described it for the nighttime period of drinking and singing in *pudáli* ceremonies. Guest men sat on a row of benches along the wall closest to the front door, with guest women settled toward the rear of the house along the same wall. Host men and women sat facing their guests from the opposite side of the house.

The setting was just like Horacio's description of the late-night period of *pudáli* ceremonies when hosts invited their guests to come inside to drink and sing together. Yet no one was singing the song dialogues, called *pákamarántakan,* that night. The next day I asked Horacio about the drinking songs, and he assured me that almost all the local men and women knew how to sing them but that they could not perform the songs without consuming a drink of rum or some other alcoholic beverage. A day or two later, I was back from Maroa with a bottle of Ron Cacique, and people gathered after the evening communal meal to drink and sing *pákamarántakan.* I recorded several of the songs, beginning with a dialogue between Antonia and a man who was visiting from a nearby village. Herminio's son, Julio, followed with a short song addressed to his brother-in-law. The next three songs were by adult women from the village, and I became acutely aware that they were directing their songs at me rather than one of the local men. Since I was the person who had provided the bottle of rum and invited people to sing, I had unknowingly put myself in the role of ceremonial host and was therefore an appropriate target for the women's singing.

> *Luisa's Song*
> I am going to speak,
> I am going to speak.
> I, an ugly woman,
> I speak here in front of you
> About my people, my family.
> Yes, mother, I speak for you.
> Thus I speak for my lazy, shameless children.
> Sadness when one goes far away.
> My children have gone away.
> Yes, mother, let us leave this sentiment.
> Thus I speak for my children.
> Thus I am speaking to you, my friend.
> You bring this kind of machine [my tape recorder and
>   microphone] for me.

My friend, look at how I am
So that you bring me a machine of this kind from your people.
From Caracas you bring me things, my friend,
In the afternoon I am in my house, my friend.
Bring things for me, my friend.
Look at how poor I am.
It's been a week since I put on these clothes, my friend.
Bring some clothes for me, since I am poor.
Then my hammock, my friend.
Thus is my hammock, tiny, my friend.
I have no money to buy soap, my friend.
Bring some for me, my friend.
I have nothing to eat with,
No money to buy dishes, my friend.
Thus we are poor here in the Guainía.
Here in this village I live, my friend.
You take with you only my words, my friend.
Thus, my friend, I have spoken to you.

Maria's Song
I am a poor woman.
I walk about among my family,
I walk about poor,
I walk about here.
Now I want from you what you are to give me.
I am a poor woman, a widow, my friend.
I am a poor woman, my friend.
With my two children and no one else, my friend.
I walk about poor, my friend.
I want some money from you
So that you will give me just a little
From your people, my friend.
I am a poor woman with these children,
These two and no more.
Here where you walk about, my friend,
We are poor here in this river.
Thus I have spoken to you, my friend.

The evening of drinking and singing gave me a personal taste of how the traditional song dialogues, or *pákamarántakan,* served as a musical channel for allowing individual men and women to express private emotions and thoughts in the public setting of ceremonial gatherings. People are generally quite reluctant to say much about the sadness they feel when friends or family members leave on or return from trips to far-off places. Asking directly or otherwise inciting a departing or returning person to speak about their trip to other places is considered to be not only impolite but even dangerous for the traveler, whose words about experiences in faraway places could cause him illness, misfortune, or death. The drinking songs, however, allow men and women to openly express their feelings of sadness about going away to or coming back from distant places.

The drinking songs are also a socially accepted means of asking other people for drinks and other things. In the mythic time of "The World Begins," drinking songs and other ceremonial music originated through *Káali*'s act of teaching his sons how to ask for more drinks in a socially appropriate manner. Although the theme of personal sadness runs through most of the songs' texts and the repetition of a descending melodic line has the feel of a lament, the drinking songs also have humorous, satirical dimensions. These comical elements depend on irony that is only felt by people who are closely familiar with the singer and the immediate context in which the song is performed. In the case of Luisa's song, her request that I bring her a machine like the one I was using to record her song evoked gales of laughter from the assembly of local people. Her requests for other things—clothing, hammock, soap, food, and money—were likewise met with ridicule. The humor of the situation was partly due to the fact that I had only recently returned from Caracas with gifts of cloth, salt, and soap for Luisa and other women in the village. More importantly, Luisa was married to a Hohódeni man who was locally regarded as a slacker and whose incompetence at gardening, hunting, fishing, or other productive activities was perceived as the real reason for Luisa's lack of sufficient money and material goods. Luisa's husband was the subject of much joking and ridicule within the village, and her drinking song gave people an opportunity to collectively express their resentment through sharing a laugh together.

When the drinking songs ended, I put away my recording equipment and returned to Horacio's house with the small acoustic guitar that I always carried with me in the field. During 1980 and 1981, I had learned to sing a number of folk songs from Venezuela, other Latin American countries, and the United States. Learning to perform songs was an enjoyable pastime, and my indigenous hosts often asked me to play a few songs after evening meals. That night it seemed particularly appropriate to sing for my hosts as a way of reciprocating the drinking songs that they had allowed me to record. I had finished strumming my way through a couple of Venezuelan *joropos* when Félix approached me with an unusual request. "We like those songs, but what we really want to hear are *your* songs." With that in mind, I started singing American folk tunes and, with help from Félix, providing a brief Curripaco translation of the English texts.

In the few days remaining before the Catfish Trumpet Festival, Horacio, Félix, and Julio led the other men in covering the woven resonators with melted resin, cutting and inserting short tubes of *máwi* into the resonators, and fastening the resonators to the palm tubes with vines and resin. After decorating the trumpets with a variety of painted designs and feathers, Horacio gathered everyone for a rehearsal on the eve of the festival (photos 12, 13, 14, and 15).

Photo 12. Attaching máwi *palm tubes (mouthpieces) to circle of vine prior to insertion into woven resonator of* kulirrína *trumpet, 1981. Photo taken by Jonathan D. Hill.*

*Photo 13. Spreading cooked resin (*máini*) on trumpet's resonator, 1981. Photo taken by Jonathan D. Hill.*

Photo 14. *Masking and painting trumpets to make black stripes. Photo taken by Jonathan D. Hill.*

Photo 15. *Testing trumpet after painting and decorating. Photo taken by Jonathan D. Hill.*

On the day of the Catfish Trumpet Festival, Antonia led a group of women in making pineapple wine and other mildly fermented drinks. Large dugout canoes filled with people from neighboring villages arrived throughout the day. By late afternoon, there were over a hundred visitors, including a large number of Guarequena from Guzman Blanco and a smaller number of

Baniwa from Maroa. There were far too many people to fit inside Horacio's house or even on the open space outside his front door, so the opening performances were held in the larger space between Horacio's house and a row of households that extended downstream along the eastern side of the island-village. A row of benches and chairs were set up as a viewing area in front of the row of houses.

The line of men carrying trumpets and flutes came to life with a shrill whistling and a loud collective shout that started in a high falsetto pitch and slithered down to the normal range of men's voices (photos 16 and 17). After the second shout, a pair of men began to play the standard, opening *máwi* flute duet, and the line of male musicians and their female dance partners began to move in circles. The catfish trumpets started up, adding their deep, rumbling, bass ostinato to the high-pitched *máwi* flutes. After performing several more large collective dances with the catfish trumpets and *máwi* flutes, Horacio led the men through the complete repertoire of stamping-tube dances and other collective songs of *pudáli*. Performances of the *dzawírra* duet and other improvisatory duets played on *máwi* flutes brought the opening stage of the festival to a conclusion.

The visitors listened respectfully to their hosts' musical performances. After sampling the pineapple wine and other locally made drinks, some of the guests returned to their boats and departed for their villages during the last hour of daylight. Many people stayed, however, and the focus shifted to drinking and dancing inside Horacio's newly renovated house. A group of young Guarequena men began carrying several large pieces of stereo equipment from the port and setting it up inside Horacio's house. As darkness fell and the small diesel generator lit up people's homes for the evening, I sat down in Horacio's house and watched the visitors plug in and test their stereo equipment.

The Guarequena were known to throw big drinking parties at which young men and women danced all night long to Colombian popular music. After a few minutes had passed by without any music being played on the stereo, one of the visitors asked me to provide the tape recordings I had made of the catfish trumpets. I brought out several hours of recorded music, and the Catfish Trumpet Festival of 1981 continued long into the night. Amplification of the catfish trumpets' sounds on the stereo filled the entire village and provided a roaring accompaniment to the *máwi* flute dances. We drank, danced, and played music together until exhaustion set in and everyone went to sleep in the wee hours of the morning.

Photo 16. Máwi *flute players,* kulirrína *trumpet players, and female dancers at the Catfish Trumpet Festival of 1981. Photo taken by Jonathan D. Hill.*

Photo 17. Máwi *flute players,* kulirrína *trumpet players, and female dancers at the Catfish Trumpet Festival of 1981. Photo taken by Jonathan D. Hill.*

Part 3

The World Opens Up

Overview

In the third and final period of mythic history, or "The World Opens Up," Made-from-Bone continues to display the same powers of omniscience and invincibility that he has wielded since his creation in primordial times and that become the basis of his fame in the period of "The World Begins." However, in "The World Opens Up," Made-from-Bone's powers of creativity are to some extent overshadowed by the powerful musical sounds and naming processes embodied in the primordial human being *Kuwái,* who is the child of incestuous sexual relations between Made-from-Bone and a paternal aunt, named *Ámaru.* Whereas the invention of ceremonial dance music (*mádzerukái*) during "The World Begins" marked a transition from an earlier time of unceasing violence to a period of balanced reciprocity between groups of people (that is, *pudáli*), "The World Opens Up" explains that controlling human life cycle transitions, aging, sexuality, and illness require special, ritually powerful ways of speaking, chanting, and singing (*malikái*).

The period of "The World Opens Up" begins when Made-from-Bone has incestuous sexual relations with First-Woman (*Ámaru*), a paternal aunt and the prototypic human mother. First-Woman becomes pregnant but has no birth canal to allow her child, *Kuwái,* to escape from her womb. So Made-from-Bone calls for a fish to jump forcefully into her vagina, allowing her to give birth to *Kuwái.* Because he is the progeny of incestuous sexual relations, *Kuwái* is banished to a corner of the sky where he does not pose any danger to Made-from-Bone and his family at Hípana. But *Kuwái* is attracted back down to earth by the buzzing, hissing sounds made by a group of boys who have captured some wasps and put them inside a vase. The boys include *Málinálieni* and two other nephews of Made-from-Bone as well as *Éeri,* Made-from-Bone's younger brother. As soon as they come into contact with *Kuwái,* the boys are ordered to begin fasting and living in a special seclusion hut outside the village. When *Kuwái* returns to the village, Made-from-Bone orders all the women to go into hiding. "*Kuwái* began to speak the word-sounds that could be heard in the entire world. The world was still very small. He began to speak, 'Heee.' The sound of his voice ran away and opened up the world."

The boys grow increasingly hungry, and *Kuwái* decides to test their willpower by dropping *guacu* fruits into their seclusion hut. *Málinálieni* and his brothers eat some of the fruits, but *Éeri* refuses to eat anything. When *Kuwái* inspects their teeth, he learns that *Éeri* is the only one of the boys to remain faithful to the mandatory period of fasting that all male initiates must endure. When a storm brings heavy rain, all the boys except for *Éeri* run inside a rock cave to seek shelter, not knowing that the cave is really the mouth of *Kuwái*. After killing and eating *Málinálieni* and the other boys, *Kuwái* vomits their remains into three *guapas* and returns to his place in the corner of the sky.

Made-from-Bone realizes that he needs *Kuwái* to return to the ground at Hípana in order to perform the sacred *malikái* word-sounds that will allow *Éeri* to complete his initiation ritual and end the period of fasting. However, *Kuwái* is ashamed of himself for killing and eating the three boys and believes that Made-from-Bone wants to kill him in revenge. Made-from-Bone makes three wooden dolls, or effigies, to represent the three dead boys and to trick *Kuwái* into believing that the boys are still alive. Then Made-from-Bone uses his powers of divination to concoct a plan that will lure *Kuwái* back to Hípana by sending him a package of sweet-smelling *seje*-palm grubs (*mútʰi*). *Kuwái* is so intoxicated by the smell of these grubs that he reveals his secret to *Káalimátu*, a wasp-person messenger sent by Made-from-Bone:

"Now take him my message. Tell him that I will come when they call for me. Tell them to prepare the sacred food and the drinks. Have them prepare manioc breads, everything. I will allow him two days for this work. On the afternoon of the third day, I will come to your village and will then blow tobacco smoke over the sacred food. Afterwards he can kill me. But there is nothing with which he can kill me. Tell him exactly this way: Logs and trees, they are my body; vines, too; my body is poison, my hair; water, I live in water; soil, it is my body; steel, my body; the only thing my body is not is fire," he said. "With this, yes, he can kill me. That is how you will speak to him," said *Kuwái*.

When *Kuwái* arrives in Hípana, he blows tobacco smoke, sings, and chants over the sacred food (*káridzámai*) for *Éeri*. *Dzúli*, a younger brother of Made-from-Bone, sits beside *Kuwái* through the entire night and carefully memorizes all the *malikái* songs and chants. Meanwhile, Made-from-Bone misses many of the songs and chants as he busies himself with keeping the bonfire lit and doling out fermented drinks to *Kuwái* and all the men. During breaks between singing and chanting, *Kuwái* joins Made-from-Bone and the men in dancing and singing a whip dance (*kápetiápani*) around the bonfire. As dawn approaches, *Kuwái* sings the closing *malikái* song of initiation rituals and blows tobacco smoke one last time over the sacred food. Tired, old, and drunk, *Kuwái* joins Made-from-Bone and the other men in whip dance, and they push him into the bonfire. "The world closes back up again after Kuwaí dies. It is tiny again. 'Okay,' they spent the night and were very sad."

With this fiery "death" and transformation, the life cycle of *Kuwái* as an autonomous being comes to an abrupt end. In the process of creating the world through musical naming power,[1] *Kuwái* also creates the developmental process through which young boys become adult men by ritual fasting. *Éeri* rejects the temptation to break his fast and to seek shelter from the rain, and in doing so he breaks the bonds of childhood dependency by transcending the need for parental nurturance and shelter. In terms of spatial imagery, the narratives outline a process of vertical movements *up* to *Kuwái*'s childhood in the corner of the sky; *down* to earth in the extrasocial space of the forest where he meets (and ultimately kills and eats) three of the boys; and *down* to the center of social space at Hípana where he has reached old age and teaches *malikái* singing and chanting to *Dzúli* before his fiery "death." A clear differentiation emerges between *Dzúli*, who memorizes all the songs and chants and becomes the first chant owner (*malikái limínali*), and Made-from-Bone, who does not learn all the sacred songs and chants. This distinction between *Dzúli* and Made-from-Bone establishes the mythic prototype for a hierarchy between more and less ritually powerful individuals. To sum up, the narratives about *Kuwái* as a living, creative being result in a vertical dimension of ritual power that is concerned with regulating the passage of developmental and generational time.

Everything changes in the second narrative about *Kuwái*. From his ashes, a tall *macanilla* tree grows until reaching the sky, and *Kuwái* returns to earth as a set of sacred flutes and trumpets made from the felled tree. *Kuwái* is no longer an autonomous being, flying through the sky and creating natural species through musical naming power, but a set of objects (wooden flutes and trumpets) that have world-transforming powers only when they are played by groups of men and women. The vertical dimension of ritual power, embodied in the tree connecting sky and earth, now becomes the background against which a second, horizontal dimension of ritual power develops as Made-from-Bone chases after First-Woman. The world opens up for a second time as First-Woman and her female companions play the sacred flutes and trumpets of *Kuwái* in various places.

> Made-from-Bone blew air with the hawk feather, and it made a sound. "Heee," and then the world opened up again, from here to there, this entire world. The sound went up into the sky above. All the sounds of Kuwaí spoke—*waliáduwa, máaliawa,* all of them. Made-from-Bone heard how this one sounds, how that one sounds, how the other ones sound. "Now," said Made-from-Bone, "These are going to belong to us men, and we will hide them from the women. This is the son of First-Woman, but we must keep it hidden from her."

First-Woman takes the sacred flutes and trumpets away from Made-from-Bone and goes to her village at a place called Palm-Grub Dance (*Mut^{h}ípani*) on a winding stream along the Aiarí River. Only women are allowed to play and see *Kuwái*'s instruments. Leading an army of men disguised as small frogs to First-Woman's village, Made-from-Bone knocks First-Woman to the ground with a bolt of lightning. The frog men shoot First-Woman's band of women with poisoned arrows and take *Kuwái* back to Hípana. Made-from-Bone invites First-Woman and the women to a "*Kuwái* dance" (*kwépani*) at Hípana and attempts to fool her into believing that the wooden instruments have transformed into animals, birds, and fish. But First-Woman does not fall for Made-from-Bone's ruse and scornfully remarks, "Made-from-Bone has shamelessly tricked us with his animals. Now let's go and take them away from him." This time First-Woman brings a very large number of women, and they run far downstream with *Kuwái*, carrying their canoes on forest pathways to circumvent the rapids that Made-from-Bone has made to block their escape. After chasing First-Woman all over the map,[2] he finally locates her at a lake near São Gabriel on the Río Negro.

To conceal his identity from First-Woman, Made-from-Bone transforms himself into a Yeral (or Geral or Nheengatú)[3] person, and his conversation with First-Woman becomes the origin of the Yeral language spoken by people in downstream areas along the Río Negro. The dialogue between Made-from-Bone and First-Woman as he arrives at the women's village provides one of the clearest examples of the trickster-creator's use of ironic humor in the course of deceiving his rivals. Speaking in Yeral, he tells First-Woman that he has come from downstream. First-Woman, addressing him as "my grandson," tells him that Made-from-Bone is chasing her and that she would gladly pay him a large sum to kill Made-from-Bone. At this point, Made-from-Bone asks First-Woman if he can stay overnight, and she shows him where he can hang his hammock in a house full of men. The men are obligated to stay in seclusion in a separate house so that they will not be able to see First-Woman and the women playing the sacred flutes and trumpets for the first female initiation ritual. When First-Woman brings him manioc beer, Made-from-Bone drinks only a little and returns the dipper to her. "You drank nothing, my grandson. That shameless Made-from-Bone, my grandson, he really drinks a lot."

Made-from-Bone's act of deception succeeds in lulling First-Woman into a false sense of security. When she and the women are holding the female initiation ritual and singing whip dance (*kápetiá-pani*), Made-from-Bone secretly puts a potion into the women's beer that drives them crazy. As the women begin fighting with one another, Made-from-Bone opens his travel bag, letting out a number of tiny creatures who transform into men. But when they enter First-Woman's house to take away *Kuwái,* they find only a hole in the ground where First-Woman had escaped with the flutes through a tunnel leading all the way to the Vaupés River. Made-from-Bone continues chasing after First-Woman and the women, and the world opens up for a second time as the sound of *Kuwái*'s flutes and trumpets is heard in all places. Finally, First-Woman and Made-from-Bone go far downstream to the mouth of the Río Negro at Manaus and all the way to the ocean at the mouth of the Amazon. There they leave for *Éenu itánhi,* the place in the sky on the eastern horizon where the sun rises and rivers run in complete circles.

The second creation, or "opening up," of the world outlines a series of expansions away from and back to the mythic center of the world at Hípana. In their collective struggles to control the flutes and trumpets of *Kuwái,* men and women play music that creates and enlarges the world into the immense region of forests and rivers inhabited by people today. Throughout this dynamic, musical process, Made-from-Bone continues to demonstrate the same powers of invincibility, omniscience, and deceit that allowed him to survive primordial bloodbaths and to create the basis for a fully human social world.

"The World Opens Up" continues with three narratives about the origins of shamanic healing practices. In one story, the mythic owner of hallucinogenic snuff teaches *Éeri,* the younger brother of Made-from-Bone who became the first male initiated into adulthood, how to use snuff, magical stones, and other curing techniques. Shamans (*malírri*) are ritual healers who use a variety of physical actions and singing (*malirríkairi*) to dramatize their journeys to and from the world of recently deceased persons and their battles against various types of disease-causing spirits and substances.

A second narrative explains the origin of honey for curing through a series of interactions between a man and a group of bee spirits, who are known as *Kuwáiñai.* The *Kuwáiñai* give the man a pot filled with flowers to take back to his village, where the flowers transform overnight into large quantities of honey. But the man's brothers are curious to learn how he manages to collect so much honey. They get the man drunk, and he dies after telling his family about the *Kuwáiñai,* which they had explicitly forbidden him to do. The third narrative about ritual healing practices tells how the *Kuwáiñai* saved the life of *Kuwaikánirri,* the first victim of witchcraft.[4] The bee spirits take *Kuwaikánirri* from São Gabriel in a canoe made of beeswax, stopping to give him flower nectar from a variety of wild and cultivated fruit trees. *Kuwaikánirri* begins to recover, so the bee spirits give him a canoe paddle made of wax. They continue traveling upstream until they go through the center of the world and eventually reach the bee spirits' village at the headwaters of the Guainía River. *Máapakwa Makákwi,* or Great Honey Place, is filled with the most powerful of flower nectars and honeys, and *Kuwaikánirri* is now able to walk on his own. The bee spirits take him on a long journey through the forest until they reach the Vaupés River, where they leave him with an old woman who keeps him hidden from the powerful jaguar-witches who will always seek to kill him.

A final narrative in "The World Opens Up" explains the fate of a man who finds himself living in a magical city, called Temedawí, where everything is made from gold. Temedawí is in the realm of the *Yópinai,* or disease-causing spirits of the forests and rivers. After marrying a white woman who lived there, the protagonist goes to a hospital filled with fish-people who have fishhooks stuck in their mouths and splinters lodged in their bodies. The man cures all the sick fish-people, and the president of Temedawí appoints him as medical doctor in charge of the hospital for the rest of his life. The story of Temedawí can be read as a tale of the individual's assimilation into the Venezuelan national society and also as an indigenous vision of the nation-state and its urban centers as a healing machine in which shamanic curing practices are writ large.

6

Narratives from "The World Opens Up"

Kuwái, the Powerful Sound that Opened Up the World

First-Woman lived in *Mutʰípani*.[1] They lived there as a single family, since there was no other group of people to live with them. Made-from-Bone was there; First-Woman [*Ámaru*] was his aunt [father's sister]. He had sexual intercourse with First-Woman, his aunt. They hid their sexual relations from the others in their family. One day First-Woman became pregnant with a child. There was no other group of people.

"Who could it be who impregnated First-Woman?" the people asked.

"I don't know," said Made-from-Bone, "it's nothing, just sperm of this world." He went into hiding to defend himself. Thus it will be for the new people in the future world. A woman without a husband becomes pregnant. It was First-Woman who started this.

The unborn child grew larger inside First-Woman's womb until it reached completion. Already there were pains as the baby began trying to come out. But First-Woman did not have any place for giving birth to the baby. She suffered until she fell unconscious. Made-from-Bone summoned a red *mataguaru* fish. "Now I want you to enter between her legs to make a hole so that the baby can be born," said Made-from-Bone.

"Okay," said the *mataguaru* fish. He jumped, entering between her legs until only his tail was sticking out. Made-from-Bone also jumped and pulled the fish out of First-Woman by its tail. Blood came from her. The blood ran on top of a stone. It ran in curves. The place where this happened is called Caño *Dzukuáli* [Curved Stream].

Already the baby was born, but First-Woman did not know when her child was born. Made-from-Bone grabbed the baby and hid him away from his mother. He left the placenta there on the ground. It transformed into a stingray, like those that we have today in all the rivers.

Made-from-Bone made a cigar and blew tobacco smoke over First-Woman. Just then she sat up. "It was not people who caused your suffering," Made-from-Bone said to her. "This here [pointing at the placenta on the ground] is all that you gave birth to."

"It's not true," she said. "I felt that it was a person, my child," she said.

"Think about what you're doing, because this is your child," Made-from-Bone said to First-Woman.

"This stingray means nothing to me, throw it out," she said. "My son was a person." Made-from-Bone threw the stingray into the river.

The baby grew up in hiding until reaching adulthood.[2] There was a group of children who played in a clearing in the forest. They grabbed a *cigarron* wasp and put it inside a vase. They closed the lid, and the *cigarron* was flying inside the vase. "Hee, hee, hee," it was sounding. "This is called our *Kuwái*," they said. The boys continued to play this way with the vase for three days. They went again on another day, giving lashes to the vase. "This is our *Kuwái*."

The child of First-Woman, the real *Kuwái*, stopped to listen to the boys. "Aaa, perhaps they want to see me," he said. "Now I will go over to them." He came out behind them. "Eee," he said. He was an enormously fat person. "Eee, my grandchildren," he said, "What are you doing?"

"We're not doing anything, just playing," they answered.

"This thing, what is it?" he said.

"Our vase," they said.

"What name did you give it?" he asked.

"It's not important; it's just our vase," they said.

"It's not so," he said. "I heard that you know a different name," he said to them. The boys laughed. "Tell me, tell me; I want to know what you call it," said *Kuwái*.

"*Kuwái*," they said. "We gave it the name *Kuwái*."

"Okay," he said, "what you are calling *Kuwái*, it is I," he said to them. "I am dangerous," he said. "You can not eat anything," he said. "You are going to hear how I speak with my entire body," he said. "You must stay hidden; it's dangerous that other people will hear how I speak; all my fingers, my head, my body," he said. "Now you can begin whipping yourselves," he said. And the boys started to whip themselves.

They finished what they were doing and returned to their house. "Come to eat," said their parents.

"We don't want to eat; our stomachs are hurting," they said. Another day passed, and it was the same. They did not want to eat.

"Why is it that now these boys don't want to eat?" asked Made-from-Bone. "I think they must have seen something strange over there." Later he said, "I'm going to wait and see how they live there, what they're doing."

He left and secretly arrived at the edge of the clearing where the boys had been playing. The boys arrived after a few minutes, and *Kuwái* came toward them. Made-from-Bone stood up so that he could see them and came out toward them. "Eeee," he said, "what are you doing?"

"No, Made-from-Bone, I've come to show myself to them, my grandsons," said *Kuwái*. "They want to see *Kuwái*, because I am the real *Kuwái*," he said to Made-from-Bone. "You are going to hear how I speak, my sound," he said. And he began to make "speak," or make sounds, for Made-from-Bone: paca,[3] white heron flutes,[4] everything of *Kuwái*, all the sounds of his body. Made-from-Bone stood up so that he could hear.

"Okay, *Kuwái*," he said, "What can we do so that these boys can eat again?"

"You must tell the boys' parents to make a shelter," said *Kuwái*. "Find a house that has no owner and make a shelter. These women must make manioc beer so that we can drink," said *Kuwái*. "Tomorrow in the afternoon I am going to show[5] them," he said to Made-from-Bone.

"I will help you," said Made-from-Bone, "because one of the boys is my younger brother, *Éeri*."

Kuwái arrived the next afternoon. "Now *Kuwái* is coming," Made-from-Bone said to the women. "You must all get out of here." And they left. *Kuwái* arrived in the village and began to show the boys. He began to "speak" the word-sounds that could be heard in the entire world. The world was still very small. He began to speak, "Heee." The sound of his voice ran away and opened up the world.

Made-from-Bone and *Kuwái* together said to the people, "Now you must care for your children by finding someone to cut their hair. When their hair has been cut, then you can call them adults. You can give them gifts, whatever little things. You women must paint these boys before they are shown." And they all entered into the shelter within the house.

He lived with them in the house. Morning arrived, then it grew dark again. Morning came again, and *Kuwái* blew tobacco smoke over *patsiáka* and manioc breads so that the boys could eat and drink.[6] The boys drank, finished. "Now I am going to stay here inside the house with them. I will teach them all the things related to work: *manare*, large baskets, *guapa*, *sebucan,* all the things necessary for making manioc breads. Thus it will be for the new people who live in the future world," said *Kuwái.*

"Let's go collect *tiríta* palms,"[7] he said. They left. He wanted them to work quickly. He taught them how to work; then they returned to the house. "Let's go now to gather firewood for the women," he said. They left and gathered firewood before returning again to the house. Made-from-Bone called for the women so that the boys could give them the firewood. The next day *Kuwái* said, "Let's go to collect soapwood for bathing so that you can all wash yourselves." They gathered some and returned again to the house. "Let's go gather vines," he said. They gathered vines and returned to the house. "Now we are going to collect palm fruits; *seje finito, guacu.* You must harvest the *seje* fruits quickly," he said. "Your wives will work quickly; that's why I am teaching you to work this way."

They returned and arrived at their house with large quantities of *seje* and *guacu* fruits. *Kuwái* carried all these fruits inside his stomach. When they arrived at the house, Made-from-Bone called the women to come and receive the *seje* and *guacu* fruits. They shared the fruits among all the women. "Now," said *Kuwái,* "there are only a few days left until you will be taken out of the house. I am going to blow tobacco smoke over your food."

"Okay," they replied, and they were happy. They finished all their work of making things to give to their family.

"Let's go gather *guacu* fruits," said *Kuwái.* They left and arrived at a waterfall called *Tsépani.*[8] *Kuwái* climbed up a *guacu* fruit tree for them. "You are going to collect fruits," he said.

"Okay," they said. *Kuwái* broke off a branch and threw it to them. They collected the *guacu* fruits.

"This hunger is hurting me," said *Málinálieni.* "I am burning to eat."

"It's not so. If you eat anything, *Kuwái* will eat us," said *Éeri.*

"No, he won't know anything. Let's eat in secret," said *Málinálieni.*

"Okay, go ahead and eat. But I will not eat," said *Éeri,* "because he warned us not to eat anything," said *Éeri.*

"He's not going to know anything," said *Málinálieni* to *Éeri. Málinálieni* lit a fire and burned some *guacu* fruits. After they were burnt, *Málinálieni* broke open one of the *guacu* fruits to smell it. It had a delicious aroma. "Let's eat it," said *Málinálieni.* And he ate the fruit. Then *Hménakʰóewa* ate some. *Tuípwa* also ate some of the fruits.

"Come on and eat with us, *Éeri,*" they said to him.

"No, you go ahead and eat," he replied.

Kuwái smelled the aroma of the fruits and sat down on a branch of the tree. The boys had wounded him, and he began drooling. The saliva transformed into vines that exist today. "He's already dead," said *Éeri*. "I told you that he said not to eat the *guacu* fruits."

After a few minutes *Kuwái* sat up and began to speak with his fingers, the white heron flutes [*máaliawa*], "tsee-tsem, . . ." he said. "*Málinálieni* ate strong food[9] with a lot of fat, *anchoa grande*."

"Now we're in bad shape," said *Éeri*, "We don't know what to do."

"Let's go." *Kuwái* climbed back down to the ground. He was very sad and asked the boys, "Were you eating strong food?"

"No, we didn't eat anything," they said.

"Okay," said *Kuwái*, "Open your mouths so I can see inside." *Éeri* opened his mouth. *Málinálieni* also opened his mouth, and *Kuwái* saw tiny pieces of *guacu* fruit. "Yes, you ate," said *Kuwái*. "And you?" he said to one of the others. The other boy opened his mouth, and it was the same. "And you?' he said to the third boy. It was the same; all three had eaten. "And you, *Éeri*?" he asked.

"I did not eat with them," said *Éeri*.

"I warned you that I am very dangerous, but you were unable to endure the hunger," he said. "I warned you and told you that there was not much longer to wait, but you didn't heed my word."

It was the season of the strong weather of *Kuwái*, rain and thunder. "Rain is coming our way," he said to the boys. "I'm going to find a shelter." He left but stayed close by. He opened his mouth as if it were a cave beneath a large rock. He called for the boys, "Come over here, where there's a hole in the rock.

"Okay," they said, and ran toward him. *Éeri*, too.

"Enter, enter, enter," he said, "You'll get wet." The boys entered the cave. *Éeri* stood beneath a bush that was pushed up against a tree trunk. "*Éeri*, come here and enter, come here and enter," *Kuwái* said to *Éeri*.

"No *Kuwái*," he said, "I will stay here beneath this bush."

"Okay," he said. The rock cave was really the mouth of *Kuwái*. It began to rain on the boys. *Kuwái* closed his mouth and ate the three boys.

Éeri turned to look, "hoo," but the hole in the rock had already disappeared. He turned to see that the belly of *Kuwái* was enormous. *Éeri* remained quiet and was frightened. In the rain, a fish fell to the ground. It was a small catfish called *híni*. "What could this be, *Kuwái*?" he said.

"Aaa, *Éeri*, this is to make the sacred food for us so that I can blow tobacco smoke and you can eat; because you did not eat the strong food. The spirit-name of this fish in *malikái* is 'the child of the anaconda of the *dozate* bush.'"[10]

The rains stopped, and the day was beautiful again. "Earlier *Kuwái* ate the boys," Made-from-Bone said to their parents. "I warned them that it was very dangerous for them." It began to rain again, and Made-from-Bone caught some of the rain in his hand. His hand filled with blood. "Didn't I tell you that he already ate them? Now we must wait and see," said Made-from-Bone.

After that *Kuwái* was afraid to return to the house. He was ashamed. Made-from-Bone stood still and listened, "Heee, heee, heee." In the late afternoon, *Kuwái* came toward the house. He stopped outside the village. Made-from-Bone stood up to look at *Kuwái*, whose stomach was swollen. *Éeri* was the only one with him. Made-from-Bone stood up to look at him from a distance. He placed three *guapas* on the ground in front of *Kuwái*, who walked in curves around them. *Kuwái* vomited the remains of the three boys into the *guapas*. As soon as he finished vomiting, he took off flying in the air. "Heee, heee," he sang.

Made-from-Bone ran to shout after him. "*Kuwái*, why are you leaving? Come here to talk with us some more. Why are you leaving?" But *Kuwái* didn't pay him any attention and left.

Made-from-Bone went back to tell the boys' parents that *Kuwái* had eaten their sons. "Earlier *Kuwái* ate your sons," he said, "but they had done wrong to *Kuwái*. They told me that they wanted to see *Kuwái*, but now look what has happened to them. I warned them that this was very dangerous. The only bad thing now is that we don't know how to allow *Éeri* to eat; there's no way for him to eat. There's no one to blow tobacco smoke so that he can eat." Night fell, and they buried the dead.

Morning came, and Made-from-Bone ate coca leaves to divine and learn what they could do. He thought and divined in all places about what could be done, but he didn't find anything. Then he returned to thinking about the *seje* palm weevil larvae [*mútʰi*] and divined that these would be very good. "Aaa, with this maybe we can invite *Kuwái* to return. Let's go look for *seje* palm weevil larvae," he said. They found a dead *seje* palm tree, split it open, and there were many larvae inside. They gathered them. "Let's return." And they all went back to the house.

Made-from-Bone packed the larvae inside a leaf so that he could roast them. Then he called for *Káalimátu*[11] and went to look for some balsa wood. He needed the balsa wood to make effigies of the three boys that *Kuwái* had eaten. He made dancing headdresses. He made dance whips[12] for them. He made everything; their eyes, their arms; everything; their mouths; the shape of people. He painted them red, then finished. He made three of them. He left them standing in a line inside the seclusion hut. "Let's go."

He called for *Káalimátu.* "Now, you must go to invite *Kuwái*," he said. "Take these *seje* palm weevil larvae to him, and tell him this: 'Made-from-Bone ordered me to come and invite you to blow tobacco smoke for the food of the students.' That's what you will say."

"Okay," said *Káalimátu,* "I'll go to see." Just then he left, following the same path where *Kuwái* had gone.

He went until he arrived at the "mouth" of the sky, a narrow place in the sky that closed and opened, closed and opened all the time. *Káalimátu* arrived there when the passage was open and thought that it was always that way. When he arrived he went slowly, and the "mouth" closed. It closed on the waist of *Káalimátu.* "Hoo," it almost cut him in half at the waist. Then it opened again and he was able to pass through. His buttocks and body were very large, but his waist had become as tiny as a thread.

He went on. He could hear *Kuwái,* "Heee, heee, heee." The sound was constant. "Now I have indeed arrived at *Kuwái*'s place," said *Káalimátu.* "Ee, *Kuwái*," he said. *Kuwái* turned toward him and saw that it was *Káalimátu.*

"Aaa, *Káalimátu,* which way did you come?"

"I came by your pathway. Made-from-Bone ordered me to come see you," he said.

"Why did you come?" he asked *Káalimátu.* "Did you come to hurt yourself?"

"Yes," said *Káalimátu,* "already I have hurt myself. Made-from-Bone sends you a greeting so that you will go to blow tobacco smoke for the students' food," *Káalimátu* said to *Kuwái.*

"It's not so," said *Kuwái,* "I am not going because earlier I ate my students."

"No, Made-from-Bone has already revived them, and now they are well again," said *Káalimátu.* "You know that Made-from-Bone is a person who knows how to do everything."

"It's not true," said *Kuwái,* "He's joking. He wants to kill me."

"It's not so," said *Káalimátu,* "He is not going to kill you. He is inviting you only because he wants you to blow tobacco smoke over the students' food. You can go back to your village."

"It's not so," said *Kuwái,* "I know that Made-from-Bone wants to kill me. But he can't trick me."

Káalimátu gave *Kuwái* the *seje* palm weevil larvae. "Here is what Made-from-Bone sent for you," he said.

"What are these?" asked *Kuwái*.

"I don't know," said *Káalimátu*, "Open them to see."

Kuwái opened the leaf to see inside. He smelled the leaf's contents. "Haaa," he said, "With this I can definitely go," said *Kuwái*. "Okay," he said, "I am going to let him kill me."

"He's not going to kill you; it's not true, *Kuwái*," said *Káalimátu*.

"He is going to kill me because I did wrong to him," said *Kuwái*. "Now take him my message. Tell him that I will come when they call for me. Tell them to prepare the sacred food and the drinks. Have them prepare manioc breads, everything. I will allow him two days for this work. On the afternoon of the third day, I will come to your village and will then blow tobacco smoke over the sacred food. Afterwards he can kill me. But there is nothing with which he can kill me. Tell him exactly this way: Logs and trees, they are my body; vines, too; my body is poison, my hair; water, I live in water; soil, it is my body; steel, my body; the only thing my body is not is fire," he said. "With this, yes, he can kill me. That is how you will speak to him," said *Kuwái*.

"Okay," said *Káalimátu*, "I will return before you."

"Good," said *Kuwái*, "Wait for me the day after tomorrow in the afternoon."

And he left. He arrived at the doorway of the sky and saw how it opened and closed. When it opened, *Káalimátu* quickly passed through it. It closed immediately behind him. "Aaa, that's how to pass through." He left, returned, and arrived in the village of Made-from-Bone.

"How are you? What did you see?" asked Made-from-Bone.

"Good; he's up there, but I was afraid," said *Káalimátu*. "Look how I am; I was screwed."

"Ooo." Made-from-Bone saw that he had a tiny waist. "It's okay," said Made-from-Bone, "you survived. Did you meet with *Kuwái*?" he asked.

"Yes, I met him," said *Káalimátu*. "He sent you a message. You must prepare the sacred food, *kapéti* whips, and drinks. He gave you two days to do all the things he wants you to do. On the third day in the afternoon, he will arrive," he said to Made-from-Bone. "He said that there is nothing you can kill him with and that his body is made of everything. The only thing that his body is not is fire; and with this you can kill him."

"Aaa, so that's how it is," said Made-from-Bone. "Let's go gather firewood." They went looking and gathered a large amount of firewood.

Kuwái arrived on the third day. Made-from-Bone placed his "students," or effigies, in a line facing *Kuwái*. *Éeri* was the head of the group. When Made-from-Bone finished, he went to greet *Kuwái*. "Eee, *Kuwái*, you've arrived," he said. "Why did you leave me before blowing tobacco smoke over the food of your students?"

"It's not so," said *Kuwái*, "I already ate them. Why should I blow tobacco smoke over their food?"

"Yes, it is true," said Made-from-Bone. "You ate them, but they had done wrong to you. They ate, and that's why you ate them. But I revived them and woke them up again. Come have a look," he said.

Kuwái stood up to look at them and saw people. They had hair, eyes, noses, mouths, ears; everything. "So it is, Made-from-Bone," said *Kuwái*. "I have come to let you kill me."

"No, *Kuwái*, I invited you only so that you could blow tobacco smoke over your students' sacred food. When you have finished, you can go back," he said.

"Is the sacred food already ready?" asked *Kuwái*.

"Yes," said Made-from-Bone, "It's all done. We made everything; drinks, sacred food, also whips."

"Okay," said *Kuwái*, "bring me the sacred food." Just then they brought it over to him. They drank beer, and *Kuwái* became happy.

"Made-from-Bone," he said, "come here to hear my customs before you kill me." Just then *Kuwái* began to blow tobacco smoke.[13]

"It's not so, *Kuwái*," said Made-from-Bone, "I am not going to kill you." Made-from-Bone sat down close to *Kuwái*. *Dzúli* sat down a little farther away so that he could listen well to the *malikái* singing and chanting.

He blew until he was tired. "That's how it is, Made-from-Bone," he said, "to blow smoke over the sacred food." He began to blow smoke again and grew tired.

"I'm going to find some drinks for us," Made-from-Bone said to *Kuwái*. He went off to the women's house, where he doled out drinks to all the women and each of them gave Made-from-Bone a drink. He was drunk.

Kuwái was waiting for Made-from-Bone, but he grew tired of waiting for him. He began blowing tobacco smoke again. *Dzúli* sat without moving, silent. *Kuwái* blew tobacco smoke and grew tired. Made-from-Bone came back over again to *Kuwái*. "You have already missed part of the *malikái*," *Kuwái* said to him. He blew tobacco smoke again.

"I'm going to find drinks for us, *Kuwái*," said Made-from-Bone. He left, and *Kuwái* continued blowing tobacco smoke.

Again he waited for Made-from-Bone, but he did not return. "It looks like Made-from-Bone doesn't want to learn," *Kuwái* said to *Dzúli*. "You, though, I believe you still haven't missed any of the *malikái*."

"Yes," said *Dzúli*, "I am the person who truly wants to know *malikái*."

"Good, come over here to sit close to my side," said *Kuwái*. He blew tobacco smoke again, this time together with *Dzúli*.

They waited for Made-from-Bone, who came to listen for a few minutes and then left again. "Aaa, it appears that Made-from-Bone does not want to learn *malikái*," said *Kuwái*. "Thus it will be for the new people in the future world," he said, "Only very few individuals are going to learn *malikái*." Some people learn a little, while others know a little more. That's how it will be with people. "Let's dance," *Kuwái* said to *Dzúli*. "Be careful not to lose this important part." They grew tired of dancing and together blew tobacco smoke again.

In the very early morning, they gave drinks to *Kuwái*. He was drunk. "Now," he said, "You, *Dzúli*, have learned very well all the *malikái*. You, Made-from-Bone, know only some parts of it. That's how you will remain," he said to Made-from-Bone. "Only *Dzúli*." They continued blowing tobacco smoke until dawn. Again they gave drinks to *Kuwái*, who became completely drunk. They gave more and more drinks to *Kuwái*. Meanwhile, the others began lighting a bonfire on the village plaza outside.

They continued giving drinks, and *Kuwái* finished blowing tobacco smoke. He gave the sacred food to Made-from-Bone. "Here it is, Made-from-Bone," he said, "I have now finished blowing tobacco smoke. Now you must make the one who has fasted lick hot pepper, then all the other men." All the men were whipping each other. They finished. "Let's dance," said *Kuwái*. He was very drunk.

"Let's go outside," Made-from-Bone said to *Kuwái*, "We will dance around our bonfire."

"Let's go," said *Kuwái*. They danced in circles around the fire. *Kuwái* had to be supported by the other people, since he was very drunk.

They pushed him from behind, and he fell into the bonfire. Then they threw more firewood on top of him, covering him up. "Come, come, come to kill *Kuwái* to revenge our sons," they shouted.

"Come stand over here near his head," said Made-from-Bone. "His penis is pointed in the other direction; be careful that he doesn't urinate and kill us." Already *Kuwái* urinated, "Ssss." It went far but on the other side of the fire. It went into the forest where it hit some of the trees. Those trees died. That is where powerful thunder and lightning began, the kind that kills people. "I warned you that if you stood over by his penis, he would surely have killed us," said Made-from-Bone.

The world closed back up again after *Kuwái* died. It was tiny again. "Okay," they spent the night and were very sad. "Now we are not well. We don't know what to do now. We have killed the only one who knows what to do. Why did we kill him?" said Made-from-Bone.

The Struggle between Made-from-Bone and First-Woman

Made-from-Bone ate coca to divine what to do. He foresaw that things were going to turn out well. "I know that he will leave some other thing for us in the place where he died," said Made-from-Bone.

After three days, Made-from-Bone went to look at the place where they had burned him. He saw a tall tree there, *kadápu* vines, and *dzámakuápi* vines. Then he saw that water was flowing out of the place. It made a sound, and Made-from-Bone listened: "Tso-wai, tso-wai, tso-wai."[14]

He returned to his house. In the early morning, he went to look again and saw an enormous tree that reached above the sky. He saw large, beautiful *kadápu* vines and large, beautiful *dzámakuápi* vines. It was beautiful how the tree rose up.

Then Made-from-Bone summoned a squirrel. "Do you know how to do this?" he asked.

"Yes," said Squirrel, "I do know how to do it. I'm a carpenter."

"Okay," said Made-from-Bone, "you go to work on this tree."

"Good," said Squirrel. Made-from-Bone left for his house. The squirrel was already working, cutting through the tree trunk but leaving a little piece uncut. The squirrel measured different lengths—*waliáduwa,* white heron flutes, *molítu* frog flutes, paca trumpets, wild chicken flutes.[15] He finished. He left the tree this way to kill Made-from-Bone, the revenge of *Kuwái.*

"I've finished what you asked me to do, Made-from-Bone," Squirrel said. "Go and push the tree so that it falls down."

"Okay," said Made-from-Bone, who went to have a look. He chewed coca to divine what to do. He had a bad feeling. "This is not right," he said, "he wants to kill me." Made-from-Bone got a long stick and struck it against the tree from a distance. "Aaa," said Made-from-Bone, "look at this. If I had pushed it with my hand, I'd be dead underneath this pile of logs."

"Let's go," Made-from-Bone said after a few days had passed. "Squirrel, let's go work on those logs."

"Let's go," said Squirrel, and they left. When they arrived, Squirrel explained to Made-from-Bone all the names. He left the logs lying down group by group.[16] He told Made-from-Bone the names of each of the logs. "This one, *waliáduwa,* comes in three. That one, *máaliawa,* comes in two." He finished explaining how all the logs are used, and they left them all lying down.

"How do you make sound with them?" Made-from-Bone tried to blow through them.

"It's not like that," said Squirrel, who took out a feather from a large hawk. "With this you can make sound," he said to Made-from-Bone.

Made-from-Bone blew air with the hawk feather, and it made a sound. "Heee," and then the world opened up again, from here to there, this entire world. The sound went up into the sky above. All the sounds of *Kuwái* spoke—*waliáduwa, máaliawa,* all of them. Made-from-Bone heard how this one sounds, how that one sounds, how the other ones sound. "Now," said Made-from-Bone, "These are going to belong to us men, and we will hide them from the women. This is the son of First-Woman, but we must keep it hidden from her," he said. Then Made-from-Bone lived with the people and began to hold *dabucurí* and *kwépani*[17] ceremonies.

First-Woman was furious. "Made-from-Bone believes that I don't know that this is my son," she said.

After a while, First-Woman took *Kuwái* away from Made-from-Bone. "In the future, he is going to stay with us women," First-Woman said to Made-from-Bone.

"Okay," said Made-from-Bone, "I don't care."

"You men cannot see him," she said.

"Okay," he said.

She lived with *Kuwái* in *Mutʰípani.* She gathered firewood and *matsítsi* fruits that were worthless. The men worked with manioc: grating, pressing, making *casabe* breads. The manioc presses were laid on top of the men's arms, and it is for this reason that today men have "flat" forearms.

"I don't agree with First-Woman," said Made-from-Bone. "It would be good if she would harvest *seje, manaca, seje finito,* or *yuku* fruits. But what First-Woman is doing now is not good. These women aren't doing anything; we men are," he said. "Let's go now and take *Kuwái* away from First-Woman so that he stays with us men."

"Okay," they said, "Let's go." There were many of them, and they left. His companions transformed themselves into little frogs. Made-from-Bone arrived at First-Woman's village. "Eee, my aunt," he said to her, "I have come to spend some time with you."

"Okay," she said, "Here I am." The little frogs, called *dzukuékue,* followed behind Made-from-Bone. "Made-from-Bone, what are those?" she asked.

"These are little frogs," he said. "They're called *dzukuékue,*" he told her. They were actually kinsmen of Made-from-Bone, but First-Woman didn't know it. Just then Made-from-Bone made a bolt of lightning that struck First-Woman, and she fell on the ground.

Immediately the little frogs, kinsmen of Made-from-Bone, transformed themselves into people. They ran to enter the house of *Kuwái.* They fought against First-Woman's kinsmen, shooting them with poisoned arrows. They took *Kuwái* and began to run away with him.

After taking *Kuwái* away from First-Woman, Made-from-Bone blew tobacco smoke over her. She sat up. "What happened to us, Made-from-Bone?" she asked.

"Lightning struck us," he said, "We both nearly died. Just now I regained consciousness.[18] Aaa," he said, "Those things have all transformed themselves into animals; fish, jaguars, all dangerous animals. Now we men are going to watch over them. You women cannot see them any longer because they are very dangerous," Made-from-Bone said to First-Woman.

"Okay," she said, "It doesn't matter; another of Made-from-Bone's tricks."

Then Made-from-Bone took skin from all the animals: *paca,* jaguar, pikurri, wild chicken, white heron, toucan, yellow curassow, crane, white monkey, *pavon grande* fish, white bocachico fish, all of them. "Tomorrow I am going to hold a *kwépani* ceremony," he said to First-Woman, "to show you how they have transformed."

"Okay," she said. Already Made-from-Bone began making the *kwépani.* First-Woman arrived at his village. "You've arrived, my aunt," he said.

"Yes, I've arrived," she said.

"Here is the women's house; here is where you will stay for the night with the women."

"Hoo, that's fine," she said.

Kuwái came during the night.[19] First-Woman sat down close to the door of the women's house. Made-from-Bone fashioned a small stick and put some sticky *peramán* resin on its point. The *paca* trumpet was already beginning to speak, or sing. "This is the *paca,* the animal *paca,*" Made-from-Bone said to First-Woman. "You are going to see," he said. He pushed the little stick until its end was outside. The men who were outside put some *paca* fur on the sticky *peramán* resin. When Made-from-Bone pulled the stick back inside, he saw that there was *paca* fur stuck to the resin. "Look, First-Woman," he said, "Just as I told you. Look at this *paca* fur." Then another one came. "This is jaguar," he said to her, "a very dangerous animal. You are going to see." The stick went outside, then he pulled it back inside. "Look, here is jaguar fur. I'm not lying to you," he told her. Another one came. "This is *pavon grande* fish," he said, "the grandfather of *pavon grande*,[20] very dangerous. You will see," he said. The stick went outside, then he pulled it back inside. "Look, scales of the *pavon grande* fish." And so it went with all the animals of *Kuwái*.

"Thus it will be, it seems," she said. "It doesn't matter. You will keep these animals."

Made-from-Bone lived for a time with *Kuwái* at Hípana. Then one day First-Woman spoke to her family of women, "Made-from-Bone has shamelessly tricked us with his animals. Now let's go and take them away from him," she said. And they left. She brought along a very large number of women.

When they arrived at the village of Made-from-Bone, he did not see the women. They approached the house, then ran and went inside. "Heee," said Made-from-Bone's men. "War has come upon us," they shouted. They fought against the women. First-Woman ran and grabbed the *máaliawa* flutes. The ones she needed the most were the *máaliawa;* jaguar-bones, too. These are primary among all the instruments of *Kuwái*. She put them inside her vagina. Then she left with her family of women.

They went to *Mutʰípani*. First-Woman evaded Made-from-Bone. As she went down Caño *Dzukuáli*, Made-from-Bone went ahead of her and set traps to catch her so that he could take *Kuwái* away from her. He made rapids. First-Woman arrived to see the stream closed off. "Aaa," she said, "That Made-from-Bone made it this way." She left. The women carried their canoes through the forest to descend to the other side of the trap. They passed through.

Made-from-Bone went to have a look, but there was nothing. "Tse," he said, "Where could she have passed through?" He went walking to see. "Hoo," there was a broad path in the forest descending to the river below. "Here is where that shameless woman passed," he said.

Made-from-Bone ran again through the forest. First-Woman traveled by canoe. Made-from-Bone went to make another trap to catch her. He stopped to listen, "Hee, hee," from downstream. "Aaa, they've already left." She went quickly. Again Made-from-Bone made a trap for her, and again he could hear that she was already downstream. He left his trap and set off again. That's how he went around.

They went and arrived in Puerto Ayacucho. Made-from-Bone made a great rapids there, and First-Woman arrived to see the Maipure rapids. She entered into the stream at Samariapo. She left the stream and went downstream to Puerto Ayacucho. The footpath turned into the paved highway of today, and they went until they arrived in Caracas. A rooster sang, "kakalewa." "Aaa, this village is going to be called Caracas," said Made-from-Bone.

Then First-Woman returned [to the Río Negro] and hid herself at a lake called Ámaru. Made-from-Bone didn't know where she was. He went until reaching the rapids at São Gabriel, where he asked people, "Have you seen First-Woman passing by here?"

"No," they said, "We don't know this First-Woman."

"Aaa, so be it," he said. "Where could she be?" He returned to *Mut^bípani* and arrived to find that no one was there, only silence. "Where might she be?" he asked. He went downstream again, arriving a second time at the rapids beside São Gabriel. Again he asked, "Have you seen First-Woman?"

"No," they told him, "we haven't seen anything around here."

"Aaa," he said, "Where might she be?"

He returned again, going back upstream until he came to a stone called Watúra. There Made-from-Bone collected a tiny medicine, called *pikáka*. It was not exactly a medicine but something that would make people crazy. Made-from-Bone took some of it and went slowly away in his canoe. He took his family with him by carrying them inside a hollowed out *yagrumo* log. He left very early in the morning.

He saw a light, which was really Crow, a friend of First-Woman. "Who could that be over there?" he said. "Now I will go little by little to see what this could be." He arrived very close to Crow and saw that Crow was fishing with a lantern. "Surely this must be one of First-Woman's companions. I am going to see where he goes." The sun was beginning to rise. Made-from-Bone watched and saw Crow run up a stream. "Aaa," said Made-from-Bone, "Look at that." He went into the stream. The sun was already up and getting hot. Made-from-Bone chased after him in the stream. As he went up the stream, Made-from-Bone saw a clearing in the distance. "What could that be?" he said. "I must go over there." He went on and on.

He came out of the stream and saw an enormous lake. He heard "Heee, heee, heee." "I can hear where that shameless First-Woman has gone. Now I am going to catch up with her," he said. Then Made-from-Bone transformed himself into a Yeral.[21] That's where the Nheengatú language began. The Yeral live downstream at the rapids of São Gabriel, until this day.

Made-from-Bone went across the lake until he arrived at the place where First-Woman was living. When he landed at the port, there was a man. "Eee," Made-from-Bone called to him, "What are you doing?"

"First-Woman is blowing tobacco smoke over the sacred food tonight," the man answered.

"Where is First-Woman?" he asked, "Would it be possible to see *Kuwái* with her?"

"That's not how it is; she doesn't want to allow anyone to see him," the man said to Made-from-Bone.

"So be it; go and call her for me. I want to speak with her," said Made-from-Bone.

"Okay," said the man. Already he left to call First-Woman.

She was already coming down to the port. "Eee, my grandson," she said, "where did you come from?"

"Aaa, I am coming from downstream, grandmother, from São Gabriel," he answered. They spoke in the Yeral language. That is how the Yeral language that is still spoken today began.

"You haven't seen Made-from-Bone there, my grandson?" she asked.

"No, I haven't seen anything, grandmother, I don't know this Made-from-Bone," he told her.

"This shameless Made-from-Bone is chasing after me, and that's why I move about in hiding," she said. "I live well in my village."

"Let's hope that he arrives here today so that I can kill him," he said. "I would kill him."

"Let's hope so, my grandson. If you kill Made-from-Bone, I will pay you well," she said.

"Would it be possible to watch with you tonight?" he asked.

"Why not, my grandson, you can watch with us tonight," she said to him. "Let's go, grab your hammock and go where there are only men like yourself."

"Okay," he said, and left with First-Woman.

He had his companions right there with him inside the *yagrumo* log in his travel bag. "Here," she said, "This is where the men stay. You will stay here with them," she said to him.

"Okay," he said. He entered the house and put away his travel bag. Then he sat down with the other men on a bench.

First-Woman came over to him. She was carrying a gourd dipper full of manioc beer for him to drink. "Yes, my grandson, drink some beer," she said to him.

"Okay, grandmother," he said. He drank a little bit, then returned the dipper to her.

She saw that it was almost full. "You already drank?" she said.

"Yes, grandmother, I already drank."

"Paaa, you haven't drunk anything, my grandson. That shameless Made-from-Bone, my grandson, he drinks a lot," she said.

"I don't do that," he said. "I don't drink that way, like Made-from-Bone."

"Now we are going to hold the fasting of the girls," she said to him. "You can watch with us, but you must stay with the men. You cannot go outside the house during the night."

"Okay," he said. He stayed with the men and drank with them. They whipped each other. The women came to whip themselves with the men.

It was very early in the morning. Already Made-from-Bone took out his potion for making people crazy, and he threw it into the women's beer. He mixed it into the beer. The women who owned the beer were already drunk. They did not know that Made-from-Bone had mixed the potion into their beer. Made-from-Bone said to them, "I am going to dole out the beer."

"Okay, that's fine," they said. Made-from-Bone doled it out. He wove in and out around them. "Hoo," already they were quite drunk, and they began to go crazy.

Morning arrived. Already Made-from-Bone took his kinsmen out of his travel bag. When he brought them out, they transformed into people so that they could fight against First-Woman and take *Kuwái* away. Already there was much fighting, and they went outside to go to the house of *Kuwái*. They realized that Made-from-Bone had arrived. "Hee, Made-from-Bone has arrived among us," they shouted. They ran to guard the door of First-Woman's house.

"Have you seen First-Woman?" he asked them.

"She is right here in this house; there's no place for her to leave."

"We are going to fight with her now to take *Kuwái* away from her," he said to them. They waited. "Good, let's go inside the house to see where First-Woman is," he said to his kinsmen.

They entered. They went in circles all through the house, but they didn't see anything. "There's nothing," they said to Made-from-Bone.

"Where is she?" he said.

"Right here, there's no sign of her."

"Okay," he said, and he opened all the doors in the house. They opened every door but still didn't see anything. "Where'd she go?" he said. Made-from-Bone walked through the house. He saw a hole. "Haaa," said Made-from-Bone, "here is where she escaped. She's already gone. There's nothing we can do. She left."

She went inside the earth and came out beside the Vaupés River at a place called *Kuwáiñai*. Made-from-Bone chased after her. When he arrived at São Gabriel, he heard, "Hee, hee, hee, hee." First-Woman had already gone downstream ahead of him. He arrived in Manaas, then Barrakuá. He asked, "Have you seen First-Woman?"

"Yes," they said. First-Woman already passed downstream. Made-from-Bone went after her.

They went until they reached the sea, which is called Éenutanhísre. There Made-from-Bone and First-Woman live together in a single village. They celebrate *kwépani* ceremonies, all the different ceremonies that we have today. There they went to live until today. Thus it ends.

The Origin of Hallucinogenic Snuff and Shamanic Healing

Great Shaman [*Dzulíhwerri*] was the first one who knew how to use hallucinogenic snuff [*dzáatu*][22] for shamanic healing. Jaguar came to the village of Great Shaman; along with him came tapir, dolphin, wild forest spirit, herb spirit, and *Éeri*. "We want to practice shamanic curing. We want you to teach us how," they said to him.

"Okay, I can teach you. Tomorrow we'll begin," he said.

He began with them at the crack of dawn. He took them to a sandy shoal behind his village and blew hallucinogenic snuff for them. He blew snuff for each one of them. When finished, he sat with them in a line. He gave each of them a shamanic rattle. Then he taught them how to use all the words. Like this, like that, like this. Night fell.

The next day he began again with them. They ran out of hallucinogenic snuff in the morning. "Let's go. Go and get the hallucinogenic snuff over there where my daughter is," he said to them. "Tell my daughter, 'I have come to get hallucinogenic snuff.'"

"Good," said one of the students. "I will go get it from her." He left right away and arrived at the woman's house. "Your father sent me to come and get hallucinogenic snuff from you," he said.

"Okay," she said. She took off her shirt and lay down on a floor mat. She opened up her vagina for him. "Here it is; take it," she said to him. But he didn't know how to get it. He copulated with her. When finished, he returned to the village of Great Shaman.

"How was it? Did you bring back the snuff?" asked Great Shaman.

"Nothing. She didn't want to give it to me," he said.

"You, go see if you can bring back snuff for us," Great Shaman said to another of the students.

"Okay," he said, "I'll go get it." But he also failed to get the snuff. The others also failed.

"Now it's your turn to go, *Éeri*," he said. "You're a man."

"Okay," said *Éeri*, "I'll go and bring back the snuff." He left and arrived at the place, where Great Shaman's daughter was lying down on a floor mat. "I've come here to get hallucinogenic snuff from you," *Éeri* said.

"Okay," she said, "here it is." *Éeri* stood up and looked at her. He sucked her stomach. Then he vomited and got the snuff.

He returned to the village of Great Shaman. "Here is the snuff," said *Éeri*.

"Aaa, that's good, now you are truly a man," said Great Shaman. "Now you must grate it," he said. *Éeri* finished grating the snuff.

"Now we're ready. Come over here so I can blow snuff for you," he said to one of the students. Just after he blew snuff for him, he went crazy.

"Heee, I want to eat people," he said.

Great Shaman grabbed his arm and threw him away. "You go to the forest on the other side of the world."

"Now you." He blew snuff for another one of the students, and this one also went crazy.

"Hee, I want to eat people."

"No, you cannot eat people," said Great Shaman. He grabbed his arm and threw him out in the river. He went away and transformed into a dolphin, like those that live in rivers today.

He blew snuff again for one of the others. This one, too, went crazy.

"Heee, I want to eat people."

"No, you cannot eat people," said Great Shaman. He grabbed his arm and threw a piece of *yagrumo*. "Go and eat this." He left, and that's how tapir would be to this day in all the world.

He blew snuff for another of the students, who also went crazy.

"Heee, I want to eat people."

"No, you cannot eat people." Great Shaman grabbed his arm and threw him into the forest. "You will live in the forest." He is called "forest spirit," and he does harm to people.

He blew snuff for another student. This one, too, went crazy.

"Heee, I want to eat people."

"No, you cannot eat people." Great Shaman grabbed his arm and threw him down in a clearing. "There you will live." He is called herb to this day and is a source of medicines.

"Now, you," Great Shaman said to *Éeri*. He blew snuff for him. "You, yes; you can withstand the snuff. You will indeed become a shaman." Thus it will be for the new people in the future world. Only very few are able to withstand the snuff.

"Let's go. Now I will teach you," Great Shaman said to *Éeri*. He gave him a small stone, and *Éeri* swallowed it. "Vomit it so I can see it," said Great Shaman. *Éeri* vomited the stone and grabbed it. "Aaa, this is good. You are capable."

Then Great Shaman ate the small stone. "Now take it out of me."

Éeri sucked on the stomach of Great Shaman. "Here it is."

"Okay, you can do it, you can cure sickness. Now this stone is yours. Eat it now so that it will remain inside your body."

"Now I am holding a sickness-causing splinter." He put it in his head. "Now take it out of me."

Éeri sucked on his head. "Here it is."

"This is good; you can do it." He put the splinter in *Éeri*'s hand, and it remained in his body. He did the same thing for all kinds of sickness: poison, rawness, wild spirits, hair. Thus it would be for the new people in the future world.

The Origin of Honey for Curing

A long time ago there was a person who liked to find honey. Every time he went into the forest, he encountered honey. Three, four, five trees; always the same. He cut them down and took out the honey; it was always like this. Then he would harvest the soft eggs. He threw one in his ear, another in his other ear.

On another day, he went again. And it was the same again; he took it out again. "He's taking too much from us," said the bees. "Now we will take him out."

On another day the man went again. As he carried his urn, he heard people talking, laughing, and playing. "Who could this be?" he asked.

It was the season when *yebaro* trees were flowering. The man approached the voices little by little. They were picking *yebaro* flowers and throwing them down to their younger sister. "Here they come; put them inside our urn," they said. The man stood up to look at them. They, too, were looking at him. Just then they said, "My friend."

"Ee," he answered.

"What are you doing?" they asked him.

"I am looking for honey," he said.

"Okay, come and gather some with us. We're also looking for honey," they said to him.

"Good," he said. He approached their sister.

"Tell him to gather honey with you," they said to her.

"Gather honey with me," she said to the man. He was already gathering honey. "This is how we gather," she said to him. She picked up all the leaves and left nothing but flowers.

"This is how it's done," they said to him. He was already gathering, and he filled his urn.

Just then they began descending towards the man. "We are bees," they told him. "We call ourselves the *Kuwáiñai*. This is how we get honey; we pick flowers from trees. You will see," they said. Then they filled up his urn with *yebaro* flowers and closed the lid, tying it down tightly. "Let's go. Take this now and leave it close to your house," they said to him. "In the early morning, open it to look inside. But do not tell anyone about us," they said. "Thus we will work for you. If you speak to anyone about us, it will be bad for you. We will kill you however it is possible. A snake will bite you. You will already be dead, and we will take you to accompany us. If you speak about us, you will always live with us."

"Okay," the man said. He returned to his village.

When he was close to his house, the man left the urn. "How are you?" they asked him as he arrived. "Did you get any honey?" they asked.

"No," he said, "I didn't arrive there. Tomorrow I will go to search for it," he told them.

"And your urn?" they asked him.

"It's still there," he told them.

They talked, grew tired. "Let's go; see you tomorrow," they said. And they went to sleep.

He went very early the next morning to open his urn and look inside it. He saw that it was filled with honey. Pure, clean honey. Then he took it inside his house. "Here is the honey," he said, "bring a gourd dipper to share it among yourselves. I was joking when I said that I didn't get any honey yesterday," he said. And he gave honey to all his kinsmen.

"How is it that he got so much honey?" they said. "Maybe he saw something, or it could be that he saw the owners of honey."

A few days later the man went again, and again he found a lot of honey. He shared it again with all his kinsmen. "How are you getting so much honey?" they asked him.

"It's always like this; it's my destiny."

"I find honey, but I never get as much as you do," said one of them. "You haven't seen anything, such as the owners of honey?" he asked.

"No, I haven't seen anything."

"Now let's make some beer," they said. "Let's give him some. When he's drunk, we'll ask him how he gets all this honey."

They finished making beer and gave some to the man. Already he was drunk, and they asked him questions. He did not want to tell them anything. They asked him again various times. Finally he told them. He spoke about all the customs of the owners of honey. "But they did not want me to tell you about them," he said. "If I tell about them, they will kill me. You asked me, gave me drinks, and got me drunk. Now I have told you everything," he said.

He told them everything about the customs of the owners of honey. He told them that the owners of honey are people like us. "Thus it will be for the new people in the future world," he said. When he went outside, a snake bit him. "Now I am dying, but I've already told you everything," he said. And he died. His heart was already with the owners of honey. He lives with them to this day. And he never gets sick.

The Origin of Witchcraft and Its Treatment [23]

There was a sick person named *Kuwaikánirri*.
A powerful witch killed him.
"Let's take him," said the *Kuwáiñainai*.
"Let's take him to see if we can cure him," they said.
"There is medicine there."
They took him to São Gabriel, Kulukuí.
"There we will begin to see if we can cure him," they said.
They gathered some *kuku* fruits and broke them open to extract the
    nectar.
They held it for him to drink.

They collected mangos and squeezed the ripe fruits.

They gathered *hóbo* fruits that were two fingers wide, then squeezed them.

They held them for him to drink.

They gathered *hémali* fruits and squeezed them.

They picked oranges and cut them in half.

The held them and squeezed them so that he could drink.

They picked lemons and cut them in half.

They squeezed them and held them for him to drink.

Then they gathered wild grapes; they squeezed them in a gourd dipper and held it for him to drink.

They gathered tiny *idzéepu* fruits and held them so that he could drink the nectar.

"We are going to take you," they said. "We'll take you there in our canoe; that is how we'll take you," they said.

"In our canoe. We are the *Kuwáiñai*," they said. The name of the canoe will be the sweetness of the *Kuwáiñai*.

"Let him lie down there; that's how we'll cure him," they said.

"We leave him lying down. Thus it will be sweet."

"We leave him lying down where it is sweet."

Then they gathered those eggs, they gathered eggs from the owners of honey.

They left the eggs there on the floor of the canoe. They left the man lying on the floor of the canoe.

"Let's go. Now we'll take him," they said. "Kurai, kurai" [sound of paddling].

They went away. There they paddled in their canoe up to the mouth of the Vaupés.

A *karápa* tree was standing there. It looked like wild *hémali*, but it is called *karápa*. There were many flowers on the *karápa* tree.

They went up to collect flowers for him, flowers of *karápa*.

They extracted a tiny bit of nectar in a gourd dipper and held it for him to drink.

They set off again. "Let's take him away." He was lying down there.

They arrived at the island of *nina* [a tree with tiny fruits]. They arrived and gathered flowers from the *nina* tree.

They squeezed a tiny bit of nectar from the flowers, *nina* flowers. They held it for him to drink.

They went away. "Let's take him."

They arrived at the place of *guama* trees.

They collected flowers from the *guama* trees, squeezed the flowers, and held the nectar for him to drink.

They arrived with him at the mouth of the Isana River. This place is called Dzáwakána Point.

There they gathered flowers from *dzáwakána* trees. Then they threw them into a gourd dipper.

"How are you feeling, *Kuwai'káni'?*" they asked.

"No," he said, "my body is feeling better, and I am tired of lying down. I want to get up so that I can sit."

"Let's take him even farther away. Far away we have another village. This village of ours is called *lítipikwá*," they said.

"It is called the place of honey and the parakeet's tail," they said. They went and arrived at a place that is called *máapawíka*.

Arriving there, they said, "Our village here is called the place of honey and the parakeet's tail, *máapawíka*."

They arrived and held fruits so that he could drink again.

They arrived and held pineapple juice for him to drink. They squeezed the fruit and gave him the juice to drink.

Then they picked cashew fruits, squeezed them, and gave him juice to drink.

Then they squeezed juice from the small *temári* fruits and gave him some to drink.

Then they gathered cultivated sugarcane, squeezed it, and gave him the juice to drink.

Then they gave him juice made from cultivated cocoa.

Then the juice of sweet cultivated mango.

Then they drank the juice of *hóbo* fruit.

Then they gave him cacao juice to drink.

Then they drank juice from wild *kokúra*.

They did this with all the cultivated trees. "Let's take him away," they said. "Let's take him again."

Then he said, "I'm tired of lying down; my body already feels better. Now give me a paddle so that I can pull with you."

"Okay, so be it, get one for him." And they took out a paddle for him.

"This paddle will be called 'the sweetness of the *Kuwáiñai*,'" they said. "We are going to sweeten the sick person's entire body when he grasps this paddle."

"Huup-aa [sound of men pulling paddles in water]," they arrived there in Mapanáririko. *Mápanári* flowers.

They gathered *mápanári* flowers and took out the nectar.

They arrived at Yuku Point and saw *yuku* flowers. They gathered *yuku* flowers and squeezed them so that he could drink the nectar.

"Let's go. Now we will take you to Dzáwakápikwá. There is the only place that is exactly in the middle of the world. It's called Dzáwaká-pi," they said.

They arrived there in Dzáwakápi, arrived there. They gathered *dzáwakápi* flowers, squeezed them, and took out the nectar so that he could drink it.

"How do you feel now?" "No, I feel very good," he said.

"Let's go. Now we will take you with us and return to our largest village. We'll keep going until we reach the headwaters of the Guainía River," they said.

"The headwaters of the Guainía River. After that we'll go to our village, the Great Honey Place," they said.

"They call this place the Great Village of Honey," they said.

"Let's go there." They went downstream along the Guainía River. The Great Village of Honey was enormous, like Caracas.

They arrived there and gathered honey from bees so that he could drink it.

They drank from all the trees that had flowers.

They walked with him. They walked and drank honey.

They walked with him. They finished with everything in that village of theirs.

"How do you feel now?" "No, I feel fine," he said.

"But they don't want to leave you alone, those who wish to kill you," they said.

"They are following us," they said.

"Now we are going to take you away again," they said. "Now we'll go up to the headwaters of the Vaupés River," they said.

"Then we'll go to my grandmother, who is called *Numiyáleru*. She will hide you from your enemies."

"She will hide you for two months. You can come back when you feel well."

"When they tire of searching for you, you can come back. They will no longer follow you."

"Okay." And they left.

"This is *Kuwaikánirri*, grandmother," they said. "We're leaving him
   with you to keep him hidden."
"Hide him from them, those powerful witches."
"Okay, you will live with me, my nephew. I will hide you from the pow-
   erful witches. When you are feeling better, I will let you return."
There was a floor mat. It was called *numiyáleru*.
"Let's go in the very early morning," she said to him. "The powerful
   witches are watching us."
She went with him to her manioc garden. She hid him beneath the
   mat, then under a log.
She gathered manioc leaves and threw them over the log.
She finished hiding him and began to dig up manioc roots. The power-
   ful witches came looking for him, but they couldn't find him.
"Now we must go back. There is a pathway of leaf-cutter ants. Let's
   return by following this pathway of leaf-cutter ants."
They returned from the manioc garden inside the pathway, which was
   like a tunnel.
When they saw a place along the pathway where jaguars had stepped,
   they covered him up.
Thus it went, day after day.
The jaguar-witches followed *Kuwaikánirri*. They went around in
   circles. They grew tired.
"Let's go back. I think he must be dead already," they said.
He was well, and those jaguar-witches no longer searched for him.
"Now you can return," she said to him, "because you are well."
He returned, arrived back in his village. There it ends.

The Origin of Enchanted Spirits and the
City of Gold

Temedawí is the village of the *Yópinai*. There was an orphaned person, a
man who had neither a father nor a mother. He heard that one could live in
Temedawí with a human body. "Now I am going there," he said. He cooked
a squash and a chicken egg and ate them early in the morning. Then he left
for Temedawí.

   He went out across a sandy shoal until he reached the middle of it. A swarm
of gnats [*lambe ojos*] fell into his eyes. He took the gnats out of his eyes,
finished, and opened his eyes. He saw that he was standing on an avenue full

of cars. He heard a lot of sound from the village. He stood motionless and heard a dog barking, "Fwe, fwe." He saw a white woman coming toward him. She was holding the dog's leash. "Eee," she said, "You've come?"

"Yes," he said, "I came to see how they live here."

She would become the man's wife. "This is my father, seven heads," she said. "He is going to greet you three times. Don't answer him. You must shoot out his eyes."

"Okay," he said.

"Now I am leaving. I'll come look for you later," she said. "Here comes my father." And she left.

He saw that an anaconda with many heads was coming toward him. When the anaconda arrived and greeted him, the man did not answer him. Already he began to shoot out his eyes. He shot one, then another. The eyes were flashing on and off, first lighting up, then going dark. The man stopped shooting, and the anaconda greeted him again. "You came," the anaconda said to him.

"Yes," he said, "I came here to see how you live," he said.

"Here people live well," the snake said to him. "Here no one is lacking anything. Now I will return ahead of you. My daughter will come to look for you," he said. And he left.

After a few minutes the woman arrived in a car. "I've come to look for you," she said. He copulated with her in the car. Then they left. She arrived with him at her house, which was very beautiful. The table was made of gold, plates of gold, benches of gold. The entire interior of the house was made of gold, walls of gold, everything in her house was made of gold. She gave him some food, and he ate it.

"Now I will show you around so that you can see our town," she said to him.

"Okay," he said. And they left. They went to the port. He saw a ship and a long dugout canoe; these were the *Yópinai* boats. He saw speedboats running on the river. These were dolphins. They finished watching and went back to her house. Then they went out again to see the town.

"Now," she said, "I will show you the hospital where there are many sick people."

"Okay," he said. They went and arrived there, entering inside the hospital. There was a large room where all the sick people were lying down. They had toothaches caused by sharp splinters stuck in their throats. The man went over to look at one of the sick people. He saw that there was a fishhook stuck in his lip. He said to his wife, "These illnesses are not serious. I can cure them."

"Okay," she said.

She took him to the place of the president [*itálikanáti*]. "My husband knows how to cure the sick people. Some of them have been lying around for a long time but without receiving any treatment," she told the president. "My husband told me that he can cure them."

"Okay," said the president. "Now you are going to work over them," he said to the man. "When you have finished curing them, come and tell me."

Immediately the man and his wife left for the hospital and began to work. He brought along all his instruments for working. He took the hook out of one person, "Hataa." "Now you will get better; I've already removed the sickness that you had." He did the same thing with all the others. Those who had fishhooks stuck in their throats were in a more serious condition.

He finished his work and left for a different room. He arrived to look at them and asked, "What do you have?"

"We have splinters in our sides," they said.

He saw that one of them had a dart stuck in his ribs. "It's not too serious," he said. "I will take it out right away. Tomorrow you will be fine." He pulled the dart out of him, then threw medicine on his wounds. When he finished, he went to another person.

There were some who had darts in their legs and in other parts of their bodies. He finished curing them. Thus he went about working over everyone who was in the hospital. He cured them, finished. "Tomorrow I will come to see," he said. Then he went with his wife back to her house.

"Let's go to see," he said to his wife early the next morning. "Let's go to see how those sick people are doing," he said. They left, arrived there, and went inside. He began curing at the room where people had toothaches. "How are you?" he asked them.

"We're already better," they said. "You've already cured us."

"Aaa, that's good," he said. They conversed and were happy. He went back and forth to see all those who he had cured. All had gotten better.

"Now let's go to tell the president to come and see," said his wife. "The president will come to see that they are all well." They went immediately to the president's house. Upon arriving, the woman said, "Now come to see how the sick people are. They have already been cured."

"Very well," said the president. And they left.

They arrived at the hospital, and the president went to look. "Good," he said; all of them were well.

They conversed and ate together peacefully. "Let's get out of this hospital," they said.

"Okay," said the president, "You may all leave; you have already recovered. From now on," the president said to the man, "you are going to be the doctor of this hospital."

"Okay," he said. And he has lived there to this day. He lives well there and works there until today.

"Now I will return," he said to his wife.

"No," she said to him, "I am going to show you how we live here in our town so that you can tell your family. We are the defenders of all the major rivers. These places are like 'states' with 'alcabalas.' The only law that we have and that we want your family to respect is the rule that a menstruating woman can eat only 'cold' foods. She must not go out to work. If she goes out, we will kill her, if she does not follow my advice. Tell this to all your family."

"Okay," he said.

"Now go and tell your family everything that I have explained to you," she said to him. "If you don't return to me, I will kill you," she told him. "Go for two days," she said. "On the third day I will expect you at twelve noon."

He left immediately. As he was walking, a swarm of *lambe ojo* gnats fell into his eyes. He closed his eyes, then opened them. He saw that he was here in this world again. He saw his canoe. He had been away from his family for five days. He got into his canoe and departed.

He arrived in his family's village. "Eeee," his family said when they saw him. "Here is the lost person." They jumped up to embrace him. "What happened to you? Where have you been? We suffered while searching for you all night."

"No, I'm fine," the man said. "Now I have come to tell you that I am going to live in Temedawí. That's what I've come to tell you," he said.

"Okay," they said, "but we don't want you to do that," they told him.

"It doesn't matter. I live well there. It's okay," he said. "I will be able to see you all the time, but you will never be able to see me," he said. "Thus we will be passing you by in ships." And he told them everything he had seen in Temedawí.

"Let's get going now. Come with me so that I can give my canoe back to you," he said to them.

"Okay," they said. They left and arrived there on the sandy shoal. The man left them. As they were arriving and tying up their canoe, he left quickly ahead of them. His family got out after him. *Lambe ojo* gnats fell into their eyes. They closed their eyes, then opened them. They saw that their kinsman had already disappeared. They followed his tracks as far as they could, but there was nothing they could do. He was already gone. They went back to their house. That's how it ends.

Ethnological Coda:
Shamanizing the State
in Venezuela

The narrative about Temedawí, the magical city of the *Yópinai*, spirits of the forest, rivers, and air, serves as a historical metaphor for the sociopolitical transformations unfolding at local, regional, and national levels in Venezuela at the time of my fieldwork in June through December 1998. The sociopolitical circumstances of indigenous peoples in the Venezuelan Amazon had dramatically changed since my fieldwork in the 1980s. In large part, these changes reflected the fact that in July 1992, the Venezuelan congress had voted to transform Amazonas from a federal territory into the twenty-second state of Venezuela. In the wake of this change, a legislative assembly was elected and charged with elaborating a new Law of Political-Territorial Division, and a protracted political struggle between indigenous peoples and the assembly developed between 1995 and 1998 over how to define and implement this new law.

Indigenous peoples, who constituted 44 percent of the state's population in 1996, organized themselves into an umbrella organization called ORPIA (*Organización Regional de Pueblos Indígenas de Amazonas*), and their cause received powerful support at the national level from several rulings of the Supreme Court. The Legislative Assembly reacted to the Court's mandate by delaying and otherwise obstructing the formulation and implementation of a new Law of Division that would protect three categories of legal rights: (1) the right to a "regime of exception" for indigenous communities, (2) the requirement that all constituents of the state's population be consulted and allowed to participate in the development of new municipios, and (3) the land rights of indigenous communities. The first of these rights, or the regime of exception, is particularly interesting and important since the Supreme Court argued that the 1994 law had created municipios based on urban criteria and had failed to consider "la especifidad indígena," the cosmovision and sociocultural organization of the ethnic groups.

In its counterargument, the Legislative Assembly portrayed the regime of exception as an unconstitutional law that would force indigenous communities to live in "political and territorial divisions separated from the rest of the country's population, or under organizational forms distinct from those of the nonindigenous population of Venezuela" (Corte Suprema de Justicia 1996:19, my translation). The Supreme Court rejected these arguments and in addition ordered the Legislative Assembly to abstain from interfering with or distorting the Court's decision. Subsequent events revealed a sustained effort by the Legislative Assembly to do everything possible to subvert or interfere with the Court's decision. The assembly's call for a referendum was a deliberate attempt to limit indigenous participation, since it would have reflected the public opinion in Puerto Ayacucho and other areas where most of the nonindigenous population resides. There is also solid evidence that the members of the Legislative Assembly had full knowledge of the Supreme Court's order against carrying out the referendum when it voted to reject the indigenous project on the Law of Division and to publicize the Law of Partial Reform in December 1997 (Informe Annual 1998:61).

This brief overview of the regional setting of my 1998 fieldwork in the Venezuelan Amazon is sufficient to demonstrate that the national context of indigenous histories cannot be understood apart from the dynamics of shifting power relations at the state level.[1] And there are certain parallels between the Supreme Court's vision of the new Law of Political-Territorial Division as a means for greater inclusion of indigenous peoples and the more poeticized imagery of a magical state developed in the narrative about Temedawí. The Supreme Court's ruling contemplated the possibility of a new political landscape in which indigenous peoples' cultural differences and land rights would become protected by law and indigenous peoples themselves would have a voice in defining the state through voting and other forms of democratic participation in the development of new political institutions. The narrative of Temedawí outlines a view of the state as a political entity that appropriates the magical healing powers of indigenous shamans but that, in doing so, also comes to define itself as a projection, or amplification, of those shamanic ritual powers.

Both nationalism and shamanism rely on symbolic transformations of human, social inventions into natural species or objects. As processes of naturalizing social being, both nationalism and shamanism are dynamic historical journeys, or pilgrimages, between the here-and-now and the there-and-then; both are ways of constructing imagined communities (Anderson 1983). Like nationalism, shamanism as a mode of political history, or the constructing of political communities, shares an ability to link with a diversity of demographic, economic, and other social and natural conditions. Far from existing as a residual practice at the margins or in the interstices of expanding colonial and national states in Latin America, shamanic traditions have proliferated as a source of cultural energies shaping the production of local histories in contexts ranging from open resistance against state authorities to covert resistance through syncretistic mergings with state-sponsored religions, to accommodation and conversion of entire indigenous societies (see, for example, Brown 1991; Civrieux 1980; Butt Colson 1971, 1985; Clastres 1995; Agüero 1992; Langdon and Baer 1992). Alongside of these studies, a growing number of scholars have documented the variety of ways in which indigenous shamanic practices are being actively absorbed into religious and political movements of nonindigenous, mestizo peoples in both rural and urban Latin America (Chameil 1992; Taussig 1987; Luna 1991; Gow 1994; Whitehead and Wright 2004).

What these studies demonstrate is that shamanism and nationalism continue to develop in Latin America and other world regions as coeval social processes in the contemporary social world. By starting from an understanding of both shamanism and nationalism as constructions of history that reflect underlying processes of naturalizing social relations, one gains a theoretical space for exploring the multiple ways in which these two political forces have become articulated with each other. However, I must emphasize from the outset that shamanism and nationalism take this naturalizing of social relations in different directions. Shamanic histories poeticize the relations between living and dead humans, or between mythic ancestors and living human descendants, and make them into objects of symbolic elaboration and remembrance.

My fieldwork with Wakuénai shamans along the Río Guainía in Venezuela has led me to the conclusion that their practices can best be interpreted as a more general process of "re-membering" the world, or repopulating the world of the living with an imagined community of mythic and deceased beings so that the past is not forgotten or reified into a dead, external thing. Nationalist histories work in a different direction since they reflect an underlying process of forgetting or reifying the past, or "a global project of modernity that claims for itself a singular universality, rationality, and morality that depend on the subordination, exclusion, or destruction of alternative forms of sociality, rationality, and values" (Coronil 1997:17).

In contrast to nationalism, shamanism rests not upon print language but upon the poeticized activities of myth and ritual, and especially the highly musical forms of ritually powerful singing and chanting. Instead of masking the relations between living and dead humans embodied in language, shamanism makes these relations the central feature of an imagined community of living and dead human descendants of mythic ancestors. Unlike nationalism, shamanism creates an imagined community through re-membering, or re-populating, the world of living people with ghosts and immortal mythic beings so that the past cannot become reduced or essentialized into an exterior, dead thing. Rather like Anderson's scholarly attempt (1983:182) to relocate the "empty time" of nationalism in real, historically traveled journeys across the political spaces between metropoles and hinterlands, shamanic practices reconnect the imagined time of ghostly and mythic beings to the places and movements of real, historical communities of living people. Shamanism accomplishes this not through language per se but with specially altered poetic and musical processes of speaking, chanting, and singing.

Mythic narratives about the primordial times or its more recent transformations are centrally important to shamanic ways of re-membering the past. Through storytelling, the Wakuénai bring a variety of mythic beings to life in the present: Made-from-Bone, Great Sickness, Grandfather Sleep, River Spirits, Vulture-People, Bat-People, Manioc-Man, First-Woman, and the primordial human being. The return from death to life, the main theme of shamanic practices, is clearly expressed at the very outset of mythic times when Made-from-Bone and his brother were created from the bones of their slain father.

To anyone who has done extensive field research with indigenous South American shamans or who has read ethnographic studies based upon such fieldwork, it comes as no surprise that shamanic beliefs and practices, along with associated genres of storytelling, are a major conduit for mediations between indigenous and nationalist histories. At a very basic level, shamanic rituals are cultural processes for transcending everyday social boundaries through sung and chanted performances that musically embody transitions and movements between "places": regions of the cosmos, bodies or body parts, social positions, and historical moments. Historical narratives about powerful shamans of the past offer richly poetic images of travel between life and death and between the worlds of the white rubber barons and indigenous communities along the Río Negro (see Wright and Hill 1986; Hill and Wright 1988).

Temedawí: The Shamanic Pathway to El Dorado

In contrast to historical narratives about heroic shamans whose actions helped indigenous peoples of the Upper Río Negro survive the horrible atrocities of the rubber boom, the story of Temedawí is a fairly simple tale in which there are neither heroic feats of returning from death nor revolutionary overturnings of oppressive power structures. Instead, an indigenous man travels to the *Yópinai* spirits' city of Temedawí, gains official recognition of his shamanic curing powers from a powerful "president," returns to this world one last time to tell his family about his new life in the other world, and leaves this world to live the rest of his life in Temedawí.

Over the several months in 1998 that Félix Oliveros and I worked on producing detailed transcriptions and Spanish translations of the narratives presented in this book, most of the narratives we transcribed and translated were made either from recordings I had made with Félix's father, Horacio, back in the early 1980s or from Félix's retellings of these same narratives. The narrative of Temedawí, however, was one of Félix's original contributions to the project, and I had never heard or recorded any version of it in my previous trips to the upper Río Negro region of Venezuela.

It is probably not coincidental that my first encounter with the Temedawí narrative came at a time when local indigenous communities were undergoing rapid changes and that these changes were along the classic lines of emerging modernity: democracy, literacy, and individualism. At one level, the Temedawí narrative is about the individual's acquisition of wealth, power, and prestige and the weakening or subordination of communal and family ties relative to the individual's pursuit of success. When looked at on a more collective, historical level of developing interethnic relations, however, the Temedawí narrative is not about the individual's embracing of modernity but about a social process of constructing an imagined state that defines itself through an institutionalizing of shamanic powers of healing.

Modernizing the Individual, Shamanizing the State

At one level, the Temedawí narrative outlines a process in which an orphaned man who initially lacks a central dimension of his humanity—a human body—

gains or completes his humanity through marrying a white woman, living with her in a golden house in the city of Temedawí, and being appointed as doctor-for-life by the president. The overall plot of the Temedawí narrative is relatively simple and consists of three general movements: (1) the protagonist's departure from this world and integration into his wife's family at Temedawí, (2) the protagonist's curing of the sick and appointment as doctor by the president, and (3) the protagonist's return to this world to explain his new life to family members prior to his final, permanent departure for Temedawí.

Although the unnamed protagonist in the Temedawí narrative is not explicitly identified with Made-from-Bone, it is impossible to overlook the striking parallels between Made-from-Bone's encounter with the *Yópinai* father-in-law during primordial times (see chapter 2, "The Origin of Cooking with Hot Peppers") and the man's first meeting with the many-headed anaconda in Temedawí. Both narratives focus on the tensions and potential dangers that arise from the forming of affinal relations with women from the world of River Spirits, or *Yópinai*. And in both narratives, the prospective son-in-law avoids the fate of being killed and eaten by the *Yópinai* father-in-law by not responding to the latter's thrice-repeated greeting.

The Temedawí narrative also bears strong resemblance to mythic narratives about individuals who leave their families and communities by unwittingly entering into relations with bee spirits, fish spirits, and other mythic beings (see chapter 4, "The Origin of Bocachico-Fish Dances," and chapter 6, "The Origin of Honey for Curing"). However, beyond the striking resemblance of its overall plot structure to these narratives, the Temedawí narrative inverts many of their most central messages. In the other stories, the protagonist is warned, under penalty of death, against speaking about what he has experienced in the other world. Violation of this injunction is the immediate cause of the protagonist's death. In contrast, the protagonist in the Temedawí narrative is not only allowed but required to tell his family in this world everything about his experiences in the other world.

In the Temedawí narrative, what has come to replace the boundary-defining function of speaking versus remaining silent is seeing versus being seen. The importance of vision and (in)visibility is woven through the entire narrative. It is through closing and opening his eyes that the protagonist travels to and from Temedawí, and it is through shooting the eyes of the seven-headed anaconda that he is able to enter into the social status of son-in-law/husband in Temedawí. When the protagonist's wife takes him to the river, his ability to see that the *Yópinai*'s boats are fish and animal species marks the completion of his integration into the world of *Yópinai* spirits. And near the end of the narrative, the protagonist explains to his family that he would be able to see them after his departure for Temedawí but that they would not be able to see him or the *Yópinai* spirits.

The increasing importance of vision and (in)visibility in the Temedawí narrative, along with the declining importance of speech taboos as boundary-defining processes, is consistent with the general tendency of modernism to privilege the visual-spatial over other sense modalities. In Wakuénai communities of Venezuela in the late 1990s, the transition from speech to vision that is hinted at in the Temedawí narrative can be most directly related to the increasing strength of literacy. The generation of elders who had died or receded into the background during the 1980s and '90s had been the last generation who had had little or no training in written language skills. In contrast, most individuals who had reached middle-aged adulthood in the late 1990s had received enough formal schooling as children to read and write, at least on a basic level.

The Temedawí narrative encapsulates changes happening in the upper Río Negro region of Venezuela in the late 1990s. Formal education and literacy were gaining the upper hand over ritual performances and oral traditions. However, this story about the modernizing individual who turns his back on his indigenous cultural roots is not the only story contained within the Temedawí narrative. The other story being told is about the construction of a new kind of state in which indigenous practices of shamanic ritual healing are centrally important. In the narrative, the *Yópinai* patients are described in terms that are identical to the traditional descriptions of the victims of witchcraft or poisoning, and the protagonist's ability to cure the patients is described in terms that are identical to the traditional rituals in which shamans sucked, vomited, and otherwise extracted splinters and other disease-causing agents from victims' bodies. In the Temedawí narrative, the protagonist demonstrates traditional shamanic healing powers, only on a larger scale: rather than curing a single patient by extracting the splinter or dart, the protagonist cures an entire hospital filled with patients.

The narrative also makes it clear that the man's curing powers are to some extent subordinated to the official power of the state via the authority of its "president." On the man's first visit to the hospital with his wife, he performs no acts of curing but only makes the claim that he can cure all the patients. The man and his wife visit the president to report his alleged ability as a healer, and the president commands the protagonist to cure the patients in the hospital and to report back to him when he has finished doing so. Only after receiving this command does the man actually cure the patients at the hospital. This sequence of events strongly implies that the man's curing powers exist independently of the state's authority but that they can only be put to use with the official authorization of the state.

After the curing has taken place, the president visits the recovered patients along with the man and his wife. The president, not the shamanic healer, authorizes their release and appoints the man as doctor of the hospital. Again, the narrative indicates that the man's healing powers are limited to curing the sick and that it is only the state that carries the authority to determine that patients are ready to be released from the hospital. The protagonist's actions outline a process of fusing shamanic and state power into a single "magical state" in which the indigenous form of healing power has become subordinate to the authority of the state.

At the same time, however, as the state's power engulfs and appropriates shamanic healing power, there is a reciprocal sense in which the state's power is portrayed as dependent upon the shamanic powers that it has harnessed. The man's remarkable ability to cure the sick is, after all, necessary to the president's powers of discharging the sick and appointing the man to serve as doctor-for-life. Looking at this fusion of shamanic and state power from this perspective reveals a magical state apparatus in which state political author-ity has not only appropriated shamanic curing powers but has come to be defined through them. In effect, the magical state of Temedawí is nothing less than an institutionalized structure for the mass production of shamanic healing. Unlike the alien, dangerous, suffocating power structures of the rub-ber boom period and their narrative representation as life-swallowing coffins (see Hill and Wright 1988; Wright and Hill 1986), the state is portrayed in the Temedawí narrative as a giant healing machine. Official state appropriation of shamanic power is balanced by an equally effective process of transforming the state from the genocidal killing machine that it had become during the rubber boom into a shamanic healing machine. As shamanic power becomes part of official state power, it also socializes, or shamanizes, the state. The protagonist of the Temedawí narrative's collective curing of sick *Yópinai* patients can be interpreted as a shamanic curing of the state, purifying it and purging its diseases.

Official state recognition of indigenous cultural practices is often a mixed blessing. State appropriations of symbols of indigenous identities have often become part of broader neonationalist or global agendas as failing liberal states desperately seek new ways of authenticating national identities. In the process, official policies and commercial interests essentialize indigenous cultural practices—dress styles, artifacts, architecture, behavioral patterns—by removing and isolating such practices from communities of real people and their histories. This process of alienating cultural practices from their producers results in the construction of "cultures without peoples" (Hill and Staats 2002), or folkloricized cultures that are no longer rooted in real political histories. Cultural markers are appropriated by national states, yet the individuals whose ancestors originally created these markers are bracketed out of national consciousness.

There are counterexamples, however, in which indigenous peoples have managed to construct understandings of their histories in ways that allow for the persistence of highly specific linguistic and cultural forms through embracing radical changes in the realm of signification (see, for example, Staats 1996; Hill and Staats 2002). From this perspective, the Temedawí narrative forms part of a broader set of mythic histories being related throughout South America that open up new spaces for meaning construction even as they reproduce received linguistic and cultural forms (Hill 1988a; Briggs 2000). This reopening of meaning construction creates not only new interpretive spaces for revitalizing indigenous communities but also new political-historical spaces for indigenous communities to move forward into the future within the broader context of globalizing national states.

There is an important linguistic clue within the Temedawí narrative that alludes to the fact that the magical state being depicted is one with deep historical and cultural roots in the Arawak-speaking communities of the Upper Río Negro. The term for "president" is not borrowed from Spanish but is an indigenous word meaning "paramount chief." As Vidal has demonstrated (1993, 2000, 2002), the term *itálikanáti* was used to refer to the leaders of multiethnic confederacies that emerged during the colonial period. These political confederacies included the Manao (Lower Río Negro, 1700–1725), Demanao (Upper Río Negro, 1725–1755), Boape-Pariana-Maniva (headwaters of Isana, Guainía, Inirida, and Guaviare Rivers, 1725–1755), Madavaka (Casiquiare River, 1725–1755), and Maipure (Middle Orinoco River, 1730–1760). Furthermore, these multiethnic confederacies relied heavily upon the support of indigenous shamans and other ritual specialists, whose specialized knowledge of the ancestral pathways connecting different peoples and regions served as a strategic resource in migrations and political mobilizations (Vidal 2002).

The image of a magical shamanic state in the Temedawí narrative resonates with this deep history of shamanic political hierarchies throughout the vast region stretching from the Lower Río Negro in Brazil to the middle Orinoco basin in Venezuela and Colombia. The ritual power of Arawak-speaking shamans from the Río Negro is not limited to the memory of their powers in the historical past but is recognized widely in the Venezuelan Amazon and adjacent regions today. In Puerto Ayacucho, the capital of the state of Amazonas, the state's governor, Bernabé Gutiérrez Parra, never made any important or difficult political decisions without first consulting a team of powerful shamans from the Río Negro (Vidal and Whitehead 2004).

Ironically, Amazonas had only recently reached the beginning of democratic statehood when Venezuelan democracy at the national level was on the verge of radical changes. As the struggle over the Law of Political-Territorial Division demonstrated in the late 1990s, the criollo majority in the state of Amazonas was strongly resistant to the creation of more inclusive forms of government that would give official recognition to "la especifidad indígena." The indigenous vision of a "shamanized" state as an instrument for magical healing was appropriate to the late 1990s, a transitional moment in Venezuelan history when the forty-year old *partidocracia,* or monopolization of power and oil wealth by the two dominant political parties, was about to give way to a new government, Hugo Chávez's *Movimiento Quinta República* (Fifth Republic Movement). Like the *Yópinai* patients caught in the state's hospital at Temedawí, indigenous peoples of the Venezuelan Amazon in the late 1990s were stuck between the Supreme Court's mandate for a "regime of exception" and the Legislative Assembly's determination to block any attempt to implement such a mandate. Along with Made-from-Bone, the invincible trickster-creator of mythic times, the Wakuénai of Venezuela are navigating into the new millennium between the historical weight of centuries of discrimination and marginalization and the promise of unprecedented political recognition for indigenous cultural and territorial rights under the constitution of 1999.

Appendix A:
A Note on Translation Methods

Translating indigenous verbal artistry from oral performances in the original language to written texts in English is a difficult process of balancing the need to preserve important features of form and meaning from the original performances against the goal of making readable English texts. Translation is always an act of transformation that can never be reduced to a mere activity of transporting static or fixed meanings from one language to another. A better way of approaching the art of translation is to understand it as a collaborative process of "attending to the indigenous experience of verbal artistry" in order to achieve "readability without compromising the integrity of the original" (McDowell 2000:211, 212). Translation requires making difficult aesthetic choices and awareness of the political implications of spoken words and written texts. Although some features of original form and meaning are inevitably lost in translation, such losses can be offset to a large extent through collaboration between researchers and indigenous performers in the making of important aesthetic decisions about how to transcribe and translate narratives.

The English translations of Wakuénai narratives about Made-from-Bone in this book result from collaborative decisions made in 1998 when Félix Oliveros and I discussed how to represent the texts in Curripaco and Spanish. One of the prominent features of these narratives is their use of quotations, dialogues, and conversations as vehicles for storytelling. In transcribing these dialogues, Félix and I decided to write them out as single lines of text that replicated the exact ordering of words in the oral performance. What became immediately apparent is that the narratives are to a considerable extent built around the verb "to say" or other speaking verbs: "their aunt asked them," "they told her," "he said to her," "tell them," "she said," "she said to them," "they said," and so forth.[1]

There are many different ways of representing these quotations and dialogues as a written text. One approach would be to write them out as if the quotations were lines in a play by indicating the speaker's identity at the start of each speech act. For example, the lines from the above example could be rendered as follows:

Boys' aunt: "How did things go with him?"
They told her about everything that had happened.
Great Sickness had made a large clearing for a new garden.
Great Sickness: "Tell them that they must accompany me while I burn
   the clearing."
Boys' aunt: "Okay, go with him to burn the new garden. Be careful
   that he does not burn you."
Cricket-brothers: "No, do not think that he will kill us."
Boys' aunt: "Okay, go with him."

This approach results in a more readable text in a visual style that is familiar to English-speaking readers, but it leaves out or moves to the background all the indigenous phrases based on the verb "to say." Félix and I both felt that it was important to leave the "say" verbs in the Spanish translation as a way of preserving the integrity of the original performances. However, we also decided that it was necessary to group together sentences into paragraphs in order to make the stories readable in the original Curripaco transcription and in the Spanish translation. At the same time, we were careful to preserve crucial features of the original texts, such as the order of phrases within clauses and the order of clauses within sentences.

For example, here is how the same lines of speech from the excerpt above appear in paragraph form in English:

"How did it go?" the boys' aunt asked. They told her about everything that had happened. Great Sickness had cleared a large area of forest for a new manioc garden. "Tell them that they must accompany me while I burn the clearing," he said to the woman.

"Okay," she replied. Later she said to her nephews, "Go with him to burn the new garden, but be careful not to let him burn you."

"No," they said to her, "don't even think about him killing us."

"Okay," she said, "Go with him."

In making sentences for the English translations, I have not altered the ordering of clauses and phrases in the original performance. In the linear translation, however, there are places where the narrator has left out information about who is speaking to whom, making it confusing to the reader. For example, when the boys' aunt responds to Great Sickness, the phrase "she said" does not specify that the following quotation is directed at the Cricket-Brothers rather than Great Sickness.

Linear translation: "Okay," she said. "Go with him to burn the new garden. Be careful that he does not burn you."

Revised translation: "Okay," she replied. Later she said to her nephews, "Go with him to burn the new garden, but be careful not to let him burn you."

In the English translation, I have also conjoined the aunt's two lines into a single sentence to improve the flow of the text.

The narratives about Made-from-Bone consist largely of these kinds of quotations and dialogues built around speaking verbs. However, the extent to which the narration relies on quoted speech acts varies greatly from one paragraph to another. In the continuation of the story of the origin of Made-from-Bone, for example, the next paragraph contains only two short quotations—a command by Great Sickness to the boys and their affirmative response—followed by a lengthy third-person description of how the boys transform themselves into leaf-cutter ants and escape from the burning garden by going underground. Before leaving the garden, the boys also spit into their wooden whistles and throw them on the ground so that Great Sickness will be tricked into believing that their bodies have exploded when the fire consumes the two whistles.

At the end of this largely descriptive paragraph, the narrator returns to a complex set of quotations as Great Sickness thinks out loud and rehearses how he will explain the boys' deaths to their aunt.

> Great Sickness saw the fire arriving at the place where the boys were dancing. "Now it is certain that they are burning up. I will return home and tell their aunt, 'I warned them, but they did not listen to me.' That's what I'll tell her. 'That is how they burned,' I will say to her." Great Sickness stood up so that he could see the fire. They are burning up. "Now their guts are going to explode." Just then one of them broke open, and he heard "Too!" "Now it is certain. His guts already broke open; one more to go." After a minute he heard again, "Too." That was all. "Now I will return."

What is interesting in this paragraph is the way quoted speech itself is made into an object of reflection through embedding quotations within quotations. The effect of this doubly quoted speaking is to take us more deeply into the consciousness of Great Sickness and to give us a vicarious perspective on his innermost thoughts and feelings. When we read "That's what I'll tell her," we can understand just how badly Great Sickness wants to kill the two Cricket-Brothers. Their deaths are already a fait accompli in his mind, and it is only a matter of putting a good spin on events so that his wife, or the boys' aunt, will quit asking him all those annoying questions. The sound of the whistles popping open in the fire only strengthens his belief that the boys have indeed perished in the flames. But the sounds—"Too," "Too"—also heighten the ironic humor of the story, since we already know that the two boys have escaped to safety outside the burning garden.

Appendix B:
AILLA Numbers for Narratives, Music, Dances, and Illustrations

v. The Origin of Witchcraft and Its Treatment KPC003R305
vi. The Origin of Enchanted Spirits and the City of Gold
   KPC003R306

AILLA numbers for instrumental music and songs, or dances, referred
   to in the story in chapter 4, "The Origin of Ceremonial Music,"
   and in chapter 5, "Ethnomusicological Interlude: The Catfish
   Trumpet Festival of 1981, or How to Ask for a Drink in Curripaco":
   p. 92: *máwi* flute duets KPC001R002I001, KPC001R004I001,
   KPC001R008I001, KPC001R009I001, KPC001R0011I001, KP-
   C001R0013I001, KPC001R0036I003, KPC001R0036I004,
   KPC001R0036I006, KPC001R0036I007, KPC001R0038, KP-
   C001R0042, KPC001R0043, KPC001R0044, KPC001R0045,
   KPC001R0047, KPC001R0048, KPC001R0049, KPC001R0050,
   KPC001R0051, KPC001R0052, KPC001R0055, KPC001R0056,
   KPC001R0060, KPC001R0062, KPC001R0063, KPC001R0072,
   KPC001R0073

p. 107: Photos of "Catfish Trumpet Festival of 1981" KPC001R102
pp. 104–5: *Kulirrína* trumpets KPC001R0069, KPC001R0070
p. 100: W*áana* dance stamping tubes KPC001R0053, KPC001R0054,
   KPC001R0057, KPC001R0058, KPC001R0067
pp. 101–2: P*ákamarántakan* KPC001R0061, KPC001R0064
p. 106: M*áwi* flute duet with *kulirrína* trumpets KPC001R0068

Notes

Preface

1. Scholars of mythic tricksters in West Africa have noted a similar contrast between African and "New World" (North American) trickster figures, arguing that the African trickster's "amorality is not that of the anomic, presocialized individual, who has not yet matured to a sense of responsibility. Suave, urbane, and calculating, the African trickster acts with premeditation, always in control of the situation" (Feldmann 1963:15).

2. Made-from-Bone's uses of verbal deception are reminiscent of the Kalapalo trickster figures in whom "deception and language go together" (Basso 1987:9). However, among the Kalapalo, the theme of verbal deception, or "language as illusion," is spread across a number of trickster characters rather than concentrated into a single, omnipotent trickster-creator as it is among the Wakuénai.

3. Made-from-Bone bears striking resemblance to the West African-derived myths about *Esu*, or the "signifying monkey" (Gates 1988). Gates's study demonstrates how Trickster's privileging of the tropes forms the cornerstone of an African American theory of language use that informs not only a variety of overtly literary oral and written genres but also many varieties of speech in everyday social life. "Signifyin(g) . . . is the figurative difference between the literal and the metaphorical, between surface and latent meaning" (Gates 1988:82).

4. Richard and Sally Price's works on oral histories, verbal art, and material culture (R. Price 1983; R. and S. Price 1991; S. Price 1999) among the Saramaká, an Afro-Surinamese community, offer a parallel example from an African American perspective.

5. There are strong parallels between Made-from-Bone's struggles against his adversaries and the ongoing violence between Wanadi and Odosha in the Watunna. There may well be historical reasons for these parallels, since Arawak-speaking peoples of the Upper Río Negro region joined the Ye'kuana-led multiethnic uprising of 1776 that resulted in the expulsion of the Spanish from the Upper Orinoco region. Also, the Ye'kuana relied on safe passage through the Casiquiare and Río Negro after the 1776 uprising in order to reach the Dutch trading post at Amenadiña on the Essequibo River (Guss 1986). Two Arawak-speaking groups, the Guarequena and the Baniwa, are

specifically mentioned in the Watunna in the list of "other tribes" made by Wanadi to help the Ye'kuana fight against Odosha and his Spanish allies (Civrieux 1980:160).

6. A Venezuelan linguist had published a collection of Guarequena mythic narratives (González Ñáñez 1980).

7. The new project was also designed to build upon methodological advances of discourse-centered approaches in Amazonian ethnology (Sherzer and Urban 1986; Basso 1985, 1990, 1995; Urban 1991; Seeger 1987; Briggs 1992; Graham 1995). Readers can view the line-by-line transcriptions and Spanish translations of the entire set of narratives at the Web site of the Archives of Indigenous Languages of Latin America (AILLA; www.ailla.utexas.edu). Digital sound files of all the narratives and musical performances discussed in this book are also available at the AILLA Web site.

Chapter 1: The Arawakan Wakuénai of Venezuela

1. These historical transformations are explored in the recent volume on *Comparative Arawakan Histories* (Hill and Santos-Granero 2002).

2. Not surprisingly, these two areas have also received the most attention from anthropological and historical researchers in recent decades. For the northwest Amazon, we now have in-depth ethnographic studies of the Wakuénai (also known as Curripaco, Kurripako, or Baniwa of Brazil) phratries living in the Isana-Guainía drainage area on all three sides of the Brazil/Colombia/Venezuela border (Wright 1981, 1998; Hill 1983, 1993; Hill and Wright 1988; Journet 1995; Wright and Hill 1986), long-term ethnohistorical analyses of the Piapoco, Baré, and other groups of the Brazilian and Venezuelan Río Negro basin (Vidal 1987, 1993, 2000), a collection of Warekena mythic narratives (Gonzalez Ñáñez 1980), a complete ethnographic documentation of the Kurripako language (Granadillo 2006), and a series of articles and papers on the archaeology of northern (Maipuran) Arawak-speaking peoples' expansions through the Negro-Casiquiare-Orinoco region (Zucchi 1991a, 1991b, 1991c, 1992, 1993). For the eastern lowlands of Peru and adjacent areas of western Brazil, recent ethnographic and historical studies include important works on the Yanesha (or Amuesha) (Smith 1977; Santos-Granero 1991, 1992, 1998), Matsiguenga (Renard-Casevitz 1985, 1991; Johnson 2003), Piro (Gow 1991, 2001), Asháninka (Brown and Fernandez 1991, 1992; Hvalkof 1986; Veber 1998), and regional ethnohistory (Renard-Casevitz and Dollfus 1988).

3. It is difficult to know how to interpret this astonishing rate of population growth, a tripling within twenty years. Some of it no doubt reflects the migration of Curripaco seeking to escape political violence in Colombian territory. It is also likely that more individuals and families are willing to count themselves as "Curripaco" or "indigenous" today than in the 1980s, when there was a stronger social stigma attached to these terms.

4. Granadillo (2006) compared these different dialects of "Kurripako" and found cognate densities ranging from 69.8 percent to 80.3 percent.

Part 1: Words from the Primordial Times: Overview

1. The two brothers are called *Duiménai* in this story. This name comes from an episode near the end of the narrative in which the boys transform into squirrels and blood flowing from wounds on their hands turns into a kind of honey used in shamanic curing rituals. In most tellings of the narrative, there are three brothers—Made-from-Bone and two younger brothers—made from the bones of the three outer fingers of their slain father's hand. However, in this telling of the narrative, there is only one younger brother.

Chapter 2: Narratives from the Primordial Times

1. *Nakuírru,* or father's sister.

2. "*Kadzuwátsa nahliú walímanai apáwali hekuápi*" is a common verse found in many of the narratives. The translation I am using here ("And thus it will be for the new people in the next world") stays close to the indigenous wording. In his work with Baniwa narratives in Brazil, Robin Wright (1998) has translated this phrase as "Thus it will be for those unborn."

3. *Káridzámai* is the sacred food prepared for the parents of newborn infants during the second part of childbirth rituals as well as for male and female initiates at puberty initiation rituals. In childbirth rituals, the food consists of a stew of hot-peppered, boiled game meat over which chant owners must sing and chant the names of all edible fish, animal, and bird spirits. The chant owner transfers the chant's protective powers to the food by blowing tobacco smoke over the pot of meat. Eating the meat marks the end of the period of fasting for the newborn infant's parents. The ritual power of the sacred food is said to be transmitted to the infant via its mother's milk. In male and female initiation rituals, chant owners name a much broader set of plant and animal species as well as the various places where First-Woman (*Ámaru*) and the women played the sacred flutes and trumpets of *Kuwái* in the second opening up of the world. For male and female initiates, eating the sacred food is an internalizing of this world-opening, historical and political space-time of fully socialized adult personhood.

4. The phrase "*ʰnete ikanúpafwa pamudzuátua*" translates as "after you all destroyed it in the middle," referring to the fact that the return to life was only halfway complete when the wife of *Mawirríkuli* violated the warning against looking at him.

5. The tree is known as *héemalipánali,* or *temari del monte* in Spanish.

6. *Dabucurí* is a *lingua geral* term for ceremonies at which men play sacred flutes and trumpets and exchange wild fruits (*yuku* and *seje*).

7. *Éeri* is the younger brother of Made-from-Bone who becomes the first male initiate during the third mythic period, "The World Opens Up."

8. *Yópinai* are dangerous spirits of the rivers, forests, and air. They are also the subjects of a narrative about Temedawí, a magical city of gold (see chapters 6 and 7).

9. *Kulírri,* or *raiao* in Spanish, is also the namesake for large trumpets in *pudáli* exchange ceremonies (see chapter 6).

10. In local Spanish, *buscar pago.* This could be literally translated as "seek payment" but is more adequately rendered as "seek revenge."

11. *Kalimátu* returns in an important role as a messenger between Made-from-Bone and *Kuwái* in the third mythic period, "The World Opens Up" (see chapter 7).

12. Counting and other verbal expressions of quantity (i.e., "large" and "small," "many" and "few") require the use of numeral classifiers in everyday speech. These classifier sets implicitly encode broader relations of mythic meaning and ritual power (Hill 1988b). In the narrative about evil omens, the woman's counting of Made-from-Bone's poisoned darts foreshadows her experience of evil omens through a variety of other ways of knowing: hearing, dreaming, touching, smelling, seeing, and speaking.

Chapter 3: Ethnohistorical Interlude

1. A full translation of the cycle of myths about the primordial human mother (*Ámaru*) and child (*Kuwái*) is provided in chapter 6 of this book.

2. In this perspective, the myth of Made-from-Bone and the Anaconda-Person forms an Arawakan equivalent of the eastern Tukanoan (Desana) myths analyzed by Reichel-Dolmatoff (1985) in an essay on "Tapir Avoidance in the Northwest Amazon," where the tapir serves as a historical metaphor for the Wakuénai phratries of the Isana-Guainía drainage area.

3. Among the Cubeo, the anaconda spirit (*Ainkü*) is considered one of the two complementary forces of mythic creation who links together all aquatic life forms. "In an elementary sense, the Anaconda, who is the primary source of ritual and ritual visions, is an agency for both death and resurrection . . . , as well as for birth and transformation" (Goldman 2004:35).

4. Comparative ethnology provides another line of evidence (see Hill 1985). As Goldman once observed, "One Cubeo phratry was, in fact, once Arawakan" (1963:26).

Chapter 4: Narratives from "The World Begins"

1. The word for this bag, *páatu,* is used only in reference to the small bags or purses made of woven palm leaves that shamans use for storing rattles, stones, tobacco, and other sacred objects imbued with ritual power.

2. First-Woman, or *Ámaru,* is a paternal aunt of Made-from-Bone and becomes the first woman to give birth to a child (see chapter 6).

3. As an aside, Félix told me that this phrase is a humorous reference to the fact that Made-from-Bone and his family were surprised that the sun was rising "from downstream" (i.e., from the east) because the last time they had seen the sun, it was setting in the west.

Chapter 5: Ethnomusicological Interlude

1. On one occasion, the musical dancing of *pudáli* became a means for creating bonds of solidarity between the Wakuénai and their Yeral neighbors as a way of expressing collective opposition to exploitative economic practices of local merchants (see Hill 1994b).

2. See Hill 1987 for a detailed description and analysis of the two-part cycle of *pudáli* exchange ceremonies.

Part 3: The World Opens Up: Overview

1. Munn (1969) coined the term "naming power" in her study of creation myths and associated ritual performances among the Murngin of Australia. I have adapted Munn's term as "musical naming power" to convey the explicitly musical quality of creation processes described in Wakuénai myths as well as the sacred chanting practices based on these myths (Hill 1993).

2. The mapping of geographic space through place-naming is a prominent feature of sacred *malikái* singing and chanting during male and female initiation rituals (see chapter 1).

3. *Lingua geral*, known as Geral or Yeral in the Upper Río Negro region today, is a Tupí-Portuguese trade language introduced into northwestern Amazonia by Jesuit missionaries in the late seventeenth or early eighteenth century.

4. This narrative is different from others because it is sung rather than spoken and forms part of the ritually powerful genre of singing and chanting known as *malikái*.

Chapter 6: Narratives from "The World Opens Up"

1. *Mutʰípani* can be translated as "dance (*-pani*) of the *seje* palm grubs (*mútʰi*)," which refers to the sacred ceremonial exchanges of wild palm fruits called *kwépani* (dance of *Kuwái*). The geographic location of *Mutʰípani* is on a stream called Dzukuáli that runs into the Aiarí River slightly downstream from Hípana.

2. The place where Made-from-Bone took *Kuwái* to hide him from the people at Hípana is referred to in sacred songs and chants (*malikái*) as *liwanápu éenu*, or "the corner of the sky." It is said that to see *Kuwái* was dangerous, even life-threatening, to the people living at Hípana because he was the child of incestuous sexual relations between Made-from-Bone and First-Woman.

3. *Dápa* refers to the paca, a large rodent that is considered to be the finest game meat. *Dápa* also is the namesake of one of the most important sacred trumpets of *Kuwái* that groups of men play in sacred dances of *Kuwái* and at male initiation rituals. In the narrative, *dápa* is one of the main voices of *Kuwái* and part of his body, which is made up of all the animals, plants, and materials.

4. *Máaliawa* is the name for pairs of sacred flutes named after white herons (*máali*) and that are said to be the thumb and index finger of *Kuwái*.

5. The verb "show" here refers principally to *Kuwái*'s act of showing the boys how his body, which will later transform into sacred flutes and trumpets with animal namesakes, makes powerful sounds. More generally, "show" refers to the various practical arts of making baskets and other material artifacts that *Kuwái* teaches to the boys, or "students." The name for male initiation rituals, *wakapéetaka iénpitipé*, or "we show our children," is based on these mythic episodes.

6. Fasting is an important part of male and female initiation rituals and other highly sacred periods, such as illness or childbirth. Manioc drinks and breads are considered the safest foods, or those that have the least ritual power (*linupanáa*). Blowing tobacco smoke and chanting *malikái* over these manioc products makes them even safer for initiates.

7. *Tiríta* (*pwáapwa*) palms are the source of long, thin strips used for weaving baskets and other artifacts. Strips of the outer bark of the palm stalks are removed using a knife.

8. *Tsépani* is the name of a dance and musical performance in sacred ceremonies, called *kwépani*, and commemorates the mythic episode in which *Kuwái* eats the three nephews of Made-from-Bone.

9. Foods considered to be "dangerous" or "powerful" are those fish species that have high fat content, such as large catfish, all bird species, and all forest animal species.

10. Each species of animal or plant food has a unique spirit name in *malikái* singing and chanting. These spirit names are composed of a generic category of mythic being coupled with a specific name (see Hill 1993).

11. *Káalimátu* is a wasp-person who plays a key role as the messenger between Made-from-Bone and *Kuwái*.

12. Dance whips (*kapéti*) are long sticks made from *dzámakuápi* (two snakes) vine that are used as percussive instruments in collective song-dances during sacred ceremonies (*kwépani*) and male initiation rituals. Groups of male dancers carry them in their right hands and make loud percussive sounds by banging the whips' handles against the ground in unison as they sing and dance. The men also use *kapéti* whips to lash one another across the back during these sacred dances. However, the *kapéti* whips are not the same as the sacred whips made from *kadápu* vines, which are only used for rhythmic accompaniment to *malikái* songs and chants in male and female initiation rituals and to strike the initiates across the back at the end of these rituals.

13. The indigenous phrase used for describing performances of *malikái* singing and chanting in rituals is *ínyapakáati dzéema*, or "to blow tobacco smoke."

14. *Tsówai* is named mainly in *malikái* chanting during male initiation rituals and refers to the sea.

15. Each of the sacred flutes and trumpets of *Kuwái* has an animal namesake and also refers to a part of the body of *Kuwái*.

16. "Groups" refers to the fact that the instruments are played in ensembles representing different animal species and parts of the body of *Kuwái*. For example, the *waliáduwa* flutes are always played in groups of three, and each of the flutes is said to be one of the three outer fingers of the hand of *Kuwái*.

17. *Dabucurí* is a *lingua geral* term for collective ceremonies at which groups of men play the sacred flutes and trumpets of *Kuwái*. *Kwépani*, or "*Kuwái* dance," is the Wakuénai term for these ceremonial events.

18. The literal translation is "returned to know the world."

19. *Kuwái* here is understood as the group of men playing sacred flutes and trumpets with animal namesakes. Since each of the musical instruments also refers to a part of the body of *Kuwái*, the assemblage of instruments being played in *kwépani* or male initiation rituals can be understood as a group of men who collectively construct the mythic body of *Kuwái* through music, dance, and other ritual activities.

20. The term "grandfather" (*ihwérrim*) is used in ritual contexts to mean "large" or "great," also "prototype."

21. *Yeral* is the Spanish term for *Geral*, or speakers of *lingua geral*.

22. *Dzáatu* is the only hallucinogenic plant used among the Curripaco and comes from the bark of a tree (*Virola calophylla*). Unlike neighboring eastern Tukanoan groups, the Curripaco do not practice collective use of *Banisteriopsis caapi* (or *ayahuasca*) in rituals and ceremonies. Only shamans (*malírri*) use hallucinogenic snuff.

23. The story of *Kuwaikánirri* is usually sung rather than spoken as a narrative. I have decided to render it as a line-by-line translation rather than in paragraph form.

Chapter 7: Ethnological Coda

1. Complicating these local and regional shifts in power relations in Amazonia was the rise of Hugo Chávez as the new Bolivarian mythic hero of Venezuelan nationalist history (see Coronil 2000 on this paradoxical political figure).

Appendix A

1. Comparable uses of verbs of speaking as building blocks for mythic narratives are found in Navajo Coyote stories (Webster 2004: 71).

Glossary

Ámaru: First-Woman, the paternal aunt of Made-from-Bone, who gave birth to the primordial human being, *Kuwái,* and who opened up the world for the second time by playing the flutes and trumpets of *Kuwái* in various places

anigua: Type of small worm that penetrates the soles of people's feet and that must be removed with a needle or other sharp object

ataraya: Curved wooden frame that holds a net for scooping up fish stunned to surface with *barbasco*

barbasco: Kind of poison made from a cultivated plant (*Tephrosia* sp.) that is used to catch fish by blocking their ability to breathe

bocachico: Species of small fish (*Leporinus* spp.) that migrates and spawns at the beginning of long wet seasons in April and provides ideal food gift for male-owned *pudáli* ceremonies (see also *kulirrína*); three varieties of bocachico—white (*táari*), spotted (*dúme*), and red-tailed (*dupári*)—serve as names for collective dances in opening stage of male-owned *pudáli* ceremonies

camahái: Poison that kills people when mixed in drinks and that originated in primordial times

Cricket-Brothers: First manifestation of Made-from-Bone and his brother after their aunt saved the bones of their slain father

curare: Poison used for hunting monkeys, birds, and other arboreal game animals with blowguns

Dáinali: Grandfather Sleep, the mythic owner of night and sleep

dápa: Paca (*Cuniculus paca*), a species of large rodent considered to be the finest game animals for human consumption

déetu: Species of black coconut-palm weevil that develops from white larvae (*mútʰi*) that have been deposited in felled or broken palm trees; also, the name of flutes played during the second, late-night stage of *pudáli* ceremonies

Duiménai: Name for the Cricket-Brothers in the story of the origin of Made-from-Bone; comes from an episode near the end of the narrative in which the boys transform into squirrels, and blood flowing from wounds on their hands turns into a kind of honey used in shamanic curing rituals

dzawírra: Viejita (Spanish), a species of small fish (*cicholasoma*); also the name for *máwi* flute dances played in the last stage of *pudáli* ceremonies

dzudzuápani: "Wheel dance" song; a collective song and dance performed with dance stamping tubes to mark the end of the second, late-night stage of a female-owned *pudáli* ceremony

Dzúli: Younger brother of Made-from-Bone who learns all of the sacred songs and chants of male initiation rituals from *Kuwái* and who becomes the first master chanter (*malikái limínali*)

Dzulíhwerri: Great Shaman, the mythic owner of hallucinogenic snuff (*dzáatu*) who taught *Éeri* to become the first shaman (*malírri*)

Éenutanhísre: Place far downstream near the sea; associated with white people and diseases

Éeri: Younger brother of Made-from-Bone and the first to go through the male initiation ritual

guapa: Circular woven tray used to carry manioc bread

Hekuápi Iʰméetakawa: "The World Opens Up," the period when the primordial human being (*Kuwái*) first created the species and objects of nature through musical naming power and First-Woman (*Ámaru*) opened up the world for a second time by playing the musical instruments of *Kuwái* in various places

Hekuápi Ikéeñuakawa: "The World Begins," the time when Made-from-Bone created night, fire, and peach-palm fruits by obtaining them from various mythic owners

Hípana: Mythic center or "navel" of the world, the place where Made-from-Bone created the ancestral spirits of various patrisibs by raising them from a hole beneath the rapids, giving them powerful names, and blowing tobacco smoke over them

Hménakʰóewa: One of three nephews of Made-from-Bone who saw *Kuwái* and who were eaten by *Kuwái* because they prematurely broke their ritual fast

Iñápirríkuli: Made-from-Bone, an invincible and omniscient trickster-creator who is the most pervasive character in Wakuénai mythic narratives

itálikanáti: "President"; paramount chief; indigenous term used to describe leaders of multiethnic confederacies during colonial period

Káali: Manioc-Man, the mythic owner of manioc and all cultivated plants; creator of ceremonial dance music (*mádzerukái*) as way of teaching his sons to ask respectfully for drinks during *pudáli* and other ceremonies

Káalimátu: Wasp-person who served as messenger between *Kuwái* and Made-from-Bone; he also helped Made-from-Bone to defeat his archenemy, Great Sickness, by plugging up his blowgun

kadápu: Species of vine for making sacred whips that are used only for striking young men and women at the end of initiation rituals

kakúri: Large, heart-shaped weir; fish trap; built on riverbanks during dry seasons to catch fish as they feed in newly flooded forests during wet seasons *kapéti:* Ceremonial whips used as rhythmic instruments by drumming handles against the ground during *kwépani* ceremonies and in male initiation rituals

kápetiápani: Whip dance; a collective song performed by men during *kwépani* ceremonies and male initiation rituals; originated in mythic times when *Kuwái* had finished teaching *malikái* songs and chants to *Dzúli* and was about to be pushed into a bonfire, marking the end of the first opening up of the world

káridzámai: Sacred food; boiled, hot-peppered meat, prepared for young men and women going through initiation rituals; food is consecrated through musically naming spirits of all species of edible animals and plants in *malikái* singing and chanting

kúlírri: Species of large catfish (*Brachyplatysoma* sp.) with large black stripes on each side

kúlirrína: Ceremonial trumpets named after *kulírri* catfish; played and exchanged in male-owned *pudáli* ceremonies to imitate sound of bocachico fish migrating and spawning in newly flooded forests

Kunáhwerrim: Great Sickness, the archenemy of Made-from-Bone who set in motion the cycles of violence and revenge during primordial times

Kuwái: Primordial human being who was born of an incestuous union between Made-from-Bone and First-Woman; body gave off "word-sounds" that created the world of animal and plant species and that became the basis for *malikái* singing and chanting

Kuwaikánirri: Younger brother of Made-from-Bone and the first victim of witchcraft; saved from death through journey to places of the bee spirits

kuwáiñai (also *kuwáiñainai*): Bee spirits who are symbols of purity, immortality, and ability to counteract witchcraft

kwépani: *Kuwái* dance; sacred ceremonial exchanges of wild palm fruits in which groups of men play flutes and trumpets of *Kuwái*

línupanáa: Ritual power or danger; all edible animal and plant species have this power to varying degrees

máaliawa: White heron flutes, pairs of sacred musical instruments played by men in *kwépani* and male initiation rituals; also, the "thumb" and "index finger" of *Kuwái*

Máapakwá Makákwi: Great Honey Place, the mythic home of the *Kuwáiñai* on the Upper Guainía River

macanilla: Species of tree (*Socretea eschorrhiza;* or *púpa* in Curripaco) used for making sacred flutes and trumpets of *Kuwái;* also, the tree that grew from the ashes where *Kuwái* had burned at the end of the first creation of the world and that connected the sky-world of mythic ancestors to the world of living human descendants below

mádzerukái: Collective dance music performed in *pudáli* and *kwépani* ceremonies; originated when Manioc-Man (*Káali*) taught his sons how to ask for drinks

Malíhwerri: Grandfather Anaconda, the mythic owner of peach-palm fruits

malikái: Genre of ritually powerful singing, chanting, and speaking performed in rituals for childbirths, puberty initiations, and curing witchcraft victims

malikái limínali: Master of sacred singing, chanting, and speaking

Málinálieni: One of three nephews of Made-from-Bone who saw *Kuwái* and who were eaten by *Kuwái* because they prematurely broke their ritual fast

malírri: Shaman; ritual healer who uses hallucinogenic snuff, tobacco, and singing to bring the souls of sick persons back to the world of living people

malirríkairi: Shamanic singing performed in curing rituals as way of traveling between the worlds of living and dead persons

máwi: Species of small palm tree (*Astrostudium schomburgkii*) used for making ceremonial flutes, blowguns, and *kakúri* weirs; also, the name of long ceremonial flutes played in "male" and "female" pairs during *pudáli* ceremonies

Máwirríkuli: Youngest brother of Made-from-Bone and first to die from poisoning

moriche: Species of palm (*Mauritia minor;* or *itewíppi* in Curripaco) used for making twine and rope

mútʰi: White, oily palm-weevil larvae found in broken or felled palm trees

Mutʰípani: Palm-Weevil Dance; also, the mythic home of First-Woman on the Caño Dzukuáli, a tributary of the Aiarí River in Brazil

Owl-Monkey (*Aotus trivirgatus;* or *ipéeku* in Curripaco): One of Made-from-Bone's many adversaries during primordial mythic times; also, the mythic owner of *camahái* poison

paca: Cuniculus paca, a species of large rodent considered to be the finest game animals for human consumption

pákamarántakan: Ceremonial drinking songs performed as dialogues between men and women, guests and hosts during the late-night period of *pudáli* ceremonies

patsiáka: Manioc beverage made by soaking granules of manioc flour in water

pavon grande: Species of fish (*Cichla* spp.; or *héemari* in Curripaco)

pípirri: Peach palm; fruits used to make thick soup

pudáli: Cycle of male- and female-owned exchange ceremonies in which food gifts are offered between affinal groups

pudalímnali: Male owner of a *pudáli* ceremony

pudalímnarru: Female owner of a *pudáli* ceremony

quirípa: Marine shells that were traded throughout the northern lowlands of South America and made into necklaces and bracelets that indicated owners' prestige; became a form of general-purpose money in the Orinoco basin during the colonial period

sebucán: Woven manioc press

Témedawí: Magical city of gold

tiríta: Species of wild palm (*Ischnosiphon obliquus;* or *pwáapwa* in Curripaco) used for weaving baskets, manioc presses, ceremonial trumpets, and other products

Tuípwa: One of three nephews of Made-from-Bone who saw *Kuwái* and who were eaten by *Kuwái* because they prematurely broke their ritual fast

Uliámali: Anaconda-Person, an enemy of Made-from-Bone during primordial mythic times and the father of Anaconda-Child

viejitas: See *dzawírra* above

wáana: Dance stamping tubes used as percussive accompaniment in collective singing during female-owned *pudáli* ceremonies

waliáduwa: "New Mother"; the name of sacred flutes of *Kuwái* played in groups of three during *kwépani* ceremonies and male initiation rituals

yagrumo: Species of secondary vegetation (*Cecropia* sp.) used for making *wáana* stamping tubes and whistles played in *pudáli* ceremonies

Yáwali: Mythic owner of fire

yokúta: Manioc beverages made by soaking manioc breads in water

yópinai: Spirits of the rivers, forests, and air that can cause sickness; adversaries of Made-from-Bone during primordial mythic times and inhabitants of the magical city of gold (Temedawí) in later mythic times

References Cited

Agüero, Oscar. 1992. *The Millennium among the Tupi-cocama*. Uppsala, Sweden: Uppsala Research Reports in Cultural Anthropology.

Anderson, Benedict. 1983. *Imagined Communities: Reflections on the Origins and Spread of Nationalism*. Thetford: Thetford Press.

Asamblea Nacional. 2000. *Decreta: Ley de Demarcación y Garantía del Habitat y Tierras de los Pueblos Indígenas*. Caracas: República Bolivariana de Venezuela. http://www.asambleanacional.gov.ve.

Basso, Ellen. 1985. *A Musical View of the Universe: Kalapalo Myth and Ritual Performances*. Philadelphia: University of Pennsylvania Press.

———. 1987. *In Favor of Deceit: A Study of Tricksters in an Amazonian Society*. Tucson: University of Arizona Press.

Basso, Ellen, ed. 1990. *Native Latin American Cultures through Their Discourse*. Bloomington, Ind.: Special Publications of the Folklore Institute.

———. 1995. *The Last Cannibals: A South American Oral History*. Austin: University of Texas Press.

Biord Castillo, Horacio. 1985. El Contexto Multingüe del Sistema de Interdependencia Regional del Orinoco. *Antropológica* 63–64:83–101.

Briggs, Charles. 1992. "Since I Am a Woman, I Will Chastise My Relatives": Gender, Reported Speech, and the (Re)Production of Social Relations in Warao Ritual Wailing. *American Ethnologist* 19(2):337–61.

———. 2000. "Emergence of the Non-Indigenous Peoples": A Warao Narrative. In *Translating Native Latin American Verbal Art,* ed. Kay Sammons and Joel Sherzer, pp. 174–96. Washington, D.C.: Smithsonian Institution Press.

Brown, Michael. 1991. Beyond Resistance: Utopian Renewal in Amazonia. *Ethnohistory* 38(4):363–87.

Brown, Michael, and Eduardo Fernandez. 1991. *War of Shadows*. Berkeley: University of California Press.

———. 1992. Tribe and State in a Frontier Mosaic: The Asháninka of Eastern Peru. In *War in the Tribal Zone: Expanding States and Indigenous Warfare,* ed. Brian

Ferguson and Neil L. Whitehead, 175–97. Santa Fe, N.M.: School of American Research.

Butt Colson, Audrey. 1971. Hallelujah among the Patamona Indians. *Antropológica* 28:25–28.

———. 1973. Inter-Tribal Trade in the Guiana Highlands. *Antropológica* 34:1–69.

———. 1985. Routes of Knowledge: An Aspect of Regional Integration in the Circum-Roraima Area of the Guiana Highlands. *Antropológica* 63–64:103–49.

Chaumeil, Jean-Pierre. 1992. Varieties of Amazonian Shamanism. *Diogenes* 40(8):101–13.

Chernela, Janet. 1988. Righting History in the Northwest Amazon: Myth, Structure, and History in an Arapaço Narrative. In *Rethinking History and Myth: Indigenous South American Perspectives on the Past,* ed. J. Hill, 35–49. Urbana: University of Illinois Press.

———. 1993. *The Wanano Indians of the Brazilian Amazon: A Sense of Space.* Austin: University of Texas Press.

Civrieux, Marc de. 1980. *Watunna: An Orinoco Creation Cycle,* trans. David Guss. Richmond, Calif.: North Point Press.

Clastres, Hélène. 1995. *The Land without Evil: Tupí-Guaraní Prophetism.* Urbana: University of Illinois Press.

Constitución. 1999. *Capitulo VIII: De los Derechos de los Pueblos Indígenas.* http://www.asambleanacional.gov.ve.

Coronil, Fernando. 1997. *The Magical State: Nature, Money, and Modernity in Venezuela.* Chicago: University of Chicago Press.

———. 2000. Magical Illusions or Revolutionary Magic: Chávez in Historical Context. In *Hugo Chávez, Venezuela's Redeemer?* NACLA Report on the Americas, 33(6):34–42.

Corte Suprema de Justicia. 1996. Corte en Pleno. Magistrado Ponente: Alfredo Ducharne Alonzo. December 5, 1996. 50 pages.

Federmann, Nicolas. 1945 [1530]. *Narración del Primer Viaje de Federmann a Venezuela.* Caracas: Lit. y Tip. Del Comercio.

Feldmann, Susan. 1963. *African Myths and Tales.* New York: Dell.

Gasson, Rafael. 2000. Quirípas and Mostacillas: The Evolution of Shell Beads as a Medium of Exchange in Northern South America. Special issue, "Colonial Transformations in Venezuela: Anthropology, Archaeology, and History," ed. B. Perez, *Ethnohistory* 47 (3–4):581–610.

Gates, Henry Louis, Jr. 1988. *The Signifying Monkey: A Theory of African-American Literary Criticism.* New York: Oxford University Press.

Gilij, P. Felipe Salvadore. 1965 [1782]. *Ensayo de Historia Americana.* Translation and preliminary study by Antonio Tovar. 3 vols. Biblioteca de la Academia Nacional de la Historia 71, 72, and 73. Caracas: Fuentes para la Historia Colonial de Venezuela.

Goldman, Irving. 1963. *The Cubeo: Indians of the Northwest Amazon*. Urbana: University of Illinois Press.

———. 2004. *Cubeo Hehénewa Religious Thought: Metaphysics of a Northwestern Amazonian People*. New York: Columbia University Press.

González Ñáñez, Omar. 1980. *Mitología Guarequena*. Caracas: Monte Avila Editores.

Gow, Peter. 1991. *Of Mixed Blood: Kinship and History in the Peruvian Amazon*. Oxford: Clarendon Press.

———. 1994. River People: Shamanism and History in Western Amazonia. In *Shamanism, History, and the State*, ed. Nicholas Thomas and Caroline Humphrey, pp. 90–114. Ann Arbor: University of Michigan Press.

———. 2001. *An Amazonian Myth and Its History*. Oxford: Oxford University Press.

Graham, Laura. 1995. *Performing Dreams: Discourses of Immortality among the Xavante of Central Brazil*. Austin: University of Texas Press.

Granadillo, Tania. 2006. An Ethnographic Account of Language Documentation among the Kurripako of Venezuela. Ph.D. dissertation, Departments of Anthropology and Linguistics, University of Arizona.

Guss, David. 1986. Keeping It Oral: A Yekuana Ethnology. *American Ethnologist* 13(3):413–29.

———. 1989. *To Weave and Sing: Art, Symbol, and Narrative in the South American Rain Forest*. Berkeley: University of California Press.

Herrera, Rafael, Carl Jordan, and Ernesto Medina. 1978. Amazonian Ecosystems: Structure and Function with Particular Emphasis on Nutrients. *Interciencia* 3:223–31.

Hill, Jonathan. 1983. Wakuénai Society. Ph.D. dissertation, Department of Anthropology, Indiana University.

———. 1985. Agnatic Sibling Relations and Rank in Northern Arawakan Myth and Social Life. In *Sibling Relations in Lowland South America*, ed. Judith Shapiro, pp. 25–33. Working Papers on South American Indians, no. 7. Bennington, Vt.: Bennington College.

———. 1987. Wakuénai Ceremonial Exchange in the Northwest Amazon Region. *Journal of Latin American Lore* 13(2):183–224.

———, ed. 1988a. *Rethinking History and Myth: Indigenous South American Perspectives on the Past*. Urbana: University of Illinois Press.

———. 1988b. The Soft and the Stiff: Ritual Power and Mythic Meaning in a Northern Arawakan Classifier System. *Antropológica* 69:3–25.

———. 1993. *Keepers of the Sacred Chants: The Poetics of Ritual Power in an Amazonian Society*. Tucson: University of Arizona Press.

———. 1994a. Alienated Targets: Military Discourses and the Disempowerment of Indigenous Amazonian Peoples in Venezuela. *Identities: Global Studies in Culture and Power* 1(1):7–34.

————. 1994b. Musicalizing the Other: Shamanistic Approaches to Ethnic-Class Competition in the Upper Rio Negro Region. In *Religiosidad y Resistencia Indígenas hacia el Fin del Milenio*, ed. Alicia Barabas, pp. 105–28. Quito: Abya-Yala.

————. 1996. Northern Arawakan Ethnogenesis and Historical Transformations. In *History, Power, and Identity: Ethnogenesis in the Americas, 1492–1992*, ed. J. Hill, pp. 142–60. Iowa City: University of Iowa Press.

————. 1999. Indigenous Peoples and the Rise of Independent Nation-States in Lowland South America. In *The Cambridge History of Native Peoples of the Americas: South America*, ed. F. Salomon and S. Schwartz, pp. 3:704–764. New York: Cambridge University Press.

————. 2002. Shamanism, Colonialism, and the Wild Woman: Fertility Cultism and Historical Dynamics in the Upper Rio Negro Region. In *Comparative Arawakan Histories: Rethinking Language Family and Culture Area in Amazonia*, ed. Jonathan Hill and Fernando Santos-Granero, pp. 223–47. Urbana: University of Illinois Press.

————. 2005. Collares de Quirípa como símbolo de la Hibridación Económica Colonial en la Región del Alto Río Negro. Proceedings of the II Congreso Nacional de Antropología, ed. Kay Tarble, Alex Mansutti, and Horacio Biord. Merida, Venezuela: Universidad de los Andes.

Hill, Jonathan, and Fernando Santos-Granero, eds. 2002. *Comparative Arawakan Histories: Rethinking Language Family and Culture Area in Amazonia*. Urbana: University of Illinois Press.

Hill, Jonathan, and Susan Staats. 2002. Redelineando el Curso de la Historia: Estados EuroAmericanos y las Culturas sin Pueblos. In *Colonización, Resistencia y Mestizaje en las Américas, Siglos XVI–XX*, ed. Guillaume Boccara, pp. 13–26. Quito: Abya Yala and Instituto Francés de Estudios Andinos.

Hill, Jonathan, and Robin Wright. 1988. Time, Narrative, and Ritual: Historical Interpretations from an Amazonian Society. In *Rethinking History and Myth: Indigenous South American Perspectives on the Past*, ed. Jonathan Hill, pp. 78–105. Urbana: University of Illinois Press.

Holmes, Rebecca. 1981. Estado Nutricional en Cuatro Aldeas de la Selva Amazonica— Venezuela: Un Estudio de Adaptación y Aculturación. M. Sc. Thesis, Instituto Venezolano de Investigaciones Científicas.

Hugh-Jones, Christine. 1979. *From the Milk River: Spatial and Temporal Processes in Northwest Amazonia*. Cambridge: Cambridge University Press.

Hugh-Jones, Stephen. 1979. *The Palm and the Pleiades: Initiation and Cosmology in Northwest Amazonia*. Cambridge: Cambridge University Press.

Humboldt, Alexander von. 1818. *Personal Narrative of Travels to the Equinoctial Regions of the New Continent during the Years 1799–1804*, trans. Helen Maria Williams. 7 vols. London: Longman, Hurst, Rees, Orme, and Brown.

Hvalkof, Soren. 1986. El Drama Actual del Gran Pajonal, Primera Parte: Recursos, Historia, Población y Producción Asháninka. *Amazonía Peruana* 6(12):22–30.

Informe Annual. 1998. *Situación de los Derechos Humanos en el Estado Amazonas.* Puerto Ayacucho, Venezuela: Oficina de Derechos Humanos del Vicariato Apostólico.

Jackson, Jean. 1983. *The Fish People: Linguistic Exogamy and Tukanoan Identity in Northwest Amazonia.* Cambridge: Cambridge University Press.

Johnson, Allen. 2003. *Families of the Forest: The Matsigenka Indians of the Peruvian Amazon.* Berkeley: University of California Press.

Journet, Nicolas. 1995. *La Paix des Jardins: Structures Sociales des Indiens Curripaco du Haut-Rio Negro, Colombie.* Paris: Institut d'Ethnologie, Musée de l'Homme.

Kane, Stephanie. 1994. *The Phantom Gringo Boat: Shamanic Discourse and Development in Panama.* Washington, D.C.: Smithsonian Institution Press.

Key, Mary Ritchie. 1979. *The Grouping of South American Languages.* Tübingen: Gunter Narr.

Langdon, E. Jean, and Gerhard Baer, eds. 1992. *Portals of Power: Shamanism in South America.* Albuquerque: University of New Mexico Press.

López Pequeira, Horacio, Felix López Oliveros, and Jonathan Hill. 1998. *Yákuti Úupi Pérri: Palabras de los Primeros Tiempos.* Manuscript submitted to Dirección de Asuntos Indígenas, Ministerio de Educación, Caracas, Venezuela.

Luna, Luis Eduardo. 1991. *Ayahuasca Visions.* Berkeley: North Atlantic Books.

Matos Arvelo, Martin. 1912. *Vida Indiana.* Barcelona: Maucci.

McDowell, John. 2000. Collaborative Ethnopoetics: A View from the Sibundoy Valley. In *Translating Native Latin American Verbal Art,* ed. Kay Sammons and Joel Sherzer, pp. 211–32. Washington, D.C.: Smithsonian Institution Press.

Morales Mendez, Filadelfo, and Nelly Arvelo-Jimenez. 1981. Hacía un Modelo de Estructura Social Caribe. *America Indígena* 41(4):603–26.

Morey, Robert, and Nancy Morey. 1975. *Relaciones Comerciales en el Pasado en los Llanos de Colombia y Venezuela.* Caracas: Instituto de Investigaciones Históricas.

Munn, Nancy. 1969. The Effectiveness of Symbols in Murngin Rite and Myth. In *Forms of Symbolic Action,* ed. R. F. Spencer, pp. 178–206. Seattle: University of Washington Press, Proceedings of the American Ethnological Society.

Nimuendajú, Kurt. 1950 [1927]. Reconhecimento dos Rios Içana, Ayarí, e Uaupés. Relatorio Apresentado ão Serviço de Proteção ãos Indios do Amazonas e Acre, 1927. *Journal de la Société des Américanistes,* n.s., 39.

OCEI (Oficina Central de Estadística e Información). 1982.Caracas, Venezuela.

Pané, Ramón. 1999. *An Account of the Antiquities of the Indians* [1496], ed. José Juan Arrom. Trans. Susan C. Giswold. Durham: Duke University Press.

Price, Richard. 1983. *First-Time: The Historical Vision of an Afro-American People.* Baltimore: Johns Hopkins University Press.

Price, Richard, and Sally Price. 1991. *Two Evenings in Saramaka.* Chicago: University of Chicago Press.

Price, Sally. 1999. *Maroon Arts: Cultural Vitality in the African Diaspora.* Boston: Beacon Press.

Programa Censal. 2001. *Población Indígena Por Operativo Censal Según Entidad Federal y Pueblo Indígena*. Caracas, Venezuela.

Radin, Paul. 1972 [1956]. *The Trickster: A Study in American Indian Mythology*. New York: Schocken Books.

Rausch, Jane. 1984. *A Tropical Plains Frontier: The Llanos of Colombia, 1531–1831*. Albuquerque: University of New Mexico Press.

Reichel-Dolmatoff, Gerardo. 1971. *Amazonian Cosmos*. Chicago: University of Chicago Press.

———. 1975. *The Shaman and the Jaguar*. Philadelphia: Temple University Press.

———. 1985. Tapir Avoidance in the Colombian Northwest Amazon. In *Animal Myths and Metaphors in South America*, ed. G. Urton, pp. 107–44. Salt Lake City: University of Utah Press.

———. 1996. *Yuruparí: Studies of an Amazonian Foundation Myth*. Cambridge, Mass.: Harvard University Press.

Renard-Casevitz, France Marie. 1985. Guerre, Violence et Identité a Partir de Sociétés du Piémont Amazonien des Andes Centrales. *Cahiers ORSTOM, Série Sciences Humaines* 21(1):81–98.

———. 1991. *Le Banquet Masqué: Une Mythologie de l'Etranger*. Paris: Lierre et Coudrier.

Renard-Casevitz, France Marie, and Olivier Dollfus. 1988. Geografia de Algunos Mitos y Creencias. Espacios Simbólicos y Realidades Geográficas de los Machinguenga del Alto Urubamba. *Amazonía Peruana* 8(16):7–40.

Rivero, Juan. 1956 [1733]. *Historia de las Misiones de los Llanos de Casanare y los Rios Orinoco y Meta*. Bogotá: Biblioteca de la Presidencia de Colombia.

Santos-Granero, Fernando. 1991. *The Power of Love: The Moral Use of Knowledge amongst the Amuesha of Central Peru*. Monographs on Social Anthropology 62. London School of Economics and Political Science. London: Athlone Press.

———. 1992. Anticolonialismo, Mesianismo y Utopía en la Sublevación de Juan Santos Atahuallpa, Siglo XVIII. In *Opresión Colonial y Resistencia Indígena en la Alta Amazonía*, ed. Fernando Santos Granero, pp. 103–34. Quito: Abya-Yala/CEDIME/FLACSO-Ecuador.

———. 1998. Writing History into the Landscape: Space, Myth, and Ritual in Contemporary Amazonia. *American Ethnologist* 25(2):128–48.

Seeger, Anthony. 1987. *Why Suyá Sing: A Musical Anthropology of an Amazonian People*. Cambridge: Cambridge University Press.

Sherzer, Joel, and Greg Urban, eds. 1986. *Native South American Discourse*. Berlin: Mouton de Gruyter.

Smith, Richard C. 1977. Deliverance from Chaos for a Song: A Social and Religious Interpretation of the Ritual Performance of Amuesha Music. Ph.D. dissertation, Department of Anthropology, Cornell University.

Staats, Susan. 1996. Fighting in a Different Way. In *History, Power, and Identity:*

Ethnogenesis in the Americas, 1492–1992, ed. Jonathan Hill, pp 161–79. Iowa City: University of Iowa Press.

Taussig, Michael. 1987. *Shamanism, Colonialism, and the Wild Man.* Chicago: University of Chicago Press.

Thomas, David. 1972. The Indigenous Trade System of Southeast Estado Bolivar, Venezuela. *Antropólogica* 33:3–37.

Uhl, Christopher. 1980. Studies of Forest Agricultural and Successional Environments in the Upper Rio Negro Region of the Amazon Basin. Ph. D. dissertation, Botany Department, Michigan State University.

Urban, Greg. 1991. *A Discourse-Centered Approach to Culture: Native South American Myths and Rituals.* Austin: University of Texas Press.

Veber, Hanne. 1998. The Salt of the Montaña: Interpreting Indigenous Activism in the Rain Forest. *Cultural Anthropology* 13:382–413.

Velásquez Runk, Julie. 2005. And the Creator Began to Carve Us of Cocobolo: Culture, History, Forest Ecology, and Conservation among Wounaan in Eastern Panama. Ph.D. dissertation, Department of Anthropology and School of Forestry and Environmental Studies, Yale University.

Vidal, Silvia. 1987. El Modelo del Proceso Migratorio Prehispánico de los Piapoco: Hipótesis y Evidencias. Master's thesis, Centro de Estudios Avanzados, Instituto Venezolano de Investigaciones Científicas.

———. 1993. Reconstrucción de los Procesos de Etnogénesis de Reproducción Social entre los Baré de Rio Negro, Siglos XVI–XVII. Ph.D. dissertation, Centro de Estudios Avanzados, Instituto Venezolano de Investigaciones Científicas.

———. 2000. Kuwé Duwákalumi: The Arawak Secret Routes of Migration, Trade, and Resistance. *Ethnohistory* 47(3):635–68.

———. 2002. Secret Religious Cults and Political Leadership: Multiethnic Confederacies from Northwestern Amazonia. In *Comparative Arawakan Histories,* ed. Jonathan Hill and Fernando Santos-Granero, pp. 248–68. Urbana: University of Illinois Press.

Vidal, Silvia, and Neil Whitehead. 2004. Dark Shamans and the Shamanic State: Sorcery and Witchcraft as Political Process in Guyana and the Venezuelan Amazon. In *In Darkness and Secrecy: The Anthropology of Assault Sorcery and Witchcraft in Amazonia,* ed. Neil Whitehead and Robin Wright, pp. 51–81. Durham: Duke University Press.

Webster, Anthony. 2004. Coyote Poems: Navajo Poetry, Intertextuality, and Language Choice. *American Indian Culture and Research Journal* 28(4):69–91.

Whitehead, Neil. 1988. *Lords of the Tiger Spirit.* Netherlands: Foris.

———. 1990. Carib Ethnic Soldiering in Venezuela, the Guianas, and the Antilles, 1492–1820. *Ethnohistory* 37(4):357–85.

Whitehead, Neil, and Robin Wright, eds. 2004. *In Darkness and Secrecy: The Anthropology of Assault Sorcery and Witchcraft in Amazonia.* Durham: Duke University Press.

Wright, Robin. 1981. History and Religion of the Baniwa Peoples of the Upper Rio Negro Valley. Ph.D. dissertation, Department of Anthropology, Stanford University.

——. 1998. *Cosmos, Self, and History in Baniwa Religion: For Those Unborn.* Austin: University of Texas Press.

Wright, Robin, and Jonathan Hill. 1986. History, Ritual, and Myth: Nineteenth-Century Millenarian Movements in the Northwest Amazon. *Ethnohistory* 33(1):31–54.

Zucchi, Alberta. 1991a. Las Migraciones Maipures: Diversas Líneas de Evidencia para la Interpretación Arqueológica. *América Negra* 1:113–38.

——. 1991b. El Negro-Casiquiare-Alto Orinoco Como Ruta Conectiva entre el Amazonas y el Norte de Suramérica. In *Proceedings of the Twelfth Congress of the International Association for Caribbean Archaeology,* pp. 1–33. Martinique.

——. 1991c. Prehispanic Connections between the Orinoco, the Amazon, and the Caribbean Area. In *Proceedings of the Thirteenth International Congress for Caribbean Archaeology,* pp. 202–20. Curaçao.

——. 1992. Lingüística, Etnografía, Arqueología y Cambios Climáticos: La Dispersión de los Arawako en el Noroeste Amazónico. In *Archaeology and Environment in Latin America,* ed. Omar R. Ortiz-Troncoso and Thomas Van der Hammen, pp. 223–52. Amsterdam: Instituut voor Pre-en Protohistorische Archeologie Albert Egges Van Giffen, Universiteit van Amsterdam.

——. 1993. Datos Recientes para un Nuevo Modelo sobre la Expansión de los Grupos Maipure del Norte. *América Negra* 6:131–48.

Index

bathing, 41, 75, 76, 80, 120
Bat-People, 21, 22, 37–38
beads, 57, 58
beer, 86–87, 125, 138; manioc, 114, 119, 132, 133
bees, 136–37, 141
bee spirits (*Kuwáiñai*), 115, 116
beeswax, 115
Bird-Person (*Dókutsiári*), 33, 34
birds, 39, 40–41, 51, 71, 78, 90; baby
    (*awádu*), 52; *dzáaliro*, 35; giant, 53; *hádzee*,
    56; *pauhwí pedrera*, 78; seen by author in
    study region, 97–98; *wanáli*, 35
birth: in mythic narratives, 36, 64; rituals of,
    165n3
birth canal, creation of, 110, 117
blood, 28, 54–55, 117; from rain, 30, 49–50,
    122
blood of *Duiménai* (honey), 28, 165n1
blowgun, 34, 52, 53, 54, 56
blowing, with a feather, 113
blowing hallucinogenic snuff, 134, 135
blowing tobacco smoke, 51, 76, 126, 168n13;
    to avert magic, 78; for the dead, 53; over
    food, 119, 120, 122, 123, 168n6; to induce
    sleep, 54; to revive a person, 29, 30, 55, 118,
    129; and sacred food, 95, 112, 124, 125, 132,
    165n3; to transform objects, 46
Boape-Pariana-Maniva, 155
bocachico fish, 10, 11, 129; dances of, 11,
    85–87
bones, 25, 26, 29, 30, 150
bonfire, 126
bow, 52, 53
bowl, cooking, 40–41
Brazil, 13, 35
butterflies, 51

cacao juice, as medicine, 140
cajaro (catfish), 41
camahái poison, 29, 31
Camico, Venancio, 14–15
canoes, 45–46, 86, 113, 131, 145, 146; as
    anacondas, 66, 68; drinks placed in, 84, 85;
    dugout, 143; made of beeswax, 115; named,
    139; of women, 130
Caño *Dzukuáli* (Curved Stream), 130;
    mythical origin of, 117
Caño San Miguel, 96, 98

Caño Tigre, 85
Caracas, 98–99; in mythic narratives, 131, 141
Carib speakers, 58, 59, 60, 61
cars, 143
casabe bread, 80
cascaradora, 45
cashew fruits, as medicine, 140
Casiquiare River region, 3, 5, 10, 61, 85; and
    rubber boom, 15; and slave trade, 60
catfish, 41, 45, 49; *bagre choro*, 40; human
    transformed into, 37, 65; as sacred food,
    121; trumpets named after, 11, 95, 166n9
Catfish Trumpet Festival of 1981, 92–107;
    ethnic groups attending, 100; preparations
    for, 96–100, 104, 105
catfish trumpets, 11, 84, 95, 96, 106; con-
    struction of, 100, 104–5. See also *Kulirrína*
    trumpets
cave, mouth of *Kuwái*, 111, 121
Cayarí (Vaupés) River, 85
ceremonial dance music, 94, 110; compared
    with ritual chanting, 93–95; mythic origin
    of, 72–73, 83–85
ceremonies: drinking, 37; female-owned,
    11–12, 94, 95–96; male-owned, 11–12, 94,
    95, 96
chant owners, 10, 64; first (*Dzúli*), 64, 112
Chávez, Hugo, 16–17, 18, 156, 169n1
Chibcha speakers, 59
chicken, wild, 78, 79, 127, 129
child of the anaconda of the *dozate* bush, 122
children of the Armadillo (*Adzanéni*) phra-
    try, 6, 9
Children of the Wild Chicken (*Hohódeni*)
    phratry, 6, 9
Christianity, 15–16
chronology, in Wakuénai narratives, xviii
cigar, 29, 37, 46, 55, 76, 78, 118
City of Gold, 116, 142–46. See also Temedawí
Civrieux, Marc de, xiv
clay, colored, 38
coca, 41; used for divining, 122, 127
cocoa, as medicine, 140
coin necklaces and bracelets, 58
Cold War, 16, 17
Colombia, 106, 156, 164n3
colonial period, 13–14, 57, 58–62, 65–66; and
    indigenous trade, 59; late, 61–62; and

Jonathan D. Hill is a professor in of the Department of Anthropology at Southern Illinois University and editor of the journal *Identities: Global Studies in Culture and Power.* He is the author of *Keepers of the Sacred Chants: The Poetics of Ritual Power in an Amazonian Society,* editor of *Rethinking History and Myth: Indigenous South American Perspectives on the Past,* and coeditor of *Comparative Arawakan Histories.*

The University of Illinois Press
is a founding member of the
Association of American University Presses.

_____

Composed in 10/13 ITC Galliard Std.
with Galliard display
by Celia Shapland
at the University of Illinois Press
Designed by Dennis Roberts
Manufactured by Cushing-Malloy, Inc.

University of Illinois Press
1325 South Oak Street
Champaign, IL 61820-6903
www.press.uillinois.edu